ISBN 978-1-330-54048-0
PIBN 10075937

This book is a reproduction of an important historical work. Forgotten Books uses
state-of-the-art technology to digitally reconstruct the work, preserving the original format
whilst repairing imperfections present in the aged copy. In rare cases, an imperfection in
the original, such as a blemish or missing page, may be replicated in our edition. We do,
however, repair the vast majority of imperfections successfully; any imperfections that
remain are intentionally left to preserve the state of such historical works.

1 MONTH OF
FREE
READING

at

www.ForgottenBooks.com

By purchasing this book you are eligible for one month membership to ForgottenBooks.com, giving you unlimited access to our entire collection of over 1,000,000 titles via our web site and mobile apps.

To claim your free month visit:

www.forgottenbooks.com/free75937

English
Français
Deutsche
Italiano
Español
Português

www.forgottenbooks.com

Mythology Photography **Fiction**
Fishing Christianity **Art** Cooking
Essays Buddhism Freemasonry
Medicine **Biology** Music **Ancient
Egypt** Evolution Carpentry Physics
Dance Geology **Mathematics** Fitness
Shakespeare **Folklore** Yoga Marketing
Confidence Immortality Biographies
Poetry **Psychology** Witchcraft
Electronics Chemistry History **Law**
Accounting **Philosophy** Anthropology
Alchemy Drama Quantum Mechanics
Atheism Sexual Health **Ancient History**
Entrepreneurship Languages Sport
Paleontology Needlework Islam
Metaphysics Investment Archaeology
Parenting Statistics Criminology
Motivational

THE RUINS;

OR

MEDITATION

ON THE

REVOLUTIONS OF EMPIRES.

BY

C? F?° VOLNEY,

COUNT AND PEER OF FRANCE ; AUTHOR OF "NEW RESEARCHES
ON ANCIENT HISTORY "

TO WHICH IS ADDED

THE LAW OF NATURE,

A SHORT BIOGRAPHICAL NOTICE,
BY COUNT DARU,

AND

THE CONTROVERSY BETWEEN DR. PRIESTLY AND VOLNEY.

NEW YORK :
PUBLISHED BY CALVIN BLANCHARD,
76 NASSAU STREET.

1857.

PREFACE OF THE EDITOR

IF books were to be judged of by their volume, the follow
ing would have but little value; if appraised by their contents,
it will perhaps be reckoned amongst the most instructive.

In general, nothing is more important than a good elementary book ; but, also, nothing is more difficult to compose and
even to read : and why ? Because, as everything in it should be
analysis and definition, all should be expressed with truth and
precision : if truth and precision are wanting, the object has not
been attained ; if they exist, its very force renders it abstract.

The first of these defects has been hitherto evident in all books
of morality : we find in them only a chaos of incoherent max-
ims, precepts without causes, and actions without a motive.
The pedants of the human race have treated it like a little child :
they have prescribed to it good behavior by frightening it with
spirits and hobgoblins. Now that the growth of the human
race is rapid, it is time to speak reason to it ; it is time to prove
to men that the springs of their improvement are to be found in
their very organization, in the interest of their passions, and in
all that composes their existence. It is time to demonstrate that
morality is a physical and geometrical science, subjected to the
rules and calculations of the other mathematical sciences : and
such is the advantage of the system expounded in this book,
that the basis of morality being laid in it on the very nature of

things, it is both constant and immutable; whereas, in all other theological systems morality being built upon arbitrary opinions, not demonstrable and often absurd, it changes, decays, expires with them, and leaves men in an absolute depravation. It is true that because our system is founded on facts and not on reveries, it will with much greater difficulty be extended and adopted : but it will derive strength from this very struggle, and sooner or later the eternal religion of Nature must overturn the transient religions of the human mind.

This book was published for the first time in 1793, under the title of The French Citizen's Catechism : it was at first intended for a national work ; but as it may be equally well entitled the Catechism of men of sense and honor, it is to be hoped that it will become a book common to all Europe. It is possible that its brevity may prevent it from attaining the object of a popular classical work ; but the author will be satisfied if he has at least the merit of pointing out the way to make a·better.

ADVERTISEMENT.

VOLNEY'S RUINS;

OR, MEDITATION ON THE REVOLUTIONS OF EMPIRES

The superior merits of this work are too well known to require commendation ; but as it is not generally known that there are in circulation three English translations of it, varying very materially in regard to faithfulness and elegance of diction, the publishers of the present edition insert the following extracts for the information of purchasers and readers :

PARIS TRANSLATION.

Now first Published in this Country by Dixon and Sickels in duodecimo and octavo.

INVOCATION.

HAIL solitary ruins ! holy sepulchres, and silent walls ! you I invoke ; to you I address my prayer. While your aspect averts, with secret terror, the vulgar regard, it excites in my heart, the charm of delicious sentiments, sublime contemplations. What useful lessons ! what affecting and profound reflections you suggest to him who knows how to consult you. When the whole earth, in chains and silence, bowed the neck before its tyrants, you had already proclaimed the truths which they abhor, and confounding the dust of the king with that of the meanest slave, had announced to man the sacred dogma of EQUALITY ! Within your pale, in solitary adoration of LIBERTY, I saw her Genius arise from the mansions of the dead; not such as she is painted by the impassioned multitude, armed with fire and sword, but under the august aspect of Justice, poising in her hand the sacred balance, wherein are weighed the actions of men at the gates of eternity.

O Tombs ! what virtues are yours ! you appal the tyrant's heart, and poison with secret alarm his impious joys ; he flies, with coward step, your incorruptible aspect, and erects afar his throne of insolence.

LONDON TRANSLATION.

INVOCATION.

Solitary ruins, sacred tombs, ye mouldering and silent walls, all hail ! To you I address my Invocation. While the vulgar shrink from your aspect with secret terror, my heart finds in the contemplation a thousand delicious sentiments, a thousand admirable recollections. Pregnant, I may truly call you, with useful lessons, with pathetic and irresistible advice to the man who knows how to consult you. Awhile ago, the whole world bowed the neck in silence before the tyrants that oppressed it; and yet in that hopeless moment you already proclaimed the truths that tyrants hold in abhorrence : mixing the dust of the proudest kings with that of the meanest slaves, you called upon us to contemplate this example of EQUALITY. From your caverns, whither the musing and anxious love of LIBERTY led me, I saw escape its venerable shade, and with unexpected felicity, direct its flight and marshal my steps the way to renovated France.

Tombs ! what virtues and potency do you exhibit ! Tyrants tremble at your aspect—you poison with secret alarm their impious pleasures—they turn from you with impatience, and, coward like, endeavour to forget you amid the sumptuousness of their palaces.

PHILADELPHIA TRANSLATION.

INVOCATION.

Hail, ye solitary ruins, ye sacred tombs, and silent walls ! 'Tis your auspicious aid that I invoke, 'tis to you my soul, wrapped in meditation, pours forth its prayer ! What though the profane and vulgar mind shrinks with dismay from your august and awe-inspiring aspect, to me ye unfold the sublimest charms of contemplation and sentiment, and offer to my senses the luxury of a thousand delicious and enchanting thoughts ! How sumptuous the feast to a being that has a taste to relish, and an understanding to consult you ! What rich and noble admonitions, what exquisite and pathetic lessons do you read to a heart that is susceptible of exalted feelings ! When oppressed humanity bent in timid silence throughout the globe beneath the galling yoke of slavery, it was you that proclaimed aloud the birthright of those truths which tyrants tremble at while they detect, and which by sinking the loftiest head of the proudest potentate, with all his boasted pageantry, to the level of mortality with his meanest slave, confirmed and ratified by your unerring testimony the sacred and immortal doctrine of EQUALITY.

Musing within the precincts of your inviting scenes of philosophic solitude, whither the insatiate love of trueborn LIBERTY had led me, I beheld her genius ascending, not in the spurious character and habit of a bloodthirsty Fury armed with daggers and instruments of murder, and followed by a frantic and intoxicated multitude, but under the placid and chaste aspect of *justice*, holding with a pure and unsullied hand the sacred scales in which the actions of mortals are weighed on the brink of eternity.

O ye tombs and emblematic images of death ! How superlative is your power, how irresistible your influence ! Your presence appals and chills the souls of tyrants with electric horror and remorse : the very remembrance of you haunts their m... a ghastly spectre in the midst of their voluptuous enjoyments, and the terror you inspire plants thorns in all their thoughts, and poisons their impious pleasures into pains.

The first translation was made and published in London soon after the appearance of the work in French, and by a late edition, is still adopted without alteration. Mr. Volney, when in this country, in 1797, expressed his disapprobation of this translation, alleging that the translator must have been overawed by the government or clergy from rendering his ideas faithfully; and accordingly an English gentleman then in Philadelphia, volunteered to correct this edition. But by his endeavours to give the true and full meaning of the author with great precision, he has so overloaded his composition with an exuberance of words, as in a great measure to dissipate the simple elegance and sublimity of the original. Mr. Volney, when he became better acquainted with the English language, perceived this defect; and, with the aid of our countryman, Joel Barlow, made and published in Paris, a new, correct, and elegant translation, of which the present edition is a faithful and correct copy

CONTENTS.

THE LAW OF NATURE.

INVOCATION.

Hail solitary ruins, holy sepulchres and silent walls ! you I invoke ; to you I address my prayer. While your aspect averts, with secret terror, the vulgar regard, it excites, in my heart, the charm of delicious sentiments, sublime contemplations. What useful lessons, what affecting and profound reflections you suggest to him who knows how to consult you ! When the whole earth, in chains and silence, bowed the neck before its tyrants, you had already proclaimed the truths which they abhor; and, confounding the dust of the king with that of the meanest slave, had announced to man the sacred dogma of Equality. Within your pale, in solitary adoration of Liberty, I saw her Genius arise from the mansions of the dead ; not such as she is painted by the impassioned multitude, armed with fire and sword, but under the august aspect of Justice, poising in her hand the sacred balance, wherein are weighed the actions of men at the gates of eternity.

O Tombs ! what virtues are yours ! you appal the tyrant's heart, and poison with secret alarm his impious joys ; he flies, with coward step, your incorruptible aspect, and erects afar his throne of insolence. You punish the powerful oppressor; you wrest from avarice and extortion their ill gotten gold, and you avenge the feeble whom they have despoiled; you compensate the miseries of the poor by the anxieties of the rich; you console the wretched, by opening to him a last asylum from distress, and you give to the soul that just equipoise of strength and sensibility which constitutes wisdom, the true science of life. Aware that all must return to you, the wise man loadeth not himself with the burdens of grandeur and of useless wealth: he restrains his desires within the limits of justice ; yet, knowing

that he must run his destined course of life, he fills with employment all its hours, and enjoys the comforts that fortune has
allotted him.   You thus impose on the impetuous sallies of cupidity a salutary rein ! you calm the feverish ardor of enjoyments
which disturb the senses ; you free the soul from the fatiguing
conflict of the passions ; elevate it above the paltry interests
which torment the crowd; and surveying from your commanding
position, the expanse of ages and nations, the mind is only ac-
cessible to the great affections, to the solid ideas of virtue and of
glory.   Ah ! when the dream of life is over, what will then
avail all its agitations, if not one trace of utility remains behind ?

   O Ruins ! to your school I will return ! I will seek again the
calm of your solitudes ; and there, far from the afflicting spectacle of the passions, I will cherish in remembrance the love of
man, I will employ myself on the means of effecting good for
him, and build my own happiness on the promotion of his.

LIFE OF VOLNEY,

BY COUNT DARU.

CONSTANTINE FRANCIS CHASSEBEUF DE VOLNEY was born
in 1757 at Craon, in that intermediate condition of life, which is of
all the happiest, since it is disinherited only of fortune's too dangerous favors, and can aspire at the social and intellectual advantages
reserved for a laudable ambition.

From his earliest youth, he devoted himself to the search after
Truth, without being disheartened by the serious studies which alone
can initiate us into her secrets. After having become acquainted
with the ancient languages, the natural sciences and history, and being admitted into the society of the most eminent literary characters,
he submitted, at the age of twenty, to an illustrious academy, the solution of one of the most difficult problems that the history of antiquity has left open to discussion. This attempt received no encouragement from the learned men who were appointed his judges; the
author's only appeal from their sentence was to his courage and his
efforts.

Soon after, a small inheritance having fallen to his lot, the difficulty
was how to spend it (these are his own words.) He resolved to
employ it in acquiring, by a long voyage, a new fund of information,
and determined to visit Egypt and Syria. But these countries could
not be explored to advantage without a knowledge of the language.
Our young traveller was not to be discouraged by this difficulty: instead of learning Arabic in Europe, he withdrew to a convent of

2

Copts, until he had made himself master of an idiom which is spoken
by so many nations of the east.   This resolution already betrayed one
of those undaunted spirits that remain unshaken amidst the trials of
life.

Although, like other travellers, he might have amused us with the
account of his hardships and the perils surmounted by his courage, he
overcame the temptation of interrupting his narrative by personal
adventures.   He disdained the beaten track ; he does not tell us the
road he took, the accidents he met with, or the impressions he received.   He carefully avoids appearing upon the stage ; he is an inhabitant of the country, who has long and well observed it, and who
describes its physical, political and moral state.   The illusion would
be entire, if an old Arab could be supposed to possess all the erudition,
all the European philosophy, which are found united and in their ma-
turity in a traveller of twenty-five.

But, though a master in all those artifices by which a narration is
rendered interesting, the young man is not to be discerned in the pomp
of labored descriptions ; although possessed of a lively and brilliant
imagination, he is never found unwarily explaining by conjectural
systems the physical or moral phenomena which he describes.   In
his observations he unites prudence with science ; with these two
guides he judges with circumspection, and sometimes confesses himself unable to account for the effects he has made known to us.

Thus his account has all the qualities that persuade, accuracy and
candor : and when, ten years later, a vast military enterprise transported forty thousand travellers to the classic ground, which he had
trod unattended, unarmed and unprotected, they all recognised a sure
guide and an enlightened observer in the writer who seemed to have
preceded them, only to remove or point out a part of the difficulties
of the way.

The unanimous testimony of all parties proved the accuracy of his
account and the justness of his observation ; and his Travels in Egypt
and Syria were recommended by universal suffrage to the gratitude
and the confidence of the public

Before it had undergone this trial, the work had obtained in the
learned world such a rapid and general success, that it found its way
into Russia.   The empress then upon the throne (in 1787) sent the
author a medal, which he received with respect, as a mark of esteem
for his talents, and with gratitude, as a proof of the approbation given
to his principles.   But when the empress declared against France,

Volney sent back the honorable present, saying; If I obtained it from her esteem, I can only preserve her esteem by returning it.

The revolution of 1789, which had drawn upon France the menaces of Catharine, had opened to Volney a political career. As deputy in the assembly of the states-general, the first words he uttered there were in favor of the publicity of their deliberations. He also supported the organization of the national guards and that of the communes and departments.

At the period when the question of the sale of the domain lands was agitated (in 1790,) he published an essay in which he lays down the following principles : " The force of a State is in proportion to its population ; population is in proportion to plenty ; plenty is in proportion to tillage, and tillage, to personal and immediate interest, that is to the spirit of property. Whence it follows that the nearer the cultivator approaches the passive condition of a mercenary, the less industry and activity are to be expected from him ; and, on the other hand, the nearer he is to the condition of a free and entire proprietor, the more extension he gives to his own forces, to the produce of his lands, and to the general prosperity of the State."

The author draws this conclusion, that a State is so much the more powerful as it includes a greater number of proprietors, that is, a greater division of property.

Conducted into Corsica, by that spirit of observation, which belongs only to men whose information is varied and extensive, he perceived at the first glance all that could be done for the improvement of agriculture in that country, but he knew that for a people firmly attached to ancient customs, there can exist no other demonstration or means of persuasion than example. He purchased a considerable estate, and made experiments on all the kinds of tillage that he hoped to naturalize in that climate : the sugar-cane, cotton, indigo and coffee soon demonstrated the success of his efforts. This success drew upon him the notice of the government, he was appointed director of agriculture and commerce in that island, where, through ignorance, all new methods are introduced with such difficulty.

It is impossible to calculate all the good that might have resulted from this peaceable magistracy ; and we know that neither instruction, zeal nor a persevering courage were wanting to him who had undertaken it : of this he had given convincing proofs. It was in obedience to another sentiment no less respectable, that he voluntarily interrupted the course of his labors. When his fellow citizens of

Angers appointed him their deputy in the constituent assembly, he resigned the employment he held under government, upon the princi ple, that no man can represent the nation and be dependent for a salary upon those by whom it is administered.

Through respect for the independence of his legislative functions, he had ceased to occupy the place he possessed in Corsica before his election; but he had not ceased to be the benefactor of that country He returned thither after the session of the constituent assembly. Invited into that island by the principal inhabitants who were anxious to put in practice his lessons, he spent there a part of the years 1792 and 1793.

On his return he published a work entitled: An account of the present state of Corsica. This was an act of courage; for it was not a physical description, but a political review of the condition of a population divided into several factions and distracted by violent animosities. Volney unreservedly revealed the abuses, solicited the interest of France in favor of the Corsicans, without flattering them, and boldly denounced their defects and vices; so that the philosopher obtained the only recompense he could expect from his sincerity; he was accused by the Corsicans of heresy.

To prove that he had not merited this reproach, he soon after published a short treatise entitled: The law of nature, or physical principles of morality.

He was soon exposed to a much more dangerous charge, and this, it must be confessed, he did merit. This philosopher, this worthy citizen, who in our first National assembly, had seconded with his wishes and his talents the establishment of an order of things which he considered favorable to the happiness of his country, was accused of not being sincerely attached to that liberty for which he had contended; that is to say, of being averse to anarchy. An imprisonment of ten months, which only ended after the 9th of Thermidor, was a new trial reserved for his courage.

The moment at which he recovered his liberty was that, when the horror inspired by criminal excesses recalled men to those noble sentiments which fortunately are one of the first necessaries of civilized life. They sought for consolations in study and literature, after so many crimes and misfortunes, and organized a plan of public instruction.

It was in the first place necessary to ensure the aptitude of those to whom education should be confided; but as the systems were vari-

ous, the best methods and an unity of doctrine were to be determined.
It was not enough to interrogate the masters, they were to be formed,
new ones were to be created, and for that purpose, a school was
opened in 1794, wherein the celebrity of the professors promised new
instruction even to the best informed. This was not, as was objected, beginning the edifice by the roof, but creating architects, who
were to superintend all the arts requisite for the construction of the
building.

The more difficult their functions were, the greater care was to be
taken in the choice of the professors; but France, though then accused of being plunged in barbarism, possessed men of transcendent
talents, already enjoying the esteem of all Europe, and we may be
bold to say, that by their labors, our literary glory had likewise extended its conquests. Their names were proclaimed by the public
voice, and Volney's was associated with those of the men most il-
lustrions in science and in literature.*

This institution however did not answer the expectations that had
been formed of it, because the two thousand students that assembled
from all parts of France were not equally prepared to receive these
transcendent lessons, and because it had not been sufficiently ascertained how far the theory of education should be kept distinct from
education itself.

Volney's lectures on history, which were attended by an immense
concourse of auditors, became one of his chief claims to literary
glory. When forced to interrupt them, by the suppression of the
Normal school, he might have reasonably expected to enjoy, in his
retirement, that consideration which his recent functions had added
to his name. But, disgusted with the scenes he had witnessed in his
native land, he felt that passion revive within him, which, in his
youth, had led him to visit Africa and Asia. America, civilized
within a century, and free only within a few years, fixed his attention. There everything was new, the inhabitants, the constitution,
the earth itself: these were objects worthy of his observation. When
embarking however for this voyage, he felt emotions very different
from those which formerly accompanied him into Turkey. Then in
the prime of life, he joyfully bid adieu to a land where peace and
plenty reigned, to travel amongst Babarians; now, mature in years,

---

* Lagrange, Laplace, Berthollet, Garat, Bernardin de Saint-Pierre,
Daubenton, Hauy, Volney, Sicard, Monge, Thouin, La Harpe, Buache,
Mentelle.

but dismayed at the spectacle and experience of injustice and persecution, it was with diffidence, as we learn from himself, that he went
to implore from a free people an asylum for a sincere friend of that
liberty that had been so profaned.

Our traveller had gone to seek for repose beyond the seas ; he there
found himself exposed to aggression from a celebrated philosopher,
Doctor Priestly.   Although the subject of this discussion was confined
to the investigation of some speculative opinions, published by the
French writer in his work entitled THE RUINS, the naturalist in
this attack employed a degree of violence which added nothing to the
force of his arguments, and an acrimony of expression not to be expected from a philosopher.   N. Volney, though accused of hottentot-
ism and ignorance, preserved in his defence, all the advantages that
the scurrility of his adversary gave over him : he replied in English,
and Priestly's countrymen could only recognise the Frenchman in
the refinement and politeness of his answer.

Whilst M. Volney was travelling in America, there had been
formed in France a literary body, which, under the name of Institute,
had attained in a very few years a distinguished rank amongst the
learned societies of Europe.   The name of the illustrious traveller
was inscribed in it at its formation, and he acquired new rights to
the academical honors conferred on him during his absence, by the
publication of his observations on the United States.

These rights were further augmented by the historical and physio-
logical labors of the Academician : an examination and justification
of Herodotus's chronology, with numerous and profound researches on
the history of the most ancient nations, occupied for a long time him
who had observed their monuments and traces in the countries they
inhabited.   The trial he had made of the utility of the Oriental languages inspired him with an ardent desire to propagate the knowledge of them, and to be propagated, he felt how necessary it was to
render it less difficult.   In this view he conceived the project of applying to the study of the idioms of Asia, a part of the grammatical
notions we possess concerning the languages of Europe.   It only
appertains to those conversant with their relations of dissimilitude
or conformity to appreciate the possibility of realizing this system ;
but already the author has received the most flattering encouragement and the most unequivocal suffrage, by the inscription of his
name amongst the members of the learned and illustrious society
founded by English commerce in the Indian peninsula.

M. Volney developed his system in three works,* which prove that this idea of uniting nations separated by immense distances and such various idioms, had never ceased to occupy him for twenty-five years. Lest those essays, of the utility of which he was persuaded, should be interrupted by his death, with the clay-cold hand that corrected his last work, he drew up a will which institutes a premium for the prosecution of his labors. Thus he prolonged, beyond the term of a life entirely devoted to letters, the glorious services he had rendered them.

This is not the place, nor does it belong to me to appreciate the merit of the writings which render Volney's name illustrious: his name had been inscribed in the list of the Senate and afterwards of the House of Peers. The philosopher who had travelled in the four quarters of the world, and observed their social state, had other titles to his admission into this body, than his literary glory. His public life, his conduct in the constituent assembly, his independent principles, the nobleness of his sentiments, the wisdom and fixity of his opinions, had gained him the esteem of those who can be depended upon, and with whom it is so agreeable to discuss political interests.

Although no man had a better right to have an opinion, no one was more tolerant for the opinions of others. In State assemblies as well as in Academical meetings, the man whose counsels were so wise voted according to his conscience, which nothing could bias; but the philosopher forgot his superiority to hear, to oppose with moderation, and to doubt sometimes. The extent and variety of his information, the force of his reason, the austerity of his manners, and the noble simplicity of his character, had procured him illustrious friends in both hemispheres; and now that this vast erudition is extinct in the tomb,† we may be allowed at least to predict that he was one of the very few whose memory shall never die.

———

A List of the Works Published by Count VOLNEY.

TRAVELS IN EGYPT AND SYRIA during the years 1783, 1784, and 1785; 2 volumes in 8vo. 1787.

---

* On the simplification of the Oriental languages, 1795.
The European alphabet applied to the languages of Asia, 1819
Hebrew simplified, 1820.

† He died in Paris on the 20th of April, 1820.

CHRONOLOGY OF THE TWELVE CENTURIES that preceded the entrance of Xerxes into Greece.

CONSIDERATIONS ON THE TURKISH WAR, in 1788.

THE RUINS, or Meditation on the Revolutions of Empires, 1791

ACCOUNT OF THE PRESENT STATE OF CORSICA, 1792.

THE LAW OF NATURE, or Physical Principles of Morality, 1793

ON THE SIMPLIFICATION OF ORIENTAL LANGUAGES, 1795.

A LETTER TO DOCTOR PRIESTLY, 1797.

LECTURES ON HISTORY delivered at the Normal school in the year 3, 1800.

ON THE CLIMATE AND SOIL OF THE UNITED STATES OF AMERICA, to which is added an account of Florida, of the French colony of Scioto, of some Canadian colonies and of the savages, 1803.

REPORT MADE TO THE CELTIC ACADEMY ON THE RUSSIAN WORK OF PROFESSOR PALLAS, entitled, A comparative vocabulary of all the languages in the world.

THE CHRONOLOGY OF HERODOTUS conformable with his text, 1808 and 1809.

NEW RESEARCHES ON ANCIENT HISTORY, 3v. in 8vo. 1814.

THE EUROPEAN ALPHABET, applied to the languages of Asia, 1819.

A HISTORY OF SAMUEL, 1819

HEBREW SIMPLIFIED, 1820.

THE RUINS, &c.

CHAPTER I.

THE JOURNEY.

In the eleventh year of the reign of Abd-ul-Hamid, son of Ahmed, emperor of the Turks; when the victorious Russians seized on the Krimea, and planted their standards on the shore that leads to Constantinople;

I was travelling in the empire of the Ottomans, and through those provinces which were anciently the kingdoms of Egypt and Syria.

My whole attention bent on whatever concerns the happiness of man in a social state, I visited cities and studied the manners of their inhabitants; entered palaces, and observed the conduct of those who govern; wandered over the fields, and examined the condition of those who cultivate them; and nowhere perceiving aught but robbery and devastation, tyranny and wretchedness, my heart was oppressed with sorrow and indignation.

I saw daily on my road fields abandoned, villages deserted, and cities in ruin. Often I met with ancient monuments, wrecks of temples, palaces and fortresses; columns, aqueducts, and tombs; and this spectacle led me to meditate on times past, and filled my mind with serious and profound contemplations.

Arrived at Hems, on the banks of the Orontes, and being at no great distance from Palmyra of the desert, I resolved to see its celebrated monuments; after three days travelling through an arid wilderness, having traversed the valley of caves and sepulchres, on

issuing into the plain, I was suddenly struck with a scene of the
most stupendous ruins: a countless multitude of superb columns,
stretching in avenues beyond the reach of sight.   Among them were
magnificent edifices, some entire, others in ruins.   The ground was
covered on all sides with fragments of cornices, capitals, shafts, en-
tablatures, pilasters, all of white marble, and of the most exquisite
workmanship   After a walk of three quarters of an hour along
these ruins, I entered the enclosure of a vast edifice, formerly a temple dedicated to the sun, and accepting the hospitality of some poor
Arabian peasants, who had built their huts on the area of the temple,
I resolved to stay some days to contemplate, at leisure, the beauty
of so many stupendous works.

Every day I visited some of the monuments which covered the
plain; and one evening, absorbed in reflection, I had advanced to
the valley of sepulchres; I ascended the heights which surround it,
and from whence the eye commands the whole group of ruins and
the immensity of the desert.—The sun had just sunk below the horizon : a red border of light still marked his track behind the distant
mountains of Syria : the full-moon was rising in the east on a blue
ground over the plains of the Euphrates ; the sky was clear, the air
calm and serene; the dying lamp of day still softened the horrors of
approaching darkness ; the refreshing breeze of night attempered the
sultry emanations from the heated earth ; the herdsmen had led the
camels to their stalls ; the eye perceived no motion on the dusky and
uniform plain ; profound silence rested on the desert ; the howlings
only of the jackal,* and the solemn notes of the bird of night were
heard at distant intervals.   Darkness now increased, and already,
brough the dusk, I could distinguish nothing more than the pale
phantasies of columns and walls.   The solitude of the place, the
tranquillity of the hour the majesty of the scene, impressed on my
mind a religious pensiveness.   The aspect of a great city deserted,
he memory of times past, compared with its present state, all elevated my mind to high contemplations.   I sat on the shaft of a column :
ad there, my elbow reposing on my knee, and head reclining on my
and, my eyes fixed, sometimes on the desert, sometimes on the ruins,
fell into a profound revery.

* A kind of fox that roves only during the night

CHAPTER II.

MEDITATION.

HERE, said I, here once flourished an opulent city; here was the seat of a powerful empire. Yes! these places now so desert, were once animated by a living multitude; a busy crowd circulated in these streets now so solitary. Within these walls, where a mournful silence reigns, the noise of the arts and shouts of joy and festivity incessantly resounded: these piles of marble were regular palaces; these prostrate pillars adorned the majesty of temples; these ruined galleries surrounded public places. Here a numerous people assembled for the sacred duties of religion, or the anxious cares of their subsistence: here industry, parent of enjoyments, collected the riches of all climates, and the purple of Tyre was exchanged for the precious thread of Serica;* the soft tissues of Kachemire for the sumptuous tapestry of Lydia; the amber of the Baltic for the pearls and perfumes of Arabia; the gold of Ophir for the tin of Thule.

And now a mournful skeleton is all that subsists of this powerful city! nought remains of its vast domination, but a doubtful and empty remembrance! To the tumultuous throng which crowded under these porticoes has succeeded the solitude of death. The silence of the tomb is substituted for the bustle of public places. The opulence of a commercial city is changed into hideous poverty. The palaces of kings are become a den of wild beasts; flocks fold on the area of the temple, and unclean reptiles inhabit the sanctuary of the gods! —Ah! how has so much glory been eclipsed?—How have so many labors been annihilated?—Thus perish the works of men, and thus do empires and nations disappear!

And the history of former times revived in my mind; I recollected those distant ages when many illustrious nations inhabited these countries; I figured to myself the Assyrian on the banks of the Ti-

---

* "Thread of Serica."—That is the silk, originally derived from the mountainous country where the great wall terminates, and which appears to have been the cradle of the Chinese empire, known to the Latins under the name of Regio Serarum, Serica.

"The tissues of Kachemire."—The shawls which Ezekiel seems to have described, five centuries before our era, under the appellation o Choud-Choud.

gris, the Kaldean on those of the Euphrates, the Persian reigning from the Indus to the Mediterranean. I enumerated the kingdoms of Damascus and Idumea, of Jerusalem and Samaria, the warlike states of the Philistines, and the commercial republics of Phœnicia. This Syria, said I, now so depopulated, then contained a hundred flourishing cities; and abounded with towns, villages and hamlets.* Everywhere were seen cultivated fields, frequented roads, and crowded habitations.—Ah! what are become of those ages of abundance and of life? How have so many brilliant creations of human industry vanished? Where are those ramparts of Nineveh, those walls of Babylon, those palaces of Persepolis, those temples of Balbeck and of Jerusalem? Where are those fleets of Tyre, those dock-yards of Arad, those work-shops of Sidon, and that multitude of sailors, of pilots, of merchants, and of soldiers? Where those husbandmen, those harvests, those flocks, and all the creation of living beings in which the face of the earth rejoiced? Alas! I have passed over this desolate land! I have visited the palaces once the theatre of so much splendor, and I beheld nothing but solitude and desolation.—I sought the ancient inhabitants and their works, and could only find a faint trace, like that of the foot of a traveller over the sand. The temples are fallen, the palaces overthrown, the ports filled up, the cities destroyed, and the earth, stripped of inhabitants, seems a dreary burying-place.—Great God! whence proceed such fatal revolutions? What causes have so altered the fortunes of these countries? Why are so many cities destroyed? Why has not this ancient population been reproduced and perpetuated?

Thus absorbed in contemplation, a crowd of new reflections continually poured in upon my mind. Everything, continued I, confounds my reason, and fills my heart with trouble and uncertainty. When these countries enjoyed what constitutes the glory and happiness of man, they were inhabited by an infidel people; it was the Phœnician, that homicide sacrificer to Molock, who gathered into his stores the riches of all climates; it was the Kaldean prostrate before a serpent,† who subjugated opulent cities, and despoiled the palaces of kings, and the temples of the gods; it was the Persian, adorer of fire, who received the tribute of a hundred nations; it was the inhabitant of this very city, worshipper of the sun and stars, who

---

* According to the calculations of Josephus and Strabo, Syria must have contained ten millions of inhabitants; there are not two at the present day.

† The dragon Bel.

erected so many monuments of prosperity and luxury.—Numerous flocks, fertile fields, abundant harvests, whatsoever should be the reward of piety, was in the hands of these idolaters: and now when a people of saints and believers occupy these fields, all is become sterility and solitude. The earth under these holy hands, produces only thorns and briars. Man sows in anguish, and reaps only vexation and tears; war, famine, pestilence, assail him in turn.—Yet, are not these the children of the prophets? the Mussulman, Christian, Jew, are they not the elect children of God, loaded with favors and miracles? Why then do these privileged races no longer enjoy the same advantages? Why are these fields, sanctified by the blood of martyrs, deprived of their ancient benefits? Why have those blessings been banished hence and transferred for so many ages to other nations and different climes?

At these words, revolving in my mind the course of vicissitudes which have transmitted the sceptre of the world successively to people so different in religion and manners, from those of ancient Asia, to the most recent of Europe, this name of a natal land revived in me the sentiment of my country: and turning my eyes towards her, I began to reflect on the situation in which I left her.*

I called to mind her fields so richly cultivated, her roads so sumptuously constructed, her cities inhabited by a countless people, her fleets spread over every sea, her ports filled with the produce of either India: and comparing with the activity of her commerce, the extent of her navigation, the magnificence of her monuments, the arts and industry of her inhabitants, what Egypt and Syria had once possessed, I was gratified to find in modern Europe the departed splendor of Asia: but the charm of my revery was soon dissolved by a last term of comparison. Reflecting that such had once been the activity of the places I was then contemplating: Who knows, said I, but such may one day be the abandonment of our countries? Who knows if on the banks of the Seine, the Thames, or the Zuyder-Zee, where now, in the tumult of so many enjoyments, the heart and the eye suffice not for the multitude of sensations: who knows if some traveller, like myself, shall not one day sit on their silent ruins and weep in solitude over the ashes of their inhabitants, and the memory of their greatness?

At these words, my eyes filled with tears: and covering my head with the fold of my garment, I sunk into gloomy meditations on hu-

* In 1782, at the close of the American war.

3

man affairs. Ah! hapless man, said I, in my grief, a blind fatality sports with thy destiny! A fatal necessity rules with the hand of chance the lot of mortals. But no: it is the justice of heaven fulfilling its decrees! A mysterious God exercising his incomprehensible judgments! Doubtless he has pronounced a secret anathema against this land: blasting with maledictions the present for the sins of the past generations. Oh! who shall dare to fathom the depths of the Divinity? *

And I remained motionless, plunged in profound melancholy

CHAPTER III

THE APPARITION.

MEANWHILE a noise struck my ear: like to the agitation of a flowing robe, or of slow footsteps on dry and rustling grass. Startled, I opened my mantle, and casting around a timid glance, suddenly on my left, by the glimmering light of the moon, through the columns and ruins of a neighbouring temple, I thought I saw a pale apparition, clothed in large and flowing robes, as spectres are represented rising from their tombs. I shuddered: and while agitated and hesitating whether to fly or to ascertain the object, a deep voice, in solemn accents, pronounced these words;

"How long will man importune heaven with unjust complaint? How long, with vain clamors, will he accuse FATE as the author of his calamities? Will he then never open his eyes to the light, and his heart to the insinuations of truth and reason? The light of truth meets him everywhere; yet he sees it not! The voice of reason strikes his ear, and he hears it not! Unjust man! if for a moment you can suspend the delusion which fascinates your senses, if your heart can comprehend the language of reason, interrogate these ruins! Read the lessons which they present to you!—And you, wit-

* Fatality is the universal and rooted prejudice of the East: "It was written," is there the answer to everything,—hence result an unconcern and apathy, the most powerful impediments to instruction and civilisation.

nesses of twenty different centuries, holy temples! venerable tombs! walls once so glorious, appear in the cause of nature herself! Approach the tribunal of sound reason, and bear testimony against unjust accusations! come and confound the declamations of a false wisdom or hypocritical piety, and avenge the heavens and the earth of man who calumniates them!

" What is that blind fatality, which without order and without law, sports with the destiny of mortals? What is that unjust necessity, which confounds the effect of actions, whether of wisdom or of folly? in what consist those anathemas of heaven over this land? Where is that divine malediction which perpetuates the abandonment of these fields? Say, monuments of past ages! have the heavens changed their laws and the earth its motion? are the fires of the sun extinct in the regions of space? do the seas no longer emit their vapors? are the rains and the dews suspended in the air? do the mountains withhold their springs? are the streams dried up? and do the plants no longer bear fruit and seed? Answer, generation of falsehood and iniquity, has God deranged the primitive and settled order of things which he himself assigned to nature? Has heaven denied to earth, and earth to its inhabitants, the blessings which once they proffered? If nothing has changed in the creation, if the same means exist now which existed before, why then are not the present what former generations were? Ah! it is falsely that you accuse fate and heaven! it is injuriously that you refer to God the cause of your evils! Say, perverse and hypocritical race! if these places are desolate, if powerful cities are reduced to solitude, is it God who has caused their ruin? Is it his hand which has overthrown these walls, destroyed these temples, mutilated these columns, or is it the hand of man? Is it the arm of God which has carried the sword into your cities, and fire into your fields, which has slaughtered the people, burned the harvests, rooted up trees, and ravaged the pastures, or is it the hand of man? And when, after the destruction of crops, famine has ensued, is it the vengeance of God which has produced it, or the mad fury of mortals? When, sinking under famine, the people have fed on impure aliments, if pestilence ensues, is it the wrath of God which sends it, or the folly of man? When war, famine, and pestilence, have swept away the inhabitants, if the earth remains a desert, is it God who has depopulated it? Is it his rapacity which robs the husbandman, ravages the fruitful fields, and wastes the earth, or is it the rapacity of those who govern? Is it his pride which excites murderous wars, or the pride of kings and their ministers? Is it the venality of his decisions which overthrows the fortunes of families, or the corruption of the organs of the law? Are they his passions which, under a thousand forms, torment individuals and nations, or are they the passions of man? And if, in the anguish of their miseries, they see not the remedies, is it the ignorance of God which is to blame, or their ignorance? Cease then mortals, to accuse the decrees of FATE, or the judgments of the Divinity! If God is good, will he be the author of your misery? if he is just, will he be the accomplice of your crimes? No, the caprice of which man complains is not the caprice of destiny; the darkness that misleads his reason is not the darkness of God; the source of his calamities is not in the distant heavens, it is beside him on the earth; it is not concealed in the bosom of the divinity; it resides in man himself, he bears it in his own heart.

"You murmur and say, How have an infidel people enjoyed the blessings of heaven and earth? Why is a holy and chosen race less fortunate than impious generations? Deluded man! where then is the contradiction which offends you? Where is the inconsistency which you impute to the justice of heaven? Take into your own hands the balance of rewards and punishments, of causes and effects. Say: when those infidels observed the laws of the heavens and of the earth, when they regulated their intelligent labors by the order of the seasons and course of the stars, ought God to have troubled the equilibrium of the universe to defeat their prudence? When their hands cultivated these fields with toil and care, should he have diverted the course of the rains, suspended the fertilizing dews, and caused thorns to spring up? When, to render these arid fields productive, their industry constructed aqueducts, dug canals, and led the distant waters across the desert, should he have dried up their sources in the mountains? Should he have blasted the harvests which art had created, wasted the plains which peace had peopled, overthrown cities which labor caused to flourish, disturbed in fine, the order established by the wisdom of man? And what is that infidelity which founded empires by prudence, defended them by valor, and strengthened them by justice; which erected powerful cities, formed capacious ports, drained pestilential marshes, covered the sea with ships, the earth with inhabitants; and, like the creative spirit, diffused life and motion through the world? If such be infidelity, what then is the true faith? Does sanctity consist in destruction? The God who peoples the air with birds, the earth with animals, the waters with fishes; the God who animates all nature, is he then a God of ruins and tombs ? Does he ask devastation for homage, and conflagration for sacrifice ? Requires he groans for hymns, murderers for votaries, a ravaged and desert earth for his temple ? Yet such, holy and believing people, are your works ! These are the fruits of your piety ! You have massacred the people, burnt their cities, destroyed cultivation, reduced the earth to a solitude ; and you ask the reward of your works ! Miracles then must be performed, the laborers whom you cut off must be recalled to life, the walls reedified which you have overthrown, the harvests reproduced which you have destroyed, the waters gathered together which you have dispersed ; the laws, in fine, of heaven and earth reversed ; those laws, established by God himself, in demonstration of his magnificence and wisdom ; those eternal laws anterior to all codes, to all the prophets ; those immutable laws, which neither the passions, nor the ignorance of man can pervert ; but that passion, which mistakes, that ignorance which observes not causes, and predicts no effect. has said in the folly of her heart : ' Everything comes from chance ; a blind fatality dispenses good and evil on the earth, so that prudence and wisdom cannot guard against it.' Or else, assuming the language of hypocrisy, she has said : 'All things are from God ; he takes pleasure in deceiving wisdom, and confounding reason ; . . . . .' and ignorance, applauding herself in her malice, has said : 'Thus I shall not be inferior to that science which I detest : I will render useless that prudence which fatigues and torments me ;' and cupidity has added : ' I will oppress the weak and devour the fruits of his labors ; and I will say : It is God who decreed and fate who ordained it so.'—But I ! I swear by the laws of heaven and earth, and by the law which is written in the heart of man, the hypocrite shall be deceived in his guile, the oppressor in his rapacity ; the sun shall change his course, before folly shall prevail over wisdom and knowledge, or stupidity surpass prudence in the delicate and sublime art of procuring to man his true enjoyments, and of building his happiness on a solid foundation "

3*

CHAPTER IV.

THE EXPOSITION.

THUS spoke the Phantom. Astonished at his discourse, and my heart agitated with different reflections, I was for sometime silent. At length, taking courage, I thus addressed him : " O Genius of tombs and ruins! your presence, your severity have disordered my senses ; but the justness of your reasoning restores confidence to my soul. Pardon my ignorance. Alas ! if man is blind, can that which constitutes his torment be also his crime ? I may have mistaken the voice of reason ; but never knowingly have I rejected her authority. Ah ! if you read in my heart, you know with what sincerity, with what enthusiasm it seeks Truth—And is it not in pursuit of her that you see me in this sequestered spot ? Alas ! I have wandered over the earth, I have visited cities and countries ; and seeing everywhere misery and desolation, a sense of the evils which oppress my fellow-men have deeply afflicted my soul. I have said with a sigh : Is man then born but for sorrow and anguish ? And I have meditated upon human miseries, that I might find out their remedy. I have said : I will separate myself from corrupt societies; I will retire far from palaces where the mind is depraved by satiety, and from the hovel where it is debased by misery. I will go into the desert and dwell among ruins ; I will interrogate ancient monuments on the wisdom of past times; I will invoke from the bosom of the tombs the spirit which once in Asia gave splendor to states, and glory to nations. I will ask of the ashes of legislators, by what secret causes do empires rise and fall; from what sources spring the prosperity and misfortunes of nations ; on what principles can the peace of society and the happiness of man be established."

I ceased; and awaited in submissive silence to the reply of the Genius. " Peace and happiness," said he, " attend on him who practises justice ! Young man! since your heart searches after truth with sincerity, since you can still recognise her through the mist of prejudice, your prayer shall not be vain: I will unfold to your view that truth you invoke ; I will teach your reason that wisdom you are in search of; I will reveal to you the wisdom of the tombs and the science of ages.—Then approaching and laying his hand on my head : " Rise, mortal," said he, " and extricate thy senses from the dust in which thou movest."—Suddenly a celestial flame seemed to dissolve the bands which fix us to the earth ; and like a light vapor, borne up on the wings of the Genius, I felt myself wafted to the regions above. Thence, from the aerial heights, looking down on the earth, I beheld a scene entirely new. Under my feet, floating in the void, a globe like that of the moon, but smaller and less luminous, presented to me one of its phases ;* and that phase had the aspect of a disk variegated with large spots, some white and nebulous, others brown, green or gray ; and while I strained my sight to distinguish what were these spots : " Disciple of truth," said the Genius, " do you know that object ? " " O Genius ! " answered I, " if I did not see the moon in another quarter of the heavens, I should have supposed that to be her globe ; it has the appearance of that planet, seen through the telescope during the obscuration of an eclipse : these variegated spots might be mistaken for seas and continents."

" They are seas and continents," said he, " and those of the very hemisphere which you inhabit.—"

" What ! " said I, " is that the earth, the habitation of man ?—"

" Yes," replied he: " that dusky space which occupies irregularly a great portion of the disk, and envelopes it almost on every side, is what you call the great Ocean, which advancing from the south pole towards the equator, forms first the great gulf of India and Africa, then extends eastward across the Malay islands to the confines of Tartary, while towards the west it encircles the continents of Africa and Europe, even to the north of Asia.

" That square peninsula under our feet is the arid country of the Arabs; the great continent on its left, almost as naked in its interior, with a little verdure only towards its borders is the parched soil inhabited by the black-men.† To the north, beyond a long, narrow and irregular sea,‡ are the countries of Europe, rich in meadows and cultivated fields ; on its right, from the Caspian, extend the snowy and naked plains of Tartary. Returning again this way, that white space is the vast and dreary desert of Cobi, which separates China from the rest of the world. You see that empire in the furrowed plain which seems by a sudden obliquity to escape from the view. On yonder coasts, those narrow

* See plate II, representing half the terrestrial globe.

† Africa.　　　‡ The Mediterranean.

necks of land and scattered points are the peninsulas and islands of the Malays, the wretched possessors of the spices and perfumes. That triangle which advances so far into the sea, is the too famous peninsula of India.* You see the winding course of the Ganges, the rough mountains of Tibet, the lovely valley of Kachemire, the briny deserts of Persia, the banks of the Euphrates, and Tygris, the deep bed of the Jordan, and the canals of the solitary Nile.—"

"O Genius," said I, interrupting him, "the sight of a mortal reaches not to objects at such a distance..." Immediately he touched my eyes, and they became piercing as those of an eagle; nevertheless the rivers still appeared like waving lines, the mountains winding furrows, and the cities little compartments like the squares of a chess-board.

And the Genius proceeding to point out the objects to me : " Those piles," said he, "which you see in that narrow valley, watered by the Nile, are the skeletons of opulent cities, the pride of the ancient kingdom of Ethiopia ; behold Thebes with her hundred palaces,†

---

* " The too famous peninsula of India." What real advantage does the commerce of India, composed entirely of articles of luxury, procure to the mass of a nation ? what are its effects, unless to export, by a marine expensive in men, objects of necessity and utility, and to import useless commodities, which only serve to mark more strongly the difference between the rich and poor, and what a mass of superstition has not India added to the general superstition.

† " Behold Thebes with her hundred palaces." The French expedition to Egypt has proved that Thebes, divided into four or five cities on both banks of the Nile, could not have the hundred gates mentioned in Homer. (See the 2nd. vol. of the commission of Egypt.) The historian Diodorus Siculus had already shown the cause of the error, by observing that the oriental word, gate, signified also a palace (on account of the public vestibule always at its entrance,) and this author seems to have understood the cause of the Greek tradition, when he adds : " From Thebes to Memphis, there were along the river a hundred royal stables, the ruins of which are still to be seen, and which contained each twelve hundred horses (for the service of the monarch :)" all these are exactly the same numbers as Homer's. (See Diodorus Siculus, book 1st. sect 11. &c of the first kings of Egypt.) The name of Ethiopians here applied to the Thebans, is justified by the example of Homer, and by the really black color of that people. The expressions of Herodotus, when he says that the Egyptians had a black skin and woolly-hair, coinciding with the head of the sphinx of the pyramids, necessarily induced the author of Travels in Syria to believe, that this ancient people was of negro race, but all the mummies and engraved heads discovered by the French expedition contradict this idea, and the traveller, yielding to evidence, has abandoned his opinion, with several others consigned in a chronological memoir, composed at the age of twenty-two, and which was erroneously inserted in the Encyclopedia in 4to. 3 vol. of Antiquities Experience and study have enabled him to correct many errors, in a late work published at Paris, in 1814 and 1815, entitled New Researches on Ancient History. (See the 3 vol. concerning the Egyptians.)

that first metropolis of the arts and sciences, the mysterious cradle of
so many opinions which still govern man without his knowledge.
Lower down, those quadrangular blocks are the pyramids whose
masses have astonished you; farther on, the coast, hemmed in between the sea and a narrow ridge of mountains, was the habitation
of the Phœnicians; there stood the powerful cities of Tyre, of Sidon,
of Ascalon, of Gaza, and of Berytus. This stream of water without
an issue is the river Jordan, and those naked rocks were once the
theatre of events which have resounded through the world. Behold
that desert of Horeb, and that Mount-Sinai, where, by means unknown to the vulgar, a profound and adventurous leader created institutions whose influence extended to the whole human race. On
that barren shore which borders it, you see no longer any trace of
splendor; yet there was an emporium of riches. There were those
famous Idumean ports,* whence the fleets of Phœnicia and Judea,
coasting the Arabian peninsula, penetrated into the Persian gulf, to
seek there the pearls of Hevila, the gold of Saba and of Ophir.
Yes, on that coast of Oman and of Bahrain was the seat of a commerce of luxuries, which, by its fluctuations and revolutions, fixed
the destinies of ancient nations: thither came the spices and precious
stones of Ceylon, the shawls of Kachemire, the diamonds of Golcou-
da, the amber of the Maldives, the musk of Tibet, the aloes of Co-
chin, the apes and peacocks of the Indian continent, the incense of
Hadramaut, the myrrh, the silver, the gold-dust and ivory of Africa:
thence passing, sometimes by the Red sea, on the vessels of Egypt
and Syria, these luxuries nourished successively the wealth of Thebes,
of Sidon, of Memphis and of Jerusalem; sometimes, ascending the
Tygris and Euphrates, they excited the activity of the Assyrians,
Medes, Kaldeans and Persians; and that wealth, according to the
use or abuse of it, raised or reversed alternately their domination.
To this is to be attributed the magnificence of Persepolis, whose
columns you still perceive; of Ecbatana, whose sevenfold wall exists no more; of Babylon, now level with the ground; of Nineveh,
whose name is scarce remembered; of Thapsacus, of Anatho, of
Gerra, and the desolated Palmyra. O names, forever glorious! fields
of renown, illustrious countries! what sublime lessons does your as-

* "There were those famous Idumean ports." The cities of Ailah
and Atsiom-Gaber, whence the Jews of Solomon, guided by the Tyrians
of Hiram, set out on their voyage to Ophir, an unknown place concerning which a great deal has been written, but which appears to have left
some traces in Ofor, an Arabian district, at the entrance of the Persian
gulf. (See New Researches, vol. 1, and Travels in Syria, vol. 2.)

peet offer! what profound truths are written on the surface of your soil! remembrances of times past, recur to my mind, places, witnesses of the life of man in so many different ages, retrace for me the revolutions of his fortune! say, what were their springs and secret causes! say from what sources he derived success and disgrace! unveil to himself the causes of his evils! correct him by the spectacle of his errors! teach him the wisdom which belongeth to him, and let the experience of past ages become a mirror of instruction, and a germ of happiness to present and future generations!"

CHAPTER V.

CONDITION OF MAN IN THE UNIVERSE.

AFTER a short silence, the Genius resumed in these words:

I have told you already, O friend of truth, that man vainly ascribes his misfortunes to obscure and imaginary agents; in vain he seeks for mysterious and remote causes of his ills.....In the general order of the universe, his condition is doubtless subject to inconveniences, and his existence overruled by superior powers: but those powers are neither the decrees of a blind fatality, nor the caprices of whimsical and fantastic beings; like the world of which he forms a part, man is governed by natural laws, regular in their course, consistent in their effects, immutable in their essence; and those laws, the common source of good and evil, are not written among the distant stars, or hidden in mysterious codes: inherent in the nature of terrestrial beings, interwoven with their existence, they are at all times and in all places present to man, they act upon his senses, they warn his understanding, and dispense to every action its reward or punishment. Let man then study these laws! let him comprehend his own nature, and the nature of the beings that surround him, and he will know the regulators of his destiny; the causes of his evils, and the remedies he ought to apply.

When the secret power, which animates the universe, formed the globe of the earth, he implanted in the beings by whom it is inhabited, essential properties which became the law of their individual motion, the bound of their reciprocal relations, the cause of the harmony of the whole; he thereby established a regular order of causes and effects, of principles and consequences, which, under an appearance of chance, governs the universe, and maintains the equilibrium of the world: thus, he gave to fire motion and activity; to air, elasticity; weight and density to matter; he made air lighter than water, metal heavier than earth, wood less cohesive than steel; he ordered the flame to ascend, stones to fall, plants to vegetate; man, who was to be exposed to the action of so many different beings, and whose frail life was nevertheless to be preserved, was endowed with the faculty of sensation. By this faculty, all action hurtful to his existence gives him a feeling of pain and evil; and every favorable action an impression of pleasure and happiness. By these sensations, man, sometimes averted from that which wounds his senses, sometimes allured towards that which soothes them, has been obliged to cherish and preserve his own life. Thus, self-love, the desire of happiness, aversion to pain, are the essential and primary laws imposed on man by NATURE herself; the laws which the directing power, whatever it be, has established for his government, and which, like those of motion in the physical world, are the simple and fruitful principle of whatever happens in the moral world.

Such then is the condition of man: on one side exposed to the action of the elements which surround him, he is subject to many inevitable evils: and if in this decree Nature has been severe, on the other hand, just and even indulgent, she has not only tempered the evils with equivalent good, she has even enabled him to augment the good and alleviate the evil: she seems to say: " Feeble work of my hands, I owe you nothing, and I give you life; the world wherein I placed you was not made for you, yet I grant you the use of it; you will find in it a mixture of good and evil; it is for you to distinguish them, and to direct your footsteps in the paths of flowers and thorns. Be the arbiter of your own lot; I put your destiny into your hands." —Yes, man is made the artisan of his own destiny; it is he who has alternately created the successes or reverses of his fortune: and if, on a review of all the pains with which he has tormented his life, he finds reason to weep over his own weakness or imprudence, yet, considering the beginnings from which he set out, and the height attained, perhaps he has more reason to presume on his strength and to pride himself on his genius.

CHAPTER VI

THE PRIMITIVE STATE OF MAN.

AT first, formed naked both in body and mind, man found himself, thrown, as it were by chance, on a confused and savage land; an orphan, abandoned by the unknown power that produced him, he saw no supernatural beings at hand to warn him of those wants which arise only from his senses, or to instruct him in those duties, which spring only from his wants. Like to other animals, without experience of the past, without foresight of the future, he wandered in the depth of the forest, guided only and governed by the affections of his nature; by the pain of hunger, he was led to seek food, and provide for his subsistence; by the inclemency of the air, he was urged to cover his body, and he made him clothes; by the attraction of a powerful pleasure, he approached a fellow being, and he perpetuated his race.

Thus, the impressions which he reecived from every object, awakening his faculties, developed by degrees his understanding, and began to instruct his profound ignorance; his wants excited industry, dangers forced his courage; he learned to distinguish useful from noxious plants, to combat the elements, to pursue his prey, to defend his life; and he thus alleviated its miseries.

Thus, self-love, aversion to pain, the desire of happiness were the simple and powerful incentives which drew man from the savage and barbarous state in which nature had placed him; and now when his life is replete with enjoyments, when he may count every day by the comforts it brings, he may applaud himself and say: "It is I who have produced the blessings that encompass me; it is I who am the fabricator of my own felicity; a safe dwelling, convenient clothing, wholesome and abundant nourishment, smiling fields, fertile hills, populous empires, all is my work; without me, this earth given up to disorder, would have been but a filthy fen, a savage forest, and a hideous desert." Yes, creative man; receive my homage! thou hast measured the expanse of the heavens, calculated the volume of the stars, arrested the lightning in its clouds, subdued seas and storms, subjected all the elements. Ah! how are so many sublime energies allied to so many errors!

CHAPTER VII.

PRINCIPLES OF SOCIETY

WANDERING in woods, and on the banks of rivers, in pursuit of game and fish, the first men, beset with dangers, assailed by enemies, tormented by hunger, by reptiles, and ravenous beasts, felt their own individual weakness; and impelled by a common need of safety and a reciprocal sentiment of like evils, they united their resources and their strength; and when one incurred a danger, many aided and relieved him; when one wanted subsistence, another shared his prey with him; thus men associated to secure their existence, to augment their powers, to protect their enjoyments; and self-love became the principle of society.

Instructed afterwards by the experience of various and repeated accidents, by the fatigues of a wandering life, by the distress of frequent scarcity, men reasoned with themselves, and said: "Why weary ourselves in search of the scattered fruits which a parsimonious soil affords? why exhaust ourselves in pursuing prey which eludes us in the woods or waters? why not collect under our hands the animals that nourish us? why not apply our cares to multiply and preserve them? We will feed on their increase, be clothed in their skins, and live exempt from the fatigues of the day, and solicitude for the morrow." And men, aiding one another, seized the nimble goat, the timid sheep; they tamed the patient camel, the ferocious bull, the impetuous horse; and, applauding their own industry, they sat down in the joy of their souls, and began to taste repose and comfort; and self-love, the principle of all reasoning, became the instigator to every art, and every enjoyment.

When men could thus pass their days in leisure, and the communication of their ideas, they began to contemplate the earth, the heavens, and their own existence, as objects of curiosity and reflection; they remarked the course of the seasons, the action of the elements, the properties of fruits and plants, and applied their thoughts to the multiplication of their enjoyments. And in some countries, having observed that certain seeds contained a wholesome nourishment in a small volume, convenient for transportation and preservation, they

4

imitated the process of nature ; they confided to the earth rice, barley, and wheat, which multiplied so as to answer their most sanguine hopes ; and having found the means of obtaining within a small compass, and without removal, plentiful subsistence and durable stores, they prepared for themselves fixed habitations; they constructed houses, villages and towns; formed societies and nations; and self-love produced all the developements of genius and of power.

Thus, by the sole aid of his faculties, man has been able to raise himself to the astonishing height of his present fortune. Too happy if, observing scrupulously the law of his being, he had faithfully fulfilled its only and true object ! But, by a fatal imprudence, sometimes mistaking, sometimes transgressing its limits, he has launched forth into a labyrinth of errors and misfortunes ; and self-love, sometimes unruly, sometimes blind, became an abundant source of calamities.

CHAPTER VIII.

SOURCE OF THE EVILS OF SOCIETIES.

In truth, scarcely were the faculties of men developed, when inveigled by the attraction of objects which gratify the senses, they gave themselves up to inordinate desires. The sweet sensations which NATURE had attached to their real wants, to endear to them their existence, no longer satisfied them : not content with the fruits offered by the earth, or produced by industry, they wished to accumulate enjoyments, and coveted those possessed by their fellow-men : and the strong man rose up against the feeble, to take from him the profit of his labor : the feeble invoked another feeble one to repel the violence ; and two strong ones then said : " Why fatigue ourselves to produce enjoyments which we may find in the hands of the weak ? Let us join and despoil them ; they shall labor for us, and we will enjoy without labor." And the strong associating for oppression, and the weak for resistance, men mutually afflicted each other ; and a general and fatal discord spread over the earth, in which the passions, assuming a thousand new forms, have never ceased to generate a continued series of calamities.

Thus the same self-love which, moderate and prudent, was a principle of happiness and perfection, becoming blind and disordinate, was transformed into a corrupting poison : and cupidity, offspring and companion of ignorance, became the cause of all the evils which have desolated the earth.

Yes, IGNORANCE and CUPIDITY ! these are the twin sources of all that torments the existence of man ! biassed by these into false ideas of happiness, he has mistaken or infringed the laws of nature in his own relations with external objects, and injuring his existence, he has violated individual morality ; shutting through these his heart to compassion, and his mind to justice, he has persecuted and afflicted his equal, and violated social morality.   Through ignorance and cupidity man has armed against man, family against family, tribe against tribe, and the earth is become a theatre of blood, of discord and of rapine ; by ignorance and cupidity, a secret war, fermenting in the bosom of every State, has separated citizen from citizen ; and the same society is constituted of oppressors and oppressed, of masters and slaves : by these, the heads of a nation, sometimes insolent and audacious, have forged its chains within its own bowels, and mercenary avarice has founded political despotism : sometimes, hypocritical and deceitful, they have called from heaven a lying power, and a sacrilegious yoke ; and credulous cupidity has founded religious despotism ; by these in fine have been perverted the ideas of good and evil, just and unjust, vice and virtue ; and nations have wandered in a labyrinth of errors and calamities.—The cupidity of man, and his ignorance ;—These are the evil genii that have laid waste the earth ! These are the decrees of fate which have overthrown empires !   These are the celestial anathemas which have smitten these walls once so glorious, and converted the splendor of a populous city into a solitude of mourning and of ruins !—But as in the bosom of man have sprung all the evils which afflict his life, there also he is to seek and to find a remedy for them.

CHAPTER IX.

ORIGIN OF GOVERNMENTS AND LAWS

In fact, the period soon arrived when men, tired of the evils they occasioned each other, began to sigh for peace; and reflecting on the nature of their misfortunes, they said : " We mutually injure each other by our passions ; and from a desire to grasp everything, we in reality possess nothing ; what one seizes to-day another robs to-morrow, and our cupidity reacts upon ourselves. Let us establish arbitrators to judge our claims, and settle our differences. When the strong rises up against the weak, the arbitrator shall restrain him, and dispose of our force to suppress violence; and the life and property of each shall be under the guarantee and protection of all, and all shall enjoy the blessings of nature."

Conventions were thus formed in society, sometimes express, sometimes tacit, which became the rule of the actions of individuals, the measure of their rights, the law of their reciprocal relations ; and persons were appointed to superintend their observance, and to these the people confided the balance of rights, and the sword to punish transgressions.

Then was established among individuals a happy equilibrium of force and action, which constituted the common security. The name of equity and of justice was recognised and revered over the earth ; every man, assured of enjoying in peace the fruits of his toil, exerted all the energies of his soul ; and industry, excited and maintained by the reality or the hope of enjoyment, developed all the treasures of nature and of art; the fields were covered with harvests, the valleys with flocks, the hills with fruits, the sea with vessels, and man was happy and powerful upon the earth.

Thus did his own wisdom repair the disorder which his imprudence had occasioned ; and that wisdom was only the effect of his own organization. It was to secure his own enjoyments that he respected those of others; and cupidity found its corrective in an enlightened self-love.

Thus the love of self, the moving principle of every individual, became the necessary basis of every association ; and on the observance of this natural law depended the fate of nations. Have the factitious and conventional laws tended to that object and accomplished its aim? Every man, impelled by a powerful instinct, has displayed all the faculties of his being; and the sum of individual felicities has constituted the general felicity. Have these laws on the contrary impeded the effort of man towards his happiness? His heart deprived of its exciting principle, has languished in inaction, and from the discouragement of the individual has proceeded the weakness of the state.

As self-love, impetuous and improvident, is ever urging man against his equal, and consequently tends to dissolve society, the art of legislation and the merit of administrators consists in attempering the conflict of individual cupidities, in maintaining an equilibrium of powers, and securing to every one his happiness, in order that, in the shock of society against society, all the members may have a common interest in the preservation and defence of the public weal.

Therefore the internal splendor and prosperity of empires, were owing to the equity of their laws and government; and their relative external powers have been in proportion to the number of individuals interested, and to the degree of their interest in the public weal.

On the other hand, the multiplication of men, by complicating their relations, having rendered the precise limitation of their rights difficult; the perpetual play of their passions having produced unforeseen incidents; their conventions having been vicious, inadequate or nugatory; in fine, the authors of the laws having sometimes mistaken, sometimes disguised their object, and their ministers, instead of restraining the cupidity of others, having been hurried away by their own; all those causes have introduced disorder and trouble into societies; and vicious laws and unjust governments, the result of cupidity and ignorance, have caused the misfortunes of nations, and the subversion of States.

CHAPTER X.

GENERAL CAUSES OF THE PROSPERITY OF ANCIENT STATES.

SUCH, O youth who seekest wisdom, have been the causes of revolution in the ancient States of which thou contemplatest the ruins! To whatever spot I direct my view, to whatever period my thoughts recur, the same principles of growth or destruction, of rise or fall, present themselves to my mind. Wherever a people is powerful, or an empire prosperous, there the conventional laws are conformable with the laws of nature: the government there procures for its citizens a free use of their faculties, equal security for their persons and property. If, on the contrary, an empire goes to ruin, or dissolves, it is because its laws have been vicious, or imperfect, or trodden under foot by a corrupt government. If the laws and government, at first wise and just, degenerate afterwards, it is because the alternation of good and evil derives from the nature of the heart of man, the succession of his propensities, his progress in knowledge, and the combination of circumstances and events, as is proved by the history of the human species.

In the infancy of nations, when men yet lived in the forest, subject to the same wants, endowed with the same faculties, all were nearly equal in strength; and that equality was a circumstance highly advantageous in the composition of society; every individual thus finding himself sufficiently independent of every other, no one was the slave, and no one thought of being the master of another. Untaught man knew neither servitude nor tyranny; furnished with resources sufficient for his existence, he thought not of borrowing from others. Owing nothing, exacting nothing, he judged the rights of others by his own, and acquired precise notions of justice; ignorant, moreover, in the art of enjoyments, unable to produce more than his necessaries, possessing nothing superfluous, cupidity lay dormant; or if excited, man, attacked in his real wants, resisted it with energy, and the very foresight of such resistance maintained a salutary equilibrium.

Thus original equality, without a compact, secured personal liberty, respect for property, morality and good order. Every man labored by himself and for himself; and his heart being occupied, wandered not to culpable desires : his enjoyments were few but his wants were satisfied ; and as indulgent nature had made them less than his resources, the labor of his hands soon produced abundance ; abundance population : the arts developed themselves, cultivation extended, and the earth, covered with numerous inhabitants, was divided into different domains.

The relations of men becoming complicated, the internal order of societies was more difficult to maintain. Time and industry having created affluence, cupidity became more vigilant, and because equality, practicable among individuals, could not subsist among families, the natural equilibrium was broken : it became necessary to substitute a factitious equilibrium in its place ; to appoint rulers, to establish laws ; and in the primitive inexperience, it necessarily happened that these laws, occasioned by cupidity, assumed its character ; but different circumstances concurred to correct the disorder, and impose on governments the necessity of being just.

States, in fact, being weak at first, and having foreign enemies to fear, the chiefs found it their interest, not to oppress their subjects ; for, by lessening the confidence of the citizens in their government, they would diminish their means of resistance ; they would facilitate foreign invasion, and, for superfluous enjoyments, endanger their very existence.

In the interior, the character of the people was repugnant to tyranny ; men had contracted too long habits of independence ; they had too few wants, and too great a consciousness of their own strength.

States being of small extent, it was difficult to divide their citizens so as to oppress some by means of others : their communications were too easy, and their interests too simple and evident. Besides, every man being at once proprietor and cultivator, no one was induced to sell himself, and the despot could find no mercenaries.

If dissensions arose, they were between family and family, faction and faction, and they interested a great number; the troubles indeed were warmer, but fears from abroad pacified discord : if the oppression of a party prevailed, the earth being still unoccupied, and man, still in a state of simplicity, finding everywhere the same advantages, the injured party emigrated, and carried elsewhere their independence.

The ancient States then enjoyed within themselves numerous means of prosperity and power : every man finding his own well-being in

the constitution of his country, took a lively interest in its preservation ; if a stranger attacked it, having to defend his field, his house,
he carried into combat all the animosity of a personal quarrel, and
devoted to his own interests, he was devoted to his country.

As every action useful to the public, attracted its esteem and gratitude, every one was eager to be useful, and self-love multiplied talents and civic virtues.

Every citizen contributing equally by his goods and his person,
armies and funds were inexhaustible, and nations displayed formidable masses of power.

The earth being free, and its possession secure and easy, every
man was a proprietor ; and the division of property preserved morals, and rendered luxury impossible.

Every one cultivating for himself, culture was more active, produce more abundant, and individual opulence constituted public
wealth.

The abundance of produce rendering subsis ence easy, population
was rapid and numerous, and States attained quickly the term of
their plenitude.

Productions increasing beyond consumption, the necessity of commerce was felt, and exchanges to k place between people and people, which augmented their activity and reciprocal advantages.

In fine, certain countries, at certain times, uniting the advantages
of good government with a position on the route of the most active
circulation, they became emporiums of flourishing commerce and
seats of powerful domination. And on the banks of the Nile and
Mediterranean, of the Tygris and Euphrates, the accumulated riches
of India and of Europe raised in successive splendor a hundred me-
tropolises.

The people, growing rich, applied their superfluity to works of
common and public use ; and this was, in every State, the epoch of
those works, whose grandeur astonishes the mind ; of those wells of
Tyre, of those dykes of the Euphrates, of those subterranean conduits
of Media,* of those fortresses of the desert, of those aqueducts of
Palmyra, of those temples, those porticos.—And such labors might
be immense, without oppressing the nations, because they were the
effect of an equal and common contribution of the force of men animated and free.

* See respecting these facts my Travels into Syria, v. II, and New
Researches on ancient history, v. III

Thus ancient States prospered, because their social institutions were conformable to the true laws of nature, and because men enjoying liberty and security for their persons and their property, could display all the extent of their faculties, all the energies of their self-love.

CHAPTER XI.

GENERAL CAUSES OF THE REVOLUTIONS AND RUIN OF ANCIENT STATES.

CUPIDITY had nevertheless excited among men a constant and universal conflict, which incessantly prompting individuals and societies to reciprocal invasions, occasioned successive revolutions, and returning agitations.

And first, in the savage and barbarous state of the first men, this inordinate and audacious cupidity produced rapine, violence, assassination ; and retarded for a long time, the progress of civilisation.

When afterwards societies began to be formed, the effect of bad habits, communicated to laws and governments, corrupted their institutions and objects, and established arbitrary and factitious rights; which depraved the ideas of justice, and the morality of the people.

Thus one man being stronger than another, their inequality, an accident of nature, was taken for her law ;* and the strong having spared the weak whose life was in his power, arrogated over his person an abusive right of property, and the slavery of individuals prepared the way for the slavery of nations.

Because the head of a family could exercise an absolute authority in his own house, he made his affections and desires the sole rule of

---

* " Thus, one man being stronger than another, their inequality, an accident of nature, was taken for her law." Almost all the ancient philosophers and politicians have laid it down as a principle that men are born unequal ; that nature has created some to be free and others to be slaves. These are the positive expressions of Aristotle in his Politics ; and of Plato, called the divine, doubtless in the same sense as the mythological reveries which he promulgated. With all the people of antiquity, the Gauls, the Romans, the Athenians, the right of the strongest was the right of nations ; and from the same principle are derived all political disorders and public national crimes.

his conduct : he gave or resumed his goods without equality, without
iustice, and paternal despotism laid the foundation of despotism in
government.* And in societies formed on such foundations, when
time and labor had developed riches, cupidity, restrained by the laws,
became more artful, but not less active. Under the mask of union
and civil peace, it fomented, in the bosom of every State, an intestine war, in which the citizens, divided into contending corps of
professions, classes and families, unremittingly struggled to appropriate to themselves, under the name of supreme power, the ability of
plundering everything and rendering everything subservient to the
dictates of their passions ; and this spirit of encroachment, disguised
under all possible forms, but always the same in its object and motives, has been the perpetual scourge of nations.

Sometimes opposing the social compact, or infringing that which
already existed, it committed the inhabitants of a country to the tumultuous shock of all their discords ; and States thus dissolved, and
reduced to the condition of anarchy, were tormented by the passions
of all their members.

Sometimes a nation, jealous of its liberty, having appointed agents
to administer, these agents assumed to themselves the powers of
which they were only the guardians : and employed the public treasures in corrupting elections, gaining partisans, and dividing the people against itself. By these means, from being temporary they
became perpetual ; from elective, hereditary : and the State agitated
by the intrigues of the ambitious, by largesses from the rich and fac-
tious, by the venality of the indolent poor, by the empiricism of ora-
tors, by the boldness of perversity, and the weakness of the virtuous,
was convulsed with all the inconveniences of democracy.

In some countries, the chiefs, equal in strength and mutually fearing
each other, formed impious pacts, nefarious associations : and portioning out power, rank and honors, arrogated to themselves privileges and immunities : erected themselves into separate orders and

* " And paternal despotism laid the foundation of despotism in government."—What is a family ? an elementary portion of that great body
called nation The spirit of this great body is but the sum of its frac
tions; as the manners of the family are, so are the manners of the whole.
The great vices of Asia are, 1, paternal despotism ; 2, polygamy, which
demoralizes the entire family, and which, among kings and princes,
causes the massacre of the brothers at each succession, and ruins the
people in appanages ; 3, the want of landed property, owing to the tyrannical right usurped by the despot ; 4, the unequal portioning of children ; 5, the abusive right of legacies and 6, the exclusion of women
from the inheritance. Change these laws, and you change Asia

distinct classes; united in enslaving the people; and under the name of aristocracy, the State was tormented by the passions of the wealthy and the great.

In other countries, tending by other means to the same object, sacred impostors have taken advantage of the credulity of the ignorant. In the gloom of their temples, behind the curtain of the altar, they made their gods act and speak, delivered oracles, worked miracles, ordered sacrifices, levied offerings, prescribed endowments, and, under the names of theocracy and religion, the States were tormented by the passions of the priests.

Sometimes a nation, weary of its dissensions or of its tyrants, to lessen the sources of evil, submitted to a single master : but, if it limited his powers, his sole aim was to enlarge them : if it left them indefinite, he abused the trust confided to him ; and, under the name of monarchy, the State was tormented by the passions of kings, and princes.

Then the factions, availing themselves of the general discontent, flattered the people with the hope of a better master, dealt out gifts and promises, deposed the despot to take his place ; and their contests for the succession, or its partition, tormented the State with the disorders and devastations of civil war.

In fine, among these rivals, one more artful or more fortunate, gained the ascendency, and concentrated all power within himself : by a strange phenomenon, a single individual mastered millions of his equals against their will or without their consent, and the art of tyranny was also the offspring of cupidity. In fact, observing the spirit of egotism which incessantly divides mankind, the ambitious man fomented it with dexterity ; flattered the vanity of one, excited the jealousy of another, favored the avarice of this, inflamed the resentment of that, and irritated the passions of all, then, placing in opposition their interests and prejudices, he sowed divisions and hatreds, promised to the poor the spoils of the rich, to the rich the subjection of the poor, threatened one man by another, this class by that ; and insulating all by distrust, created his strength by their weakness, and imposed the yoke of opinion, which they mutually rivetted on each other. With the army he levied contributions, and with contributions he disposed of the army ; lavishing wealth and office on these principles, he enchained a whole people in indissoluble bonds, and they languished under the slow consumption of despotism.

Thus did a same principle, varying its action under every possible form, unremittingly attenuate the consistence of States, and an eternal circle of vicissitudes flowed from an eternal circle of passions.

And this constant spirit of egotism and usurpation produced two principal effects equally destructive : the one, a division and subdivision of societies into their smallest fractions, inducing a debility which facilitated their dissolution ; the other, a persevering tendency to concentrate power in a single hand,* which, by a successive absorption of societies and States, was fatal to their peace and social existence.

Thus, as in a State, a party absorbed the nation, a family the party, and an individual the family ; so a movement of absorption took place between State and State, and exhibited on a larger scale in the political order, all the particular evils of the civil order. Thus a state having subdued a state, held it in subjection in the form of a province ; and two provinces, one of which had swallowed up the other, formed a kingdom : finally, two kingdoms being united by conquest, gave birth to empires of gigantic size ; and in this conglomeration, the internal strength of States, instead of increasing, diminished ; and the condition of the people, instead of ameliorating, became daily more irksome and wretched, from causes constantly derived from the nature of things.

Because, in proportion as States increased in extent, their administration becoming more difficult and complicated, greater energies of power were necessary to move such masses, and there was no longer any proportion between the duties of sovereigns and their ability to perform their duties :

Because despots, feeling their weakness, feared whatever might develope the strength of nations, and studied only how to enfeeble them :

Because nations, divided by the prejudices of ignorance and hatred, seconded by the perversity of governments ; and availing themselves reciprocally of satellites, aggravated their mutual slavery :

---

* " The other, a persevering tendency to concentrate power in a single hand."—It is remarkable that this has in all instances been the constant progress of societies ; beginning with a state of anarchy or democracy, that is with a great division of power, they have passed to aristocracy, and from aristocracy to monarchy ; does it not follow from this historical fact that those who constitute States under the democratic form, destine them to undergo all the intervening troubles between that and monarchy : but it should at the same time be proved that social experience is already exhausted for the human race, and that this spontaneous movement is not solely the effect of ignorance

Because, the balance between States being destroyed, the strong more easily oppressed the weak :

Finally, because in proportion as States were concentrated, the people, despoiled of their laws, of their usages, and of the governments that suited them best, lost that spirit of personal identification with the government which gave them energy.

And despots, considering empires as their private domains, and the people as their property, abandoned themselves to depredations and to all the licentiousness of the most arbitrary authority.

And all the strength and wealth of nations were diverted to private expense and personal caprice ; and kings, fatigued with gratification, launched into all the extravagances of a factitious and depraved taste ; they must have gardens erected upon arcades, rivers raised over mountains, fertile fields converted into haunts for wild beasts, lakes scooped in dry lands, rocks elevated in lakes, palaces built of marble and porphyry, furniture of gold and diamonds. Under the cloak of religion, their pride founded temples, endowed indolent priests, built, for vain skeletons, extravagant tombs, mausoleums and pyramids ; * millions of hands were employed in sterile labors ; and the luxury of princes, imitated by their parasites, and descending step by step to the lowest ranks, became a general source of corruption and impoverishment.

And, in the insatiable thirst of enjoyment, the ordinary revenues no longer sufficing, they were augmented ; the cultivator seeing his labors increase without retribution, was disheartened ; the merchant despoiled, was disgusted with industry ; the multitude condemned to

* " Extravagant tombs, mausoleums and pyramids."—The learned Dupuis could not be persuaded that the pyramids were tombs ; but besides the positive testimony of historians, read what Diodorus says of the religious and superstitious importance every Egyptian attached to building his eternal dwelling, b. 1.

During twenty years, says Herodotus, a hundred thousand men labored every day to build the pyramid of the Egyptian king Cheops.—Supposing only three hundred days a year, on account of the sabbath, there will be 30 millions of dayswork in a year, and 600 millions in twenty years ; at 15 sous a day, this makes 450 millions of franks lost without any further benefit.—With this sum, if the king had shut the isthmus of Suez by a strong wall, like that of China, the destinies of Egypt might have been entirely changed. Foreign invasions would have been stopped, prevented, and the Arabs of the desert would have neither have conquered nor harassed that country.—Sterile labors ! how many millions lost in putting one stone upon another, under the form of temples and churches ! Alchymists convert stones into gold ; but architects change gold into stone. Wo to the kings (as well as subjects) who trust their purse to these two classes of empirics !

eternal poverty, restrained their labor to simple necessaries, and all productive activity vanished.

The surcharge of taxes rendering lands a burdensome possession, the poor proprietor abandoned his field, or sold it to the powerful; and fortune became concentrated in a few hands. All the laws and institutions favoring this accumulation, the nation became divided into a group of indolent rich, and a multitude of mercenary poor. The people were degraded with indigence, the great depraved with satiety, and the number of those interested in the preservation of the State decreasing, its strength and existence became proportionably precarious.

On the other hand, emulation finding no object, science no encouragement, the mind sunk into profound ignorance.

The administration being secret and mysterious, there existed no means of reform or amelioration; the chiefs governing by force or fraud, the people viewed them as a faction of public enemies, and all harmony ceased between the governors and governed.

All these vices having enervated the States of opulent Asia, the vagrant and indigent inhabitants of the adjacent deserts and mountains coveted the enjoyments of the fertile plains; and, urged by a cupidity common to all, attacked the polished empires, and overturned the thrones of their despots; and these revolutions were rapid and easy, because the policy of tyrants had enervated the subjects, razed the fortresses, destroyed the warriors; and because the oppressed subjects remained without personal interest, and the mercenary soldiers without courage.

And hordes of barbarians having reduced entire nations to slavery, the empires formed of conquerors and conquered, united in their bosom two classes essentially opposite and hostile. All the principles of society were dissolved; there was no longer any common interest, any public spirit; and there arose a distinction of casts and races, which reduced into a regular system the maintenance of disorder; and according as a man was born of this or that blood, he was born a slave or a tyrant, property or proprietor.

The oppressors being less numerous than the oppressed, it was necessary to perfect the science of oppression, in order to support this false equilibrium. The art of governing became the art of subjecting the many to the few. To enforce an obedience so contrary to instinct, the severest punishments were established; and the cruelty of the laws rendered manners atrocious. The distinction of persons estabishing in the State two codes, two orders of justice, two sets of laws; the people, placed between the propensities of the heart, and the oath uttered from the mouth, had two consciences in contradiction with each other; and the ideas of justice and injustice had no longer any foundation in the understanding.

Under such a system, the people fell into dejection and despair. And the accidents of nature being added to the other evils which assailed them, in the despondency caused by so many calamities, they attributed their causes to superior and hidden powers; and because they saw tyrants on earth, they fancied others in heaven; and superstition aggravated the misfortunes of nations.

Hence originated fatal doctrines, gloomy and misanthropic systems of religion, which painted the gods malignant and envious, like their despots. Man, to appease them, offered up the sacrifice of all his enjoyments: he environed himself in privations, and reversed the laws of nature. Conceiving his pleasures to be crimes, his sufferings expiations, he endeavoured to love pain, and to abjure the love of self; he persecuted his senses, hated his life; and a self-denying and anti-social morality plunged nations into the apathy of death.

But provident nature having endowed the heart of man with inexhaustible hope, when he found his desires of happiness all baffled on this earth, he pursued it into another world: by a sweet illusion he created for himself another country, an asylum where, far from tyrants, he should recover the rights of his nature; and thence resulted new disorders: smitten with an imaginary world, man despised that of nature: for chimerical hopes, he neglected the reality. His life began to appear a toilsome journey, a painful dream; his body a prison, the obstacle to his felicity; and the earth, a place of exile and of pilgrimage, not worthy of culture. Then a holy indolence spread over the political world; the fields were deserted, empires depopulated, monuments neglected and deserts multiplied; ignorance, superstition and fanaticism combining their operations, overwhelmed the earth with devastation and ruin.

Thus agitated by their own passions, men, whether collectively or individually taken, always greedy and improvident, passing from slavery to tyranny, from pride to servility, from presumption to despondency, have made themselves the perpetual instruments of their own misfortunes.

These then are the principles, simple and natural, which regulated the destiny of ancient States; by this regular and connected series of causes and effects, they rose or fell, in proportion as the physical laws of the human heart were respected or violated; and in the course of their successive changes, a hundred different nations, a hundred empires, by turns humbled, elevated, conquered, overthrown, have repeated for the earth their instructive lessons.—Yet these lessons were lost for the generations which have followed ! The disorders of times past have reappeared in the present age ! The chiefs of the nations have continued to walk in the paths of falsehood and tyranny ! the people to wander in the darkness of superstition and ignorance !

Since then, continued the Genius, with new collected energy, since the experience of past ages is lost for the living, since the errors of progenitors have not instructed their descendants, the ancient examples are about to reappear; the earth will see renewed the tremendous scenes it has forgotten. New revolutions will agitate nations and empires; powerful thrones will be again overturned, and terrible catastrophes will teach mankind that the laws of nature and the precepts of wisdom and truth can never be infringed with impunity.

CHAPTER XII.

LESSONS OF TIMES PAST REPEATED ON THE PRESENT

THUS spoke the Genius : struck with the justice and coherence of his discourse, assailed with a crowd of ideas, repugnant to my habits, yet convincing to my reason, I remained absorbed in profound silence.—At length, while with serious and pensive mien, I kept my eyes fixed on Asia, suddenly in the north, on the shores of the Black sea and in the fields of the Krimea clouds of smoke and flame attracted my attention : they appeared to rise at the same time from all parts of the peninsula ; and passing by the isthmus into the continent, they ran, as if driven by a westerly wind, along the muddy lake of Azof, and disappeared in the grassy plains of Kouban ; and following more attentively the course of these clouds, I observed that they were preceded or followed by swarms of moving creatures, which, like ants or grasshoppers disturbed by the foot of a passenger, agitated themselves with vivacity : sometimes these swarms appeared to advance and rush against each other ; and numbers, after the concussion, remained motionless.—While disquieted at this spectacle, I strained my sight to distinguish the objects :—Do you see, said the Genius, those flames which spread over the earth, and do you comprehend their causes and effects ?—O Genius, I answered, I see those columns of flame and smoke, and something like insects accompanying them ; but when I can scarcely discern the great masses of cities and monuments, how should I discover such little creatures ? only it should seem that these insects mimic battles, for they advance, retreat, attack and pursue.—It is no mockery, said the Genius, these are real battles.—And what mad animalcules, said I, are those which destroy each other ? beings of a day ! will they not perish soon enough ?—Then the Genius, again touching my sight and hearing, Look, said he, and hear.—Immediately directing my sight towards the same objects : Ah ! wretches, cried I, oppressed with grief, these columns of flame ! these insects ! O Genius, they are men, these are the ravages of war !—These torrents of flame rise from towns and villages ! I see the squadrons who kindle them, and who sword in hand overrun the country; they drive before them crowds of old men, women, and children, fugitive and desolate : I perceive other horsemen, who with shouldered lances, accompany and guide them. I even recognise them to be Tartars by their led horses, their kalpaks, and tufts of hair : and doubtless they who pursue, in triangular hats and green uniforms, are Muscovites—Ah ! I now comprehend, a war is kindled between the empire of the tsars and that of the sultans. " Not yet," replied the Genius : " this is only a preliminary. These Tartars have been, and might still be troublesome neighbours. The Muscovites are driving them off, finding their country would be a convenient extension of their own limits ; and as a prelude to another revolution, the throne of the Guerais is destroyed."

And in fact, I saw the Russian standards floating over the Krimea : and soon after their flag waving on the Euxine.

Meanwhile, at the cry of the flying Tartars, the mussulman empire was in commotion. " They are driving off our brethren," cried the children of Mahomet : " the people of the prophet are outraged ! infidels occupy a consecrated land, and profane the temples of Islamism. Let us arm ; let us rush to combat, to avenge the glory of God and our own cause."

And a general movement of war took place in both empires
Armed men, provisions, stores, and all the murderous apparatus of
battle were everywhere assembled; and the temples of both nations,
besieged by an immense multitude, presented a spectacle which fixed
all my attention. On one side, the Mussulmen assembled before
their mosques, washed their hands and feet, pared their nails, and
combed their beards : then spreading carpets upon the ground, and
turning towards the south, with their arms sometimes crossed and
sometimes extended, they made genuflexions and prostrations, and
recollecting the disasters of the late war, they exclaimed : " God of
mercy and clemency ! hast thou then abandoned thy faithful people ?
Thou who hast promised to thy Prophet the empire over nations, and
stamped his religion by so many triumphs, dost thou deliver thy true
believers to the swords of infidels?" And the Imams and the Santons
said to the people : " It is in chastisement of your sins. You eat
pork, you drink wine ; you touch unclean things : God hath punished
you. Do penance therefore, purify, repeat the profession of faith :*
fast from the rising to the setting sun, give the tenth of your goods to
the mosques : go to Mecca : and God will render you victorious."
And the people, recovering courage, uttered loud cries : There is but
one God, said they transported with fury, and Mahomet is his prophet : cursed be the man who believeth not !

" God of mercy, grant us to exterminate these Christians : it is
for thy glory we fight, and our death is a martyrdom for thy name."—
And then, offering victims, they prepared for battle.

On the other side, the Russians, kneeling, said : " Render thanks to
God, and celebrate his power; he hath strengthened our arm to humble
his enemies. Hear our prayers, O merciful God : to please thee, we
will pass three days without eating either meat or eggs. Grant us to
exterminate these impious Mahometans, and to overturn their empire:
to thee we will consecrate the tenth of our spoils ; to thee we will
raise new temples." And the priests filled the churches with a cloud
of smoke, and said to the people :   " We pray for you ; God accept-
eth our incense, and blesseth our arms. Continue to fast and to fight ;
confess to us your secret crimes ; give your wealth to the Church :
we will absolve you from your sins, and you shall die in a state of
grace." And they sprinkled water upon the people, distributed
among them, as amulets and charms, small relics of the dead ; and the
people breathed nothing but war and slaughter.

* There is but one God, and Mahomet is his prophet.

Struck with this contrasting picture of the same passions, and lamenting their baneful consequences, I was considering how difficult it would be for the common judge to comply with such contradictory demands, when the Genius, inflamed with anger, indignantly exclaimed :

" What accents of madness strike my ear: what blind and perverse delirium disorders the spirits of the nations ? Sacrilegious prayers, rise not from the earth ! and you, oh Heavens, reject their homicide vows and impious thanksgivings ! Deluded mortals ! is it thus you revere the Divinity ? Say, how should he, whom you call your common father, receive the homage of his children murdering one another ? Ye victors ! with what eye should he view your hands reeking in the blood he has created ? And what do you expect, oh vanquished, from unavailing groans ? Hath God the heart of a mortal, with passions ever changing ? Is he, like you, agitated with vengeance or compassion, with wrath or repentance ? What base conception of the most sublime of beings ! According to them, it would seem that God, whimsical and capricious, is irritated or appeased as a man ; that he loves and hates alternately ; that he punishes or favors ; that, weak or wicked, he broods over his hatred ; that contradictory or perfidious ne lays snares to entrap ; that he punishes the evils he permits : that he foresees but hinders not crimes ; that, like a corrupt judge, he is bribed by offerings ; like an ignorant despot, he makes laws and revokes them ; that, like a savage tyrant, he grants or resumes favors without reason, and can only be appeased by servility. . . . . Ah ! now I know the lying spirit of man ! Contemplating the picture he hath drawn of the Divinity, No, said I, it is not God who hath made man, but man who hath made God after his own image ; he hath given him his own mind, clothed him with his own propensities, ascribed to him his own judgments. . . . . And when in this medley he finds the contradiction of his own principles, affecting hypocritical humility, he imputes weakness to his reason, and names the absurdities of his own mind mysteries of God.

" He hath said : God is immutable, yet he offers prayers to change him. He hath pronounced him incomprehensible, yet he is never without interpreters.

" Impostors have arisen on the earth who have called themselves the confidants of God, and who, erecting themselves into teachers of the people, have opened the ways of falsehood and iniquity : they have ascribed merit to practices indifferent or ridiculous ; they have supposed a virtue in certain postures, in pronouncing certain words, articulating certain names : they have transformed into a crime the eating of certain meats, the drinking of certain liquors, on one day rather than on another. The Jew would rather die than labor on the sabbath : the Persian would endure suffocation, before he would blow the fire with his breath ; the Indian places supreme perfection in besmearing himself with cow dung, and pronouncing mysteriously Aum ;* the Mussulman believes he has expiated everything in washing his head and arms ; and disputes, sword in hand, whether the ablution should commence at the elbow or finger ends ;† the Christian would think himself damned, were he to eat flesh instead of milk or butter. Oh sublime doctrines ! Doctrines truly from heaven ! Oh perfect morals, and worthy of martyrdom or the apostolate ! I will cross the seas to teach these admirable laws to the savage people, to distant nations ; I will say unto them, Children of nature, how long will you walk in the paths of ignorance ? how long will you mistake the true principles of morality and religion ? Come and learn its lessons from nations truly pious and learned, in civilized countries : they will inform you, how, to gratify God, you must in certain months of the year, languish the whole day with hunger and thirst ; how you may shed your neighbour's blood, and purify yourself from it by professions of faith and methodical ablutions ; how you may steal his property and be absolved on sharing it with certain persons, who devote themselves to its consumption.

"Sovereign and invisible power of the Universe ! mysterious mover of nature ! universal soul of beings ! thou who art unknown, yet revered by mortals under so many names ; being incomprehensible and infinite ; God, who in the immensity of the heavens, directest the movement of worlds, and peoplest the abyss of space with millions of suns ; say, what do these human insects which my sight no longer

---

* " Pronouncing mysteriously Aum."—This word, in signification, and nearly in sound, resembles the Aeuum (ævum) of the Latins, eternity, unbounded time. According to the Indians, this word is the emblem of the tripartite divinity ; A denotes Biamah (the time past that created) U Vichenou (the time present that preserves,) M, Chiven (the time future that shall destroy.)

† " Should commence at the elbow."—This is one of the grand points of schism between the partisans of Omar and those of Ali. Suppose two Mahometans to meet on a journey and to accost each other with brotherly affection ; the hour of prayer arrives, one begins his ablution at his fingers, the other at the elbow ; and instantly they are mortal enemies In other countries, if a man eats meat on one day rather than on another, a cry of indignation will be raised against him   By what name are we to call such fools !

discerns on the earth, appear in thy eye? To thee who art guiding stars in their orbits, what are those wormlings writhing themselves in the dust? Of what import to thy immensity, their distinctions of parties and sects? And, of what concern the subtleties with which their folly torments itself?

"And you, credulous men, show me the effect of your practices! In so many centuries, during which you have been following or altering them, what changes have your prescriptions wrought in the laws of nature? Is the sun brighter? is the course of the seasons varied? Is the earth more fruitful or its inhabitants more happy? If God is good, can your penances please him? If infinite, can your homage add to his glory? If his decrees have been formed on foresight of every circumstance, can your prayers change them? Answer, inconsistent men!

"Ye conquerors of the earth, who pretend you serve God, doth he need your aid? If he wishes to punish, hath he not earth-quakes, volcanoes, and thunder at command? and cannot a merciful God correct without extermination?

"Ye Mussulmen, if God chastiseth you for violating the five precepts, how hath he raised up the Franks who ridicule them? If he governeth the earth by the Coran, on what principles did he judge before the days of the prophet, so many nations who drank wine, eat pork, went not to Mecca, and whom he nevertheless permitted to raise powerful empires? How did he judge the Sabeans of Nineveh and of Babylon; the Persian, worshipper of fire; the Greek and Roman idolaters; the ancient kingdoms of the Nile, and your own ancestors the Arabians and Tartars? How doth he yet judge so many nations who deny, or know not your worship? The numerous casts of Indians, the vast empire of the Chinese, the sable race of Africa, the islanders of the Ocean, the tribes of America?

"Presumptuous and ignorant men, who arrogate the earth to yourselves! if God were to unite together all the generations past and present, what would be, in their Ocean, the sects, calling themselves universal, of Christians and Mussulmen? What would be the judgments of his equal and common justice over the real universality of mankind? Therein it is that your knowledge loseth itself in incoherent systems; it is there that truth shines with evidence; and there are manifested the powerful and simple laws of nature and reason: laws of a common and general mover; of an impartial and just God, who sheds rain on a country, without asking who is its

crophet; who causeth his sun to shine alike on all the races of men,
on the white as or the black, on the Jew, the Mussulman, the Christian and the Idolater; who reareth the harvest wherever cultivated
with care; who prospereth every empire where justice is practised,
where the powerful man is restrained, and the poor protected by the
laws; where the weak live in safety, and every one enjoys the rights
given him by nature and a compact formed in justice.

"These are the principles by which people are judged! this is
the true religion which regulates the destiny of empires, and which,
O Ottomans, has governed yours! Interrogate your ancestors, ask
of them by what means they rose to greatness, when few, poor, and
idolaters, they came from the deserts of Tartary and encamped in
these fertile countries; ask if it was by Islamism, till then unknown
to them, that they conquered the Greeks and the Arabs; or, by
their courage, their prudence, moderation, spirit of union, the true
powers of the social state. Then the Sultan himself dispensed justice, and maintained discipline; the prevaricating judge, the extortionate governor were punished, and the multitude lived at ease; the
cultivator was protected from the rapine of the janissary, and the
fields prospered; the high roads were safe, and commerce produced
abundance. You were a band of plunderers, but just among yourselves; you subdued nations, but did not oppress them. Harassed
by their own princes, they preferred being your tributaries. What
matters it, said the Christian, whether my master breaks or adores
images, if he renders justice to me? God will judge his doctrine in
heaven.

"You were sober and hardy; your enemies timid and effeminate;
you were expert in battle, your enemies unskilful; your leaders experienced, your soldiers warlike, and obedient; booty excited ardor,
bravery was rewarded; cowardice and indiscipline punished; and
all the springs of the human heart were in action: thus you vanquished a hundred nations, and of a mass of conquered kingdoms
compounded an immense empire.

"But other manners have succeeded; and in the reverses attending them, the laws of nature have still exerted their force. After
devouring your enemies, your cupidity, always insatiable, has reacted
on itself, and, concentrated in your own bowels, has consumed you.
Having become rich, you have quarrelled for partition and enjoyment; and disorder arose in every class of society. The Sultan, intoxicated with grandeur, has mistaken the object of his functions;

and all the vices of arbitrary power have been developed. Meeting no obstacle to his appetites, he has become a depraved being; weak and arrogant, he has kept the people aloof, and the voice of the people has no longer instructed and guided him. Ignorant, yet flattered, neglecting all instruction, all study, he has fallen into imbecility; unfit for business, he has thrown its burden on hirelings, and these have deceived him. To gratify their own passions, they have stimulated and nourished his; they have multiplied his wants; and his enormous luxury has consumed everything; the frugal table, plain cloathing, and simple dwelling of his ancestors no longer sufficed; to supply his pomp, earth and sea were exhausted; the rarest furs were brought from the poles; the most costly tissues from the equator; he has devoured at a meal the tribute of a city, and expended in a day the revenue of a province. He is surrounded with an army of women, eunuchs, and satellites. They tell him that liberality and munificence are the virtues of kings, and the treasures of the people have been delivered into the hands of flatterers; in imitation of their master, his servants also must have splendid houses, the most exquisite furniture, carpets embroidered at great cost, vases of gold and silver for the vilest purposes, and all the riches of the empire have been swallowed up in the Serai.

"To supply this inordinate luxury, the slaves and women have sold their influence, and venality has introduced a general depravation; the favor of the sovereign has been sold to the vizier, and the vizier has sold the empire. The law has been sold to the cadi, and the cadi has made sale of justice. The altar has been sold to the priest, and the priest has sold the kingdom of heaven; and gold obtaining everything, they sacrificed everything to obtain gold; for gold, the friend betrayed his friend; the child, his parent; the servant, his master; the wife, her honor : the merchant, his conscience; and good faith, morals, concord and strength were banished from the State.

"The Pacha, who purchased the government of his province, considered it as his farm, and practised in it every species of extortion. He sold in turn the collection of the taxes, the command of the troops, the administration of the villages, and as every employ has been transient, rapine spread from rank to rank, has been greedy and precipitate. The revenue officer has fleeced the merchant, and commerce was annihilated; the aga has plundered the husbandman, and culture declined. The laborer, deprived of his stock, has been unable to sow; when the tax-gatherer came he was unable to pay; threatened with the bastonado he was forced to borrow; money, from want of security, being locked up from circulation, bore an enormous interest, and the usury of the rich has aggravated the misery of the laborer.

" When excessive droughts and accidents of seasons have blasted the harvest, the government admitted no delay, no indulgence for the tax : and distress bearing hard on the village, a part of its inhabitants have taken refuge in the cities; and their burdens falling on those who remained, has completed their ruin, and depopulated the country.

" If driven to extremity by tyranny and outrage, the villages have revolted, the Pacha rejoices : he wages war on them, assails their houses, pillages their property, carries off their stock ; and when the fields have become a desert, What care I, says he, I go away to-morrow.

" The earth wanting laborers, the rains of heaven and overflowings of torrents have stagnated in marshes, and their putrid exhalations, in a warm climate, have caused epidemics, plagues, and diseases of all sorts; from whence have flowed additional depopulation, penury and ruin.

" Oh, who can enumerate all the calamities of tyrannical government !

" Sometimes the Pachas make war on each other, and for their personal quarrels, the provinces of the same State are laid waste. Sometimes, fearing their masters, they attempt independence, and draw on their subjects the chastisement of their revolt. Sometimes, dreading their subjects, they call in and subsidize strangers, and to ensure their fidelity, set no bounds to their depredations. Here they persecute the rich and despoil them under false pretences : there they suborn false witnesses, and impose penalties for supposititious offences : everywhere they excite the hatred of parties, encourage informations to obtain amercements, extort property, seize persons : and when their shortsighted avarice has accumulated into one mass all the riches of a country, the government, under pretence of avenging the oppressed people, takes to itself by an execrable perfidy all their spoils with those of the culprit, and sheds useless blood for a crime of which it is the accomplice.

" Oh wretches, monarchs or ministers, who sport with the lives and fortunes of the people ! Is it you who gave breath to man, that you dare take it from him? do you give growth to the plants of the earth, that you may waste them? do you toil to furrow the field? do you endure the ardor of the sun, and the torments of thirst, to reap the harvest or thresh the sheaf? do you watch like the shepherd in the nocturnal dew? do you traverse deserts like the merchant? Ah! on beholding the pride and cruelty of the powerful, I was transported with indignation, and have said in my wrath: Will there never arise on the earth men who will avenge the people and punish tyrants! a handful of brigands devour the multitude, and the multitude submits to be devoured! Oh! degenerate people, know you not your rights! All authority is from you, all power is yours. In vain kings command you on the authority of God and of their lance; soldiers be still: if God supports the sultan, he needs not your aid; if his sword suffices, he wants not yours: let us see what he can do alone.—The soldiers grounded their arms; and behold these masters of the world feeble as the meanest of their subjects! People! know that those who govern are your chiefs, not your masters; your agents, not your owners; that they have no authority over you, but by you, and for you; that your wealth is yours, and they accountable for it; that, kings or subjects, God has made all men equal; and no mortal has a right to oppress his fellow creature.

" But this nation and its chiefs have mistaken these holy truths.—They must abide then the consequences of their blindness.—The decree is past; the day approaches when this colossus of power shall be crushed and crumbled under its own mass: yes, I swear by the ruins of so many empires destroyed! the empire of the crescent shall share the fate of the despotism it imitated. A nation of strangers shall drive the sultan from his metropolis; the throne of Orkhan shall be overturned, the last shoot of his trunk shall be broken off; and the horde of Oguzians,* deprived of their chief, shall disperse like that of the Nogais; in this dissolution, the people of the empire, loosened from the yoke which united them, shall resume their ancient distinctions, and a general anarchy shall follow as happened in the empire of the Sophis, until there shall arise among the Arabians, Armenians, or Greeks, legislators who may compose new States.—Oh! if there were on earth men profound and bold! what elements of grandeur and glory!—But already the hour of destiny approaches.

* " The horde of Oguzians."—Before the Turks took the name of their chief, Othman 1st. they bore that of Oguzians; and it was under this appellation that they were driven out of Tartary by Gengiz, and came from the borders of the Gihoun to settle in Anadoli.

The cry of war strikes my ear, and the catastrophe begins. In vain the sultan leads forth his armies; his ignorant warriors are beaten and dispersed: in vain he calls his subjects; their hearts are ice; it is written, say they, what matters who is our master? we cannot lose by the change. In vain the true believers invoke heaven and the prophet: the prophet is dead, and relentless heaven answers: ' Cease to invoke me; you have caused your own misfortunes, cure them yourselves. Nature has established laws, your part is to obey them; observe, reason, and profit by experience. It is the folly of man which ruins him, let his wisdom save him. The people are ignorant, let them acquire instruction; their chiefs are wicked, let them correct and amend, for such is nature's decree:' since the evils of society spring from cupidity and ignorance, men will never cease to be persecuted, till they become enlightened and wise; till they practise justice, founded on a knowledge of their relations and of the laws of their organization."

CHAPTER XIII.

WILL THE HUMAN RACE IMPROVE?

AT these words, oppressed with the painful sentiment with which their severity overwhelmed me : " Wo to the nations!" cried I, bursting into tears, " wo to myself! Ah! now it is that I despair of the happiness of man. Since his miseries proceed from his heart, since he himself must apply the remedy, wo forever to his existence! Who, indeed, will ever be able to restrain the lust of wealth in the strong and powerful! Who can enlighten the ignorance of the weak? Who can teach the multitude to know their rights, and force their chiefs to perform their duties? Thus, the race of man is always doomed to suffer! Thus, the individual will not cease to oppress the individual, a nation to attack a nation, and days of prosperity, of glory, for these regions, shall never return. Alas! conquerors will come; they will drive out the oppressors and fix themselves in their place; but, inheriting their power, they will inherit their rapacity; and the earth will have changed tyrants, but not the tyranny."

Then turning to the Genius : " O Genius ! said I, despair has sunk into my soul : knowing the nature of man, the perversity of those who govern, and the debasement of the governed, have disgusted me with life ; and since there is no choice but to be the accomplice or the victim of oppression, what remains to the man of virtue but to join his ashes to those of the tomb !''

The Genius fixing on me a look of severity mixed with compassion, replied after a few moments silence : " Does virtue then consist in dying ? The wicked man is indefatigable in consummating his crime, and the just is discouraged from doing good at the first obstacle he meets !—But such is the heart of man ; success intoxicates him with confidence, a reverse overturns and confounds him : always given up to the sensation of the moment, he never judges things by their nature, but by the impulse of passion. Mortal, who despairest of the human race, on what profound combinations of facts and of reasoning hast thou established thy conclusion ? Hast thou scrutinized the organization of sensible beings, to determine with precision whether the instinctive force which moves them on to happiness is essentially weaker than that which repels them from it ? or, embracing in one glance the history of the species, and judging the future by the past, hast thou shown that all improvement is impossible ? Say ! has human society, since its origin, made no progress towards knowledge and a better state ? Are men still in their forests, destitute of everything, ignorant, stupid, and ferocious ? Are all the nations still in that age when nothing was seen upon the globe, but brutal robbers and brutal slaves ? If at any time, in any place, individuals have ameliorated, why shall not the whole mass ameliorate ? If partial societies have improved, what shall hinder the improvement of society in general ? And if the first obstacles are overcome, why should the others be insurmountable ?

" Are you of opinion that the human race is degenerating ? Guard against the illusion and the paradoxes of the misanthrope : man dissatisfied with the present, ascribes to the past a perfection which never existed, and which only serves to cover his chagrin. He praises the dead out of hatred to the living, and beats the children with the bones of their fathers.

" To prove this pretended retrograde progress from perfection, we must contradict the testimony of reason and of fact ; and if the facts of history are in any measure uncertain, we must contradict the living fact of man's organization ; we must prove that he is born with the enlightened use of his senses; that without experience he can distinguish aliment from poison; that the child is wiser than the old man; that the blind walks with more safety than the clearsighted; that the civilized man is more miserable than the cannibal; in a word, that there is no ascending scale in experience and instruction.

"Young man, believe the voice of tombs, and the testimony of monuments: some countries have doubtless fallen from what they were at certain epochs; but if we weigh the wisdom and happiness of their inhabitants, even in those times, we shall find more of splendor than of reality in their glory; we shall find, in the most celebrated of ancient States, enormous vices and cruel abuses, the true causes of their decay; we shall find in general that the principles of government were atrocious; that insolent robberies, barbarous wars, and implacable hatreds were raging from nation to nation;* that natural right was unknown; that morality was perverted by senseless fanaticism and deplorable superstition; that a dream, a vision, an oracle were constantly the causes of vast commotions: perhaps the nations are not yet entirely cured of all these evils; but their intensity at least is diminished, and the experience of the past has not been wholly lost. For the last three centuries, especially, knowledge has increased and been extended; civilisation, favored by happy circumstances, has made a considerable progress, inconveniences and abuses have even turned to its advantage: for if States have been too much extended by conquest, the people, by uniting under the same yoke, have lost the spirit of estrangement and division which made them all enemies one to the other: if the powers of government have been more concentrated, there has been more system and harmony in their exercise: if wars have become more extensive in the mass, they are less bloody in the detail: if men have gone to battle with less personality, less energy, their struggles have been less sanguinary and less ferocious, they have been less free, but less turbulent, more effeminate but more pacific. Despotism itself has rendered them some service; for if governments have been more absolute, they have been more quiet and less tempestuous; if thrones have become a property and hereditary, they have excited less dissensions, and the people have suffered fewer convulsions; finally, if the despots, jealous and mysterious, have interdicted all knowledge of their administration, all concurrence in

* "Implacable hatreds were raging from nation to nation."—Read the history of the wars of Rome and Carthage, of Sparta and Messina, of Athens and Syracuse, of the Hebrews and the Phenicians; yet these are the nations which antiquity celebrates as being most polished!

the management of public affairs, the passions of men, drawn aside from politics, have attended to the arts, and the sciences of nature, and the sphere of ideas in every direction has been enlarged : man, devoted to abstract studies, has better understood his place in the system of nature, and his relations in society; principles have been better discussed, final causes better explained, knowledge more extended, individuals better instructed, manners more social, and life more happy; the species at large, especially in certain countries, has gained considerably; and this amelioration cannot but increase in future, because its two principal obstacles, those even which, till then, had rendered it so slow and sometimes retrograde, the difficulty of transmitting ideas and of communicating them rapidly, have been at last removed.

"Indeed, among the ancients, each canton, each city, having a peculiar language, the consequence was favorable to ignorance and anarchy. There was no communication of ideas, no participation of discoveries, no harmony of interests or of wills, no unity of action or design : besides the only means of transmitting and of propagating ideas being that of speech, fugitive and limited, and that of writing, tedious of execution, expensive and scarce, the consequence was a hinderance of present instruction, loss of experience from one generation to another, instability, retrogradation of knowledge and a perpetuity of confusion and childhood.

"But in the modern world, especially in Europe, great nations having allied themselves in language, and established vast communities of opinions; the minds of men are assimilated, and their affections expanded; there is a sympathy of opinion and an unity of action : then that gift of heavenly genius, the holy art of Printing, having furnished the means of communicating in an instant the same idea to millions of men, and of fixing it in a durable manner, beyond the power of tyrants to arrest or annihilate, there arose a mass of progressive instruction, an expanding atmosphere of science, which assures to future ages a solid amelioration. This amelioration is a necessary effect of the laws of nature ; for by the law of sensibility, man as invincibly tends to render himself happy as the flame to mount, the stone to descend, or the water to find its level. His obstacle is his ignorance, which misleads him in the means, and deceives him in causes and effects. He will enlighten himself by experience, go right by dint of errors, grow wise and good because it is his interest to be so; and in a nation, ideas being communicated, whole classes will gain instruction; science will become a vulgar possession, and all men will know what are the principles of individual happiness and of public prosperity; they will know the relations they bear to society, their duties and their rights; they will learn to guard against the illusions of the lust of gain; they will perceive that morality is a physical science, composed indeed of elements complicated in their operation, but simple and invariable in their nature, since they are only the elements of the organization of man. They will see the propriety of being moderate and just, because in that is found the advantage and security of each; they will perceive that the wish to enjoy at the expense of another is a false calculation of ignorance, because it gives rise to reprisal, hatred and vengeance, and that dishonesty is the never failing offspring of folly.

" Individuals will feel that private happiness is allied to public good;

" The weak, that instead of dividing their interests, they ought to unite them, because equality constitutes their force.

" The rich, that the measure of enjoyment is bounded by the constitution of the organs, and that lassitude follows satiety;

" The poor, that the employment of time, and the peace of the heart, compose the highest happiness of man.

" And public opinion, reaching kings on their thrones, will force them to confine themselves within the limits of regular authority.

" Even chance itself, serving the cause of nations, will sometimes give them feeble chiefs, who, from weakness, will suffer them to become free; and sometimes enlightened chiefs, who from a principle of virtue will free them.

" And when nations, free and enlightened, shall become like great individuals, the whole species will have the same facilities as particular portions have now: the communication of knowledge will extend from one to another, and reach the whole. By the law of imitation, the example of one people will be followed by others, who will adopt its spirit and its laws. Even despots, perceiving that they can no longer maintain their authority without justice and beneficence, will soften their sway from necessity, from rivalship; and civilisation will become universal.

" There will be established among the several nations an equilibrium of force, which, restraining them all within the bounds of a just respect for their reciprocal rights, shall put an end to the barbarous practice of war, and submit their disputes to civil arbitration; the human race will become one great society, one individual family, governed by the same spirit, by common laws, and enjoying all the happiness of which their nature is susceptible.

" Doubtless this great work will be long accomplishing, because the same movement must be given to an immense body ; the same leaven must assimilate an enormous mass of heterogeneous parts ; but this movement shall be effected; its presages are already to be seen. Already the great society, assuming in its course the same characters as partial societies have done, is evidently tending to a like result. At first disconnected in all its parts, it saw its members for a long time without cohesion ; and this general solitude of nations formed its first age of anarchy and childhood; divided afterwards by chance into irregular sections, called states and kingdoms, it has experienced the fatal effects of an extreme inequality of wealth and rank ; and the aristocracy of great empires has formed its second age ; then, these lordly states disputing for preeminence, have exhibited the period of the shock of factions. At present the contending parties, wearied with their discord, feel the want of laws, and sigh for the age of order and peace. Let but a virtuous chief appear ! a just, a powerful people arise ! and the earth will raise them to supreme power ; the world is waiting for a legislative people ; it wishes and demands it ; and my heart hears its voice.—Then turning towards the West ; Yes, continued he, a hollow sound already strikes my ear : a cry of liberty, proceeding from far distant shores, resounds on the ancient continent. At this cry, a secret murmur against oppression is raised in a powerful nation ; a salutary inquietude alarms her respecting her situation, she inquires what she is, and what she ought to be, while, surprised at her own weakness, she interrogates her rights, her resources, and what has been the conduct of her chiefs. Yet another day, a little more reflection—and an immense agitation will begin ; a new born age will open ! an age of astonishment to vulgar minds, of surprise and terror to tyrants, of emancipation to a great nation, and of hope to the human race."

CHAPTER XIV.

THE GREAT OBSTACLE TO IMPROVEMENT

THE Genius ceased.—But preoccupied with melancholy thoughts, my mind resisted persuasion; fearing however to shock him by my resistance, I remained silent.—After awhile, turning to me with a look which pierced my soul—You are silent, said he, and your heart is agitated with thoughts which it dares not utter !—Confused and terrified; " O Genius !" I made answer, " pardon my weakness : doubtless your mouth can utter nothing but truth; but your celestial intelligence can seize its rays, where my grosser faculties discern nothing but clouds. I confess it : conviction has not penetrated my soul, and I feared that my doubts might offend you."

"And what is doubt," replied he, " that it should be a crime ? can man feel otherwise than as he is affected ? If a truth be palpable and of importance in practice, let us pity him who misconceives it : his blindness will bring on its own punishment. If it be uncertain or equivocal, how is he to find in it what it has not ? To believe without evidence or proof, is an act of ignorance and folly : the credulous man loses himself in a labyrinth of contradictions : the man of sense examines and discusses, that he may be consistent in his opinions : the honest man will bear contradiction, because it gives rise to evidence. Violence is the argument of falsehood ; and to impose a creed by authority is the act and indication of a tyrant."

Encouraged by these words, "O Genius !" said I, "since my reason is free, I strive in vain to entertain the flattering hope with which you endeavour to console me : the sensible and virtuous soul is easily caught with dreams of happiness ; but a cruel reality constantly awakens it to suffering and wretchedness : the more I meditate on the nature of man, the more I examine the present state of societies, the less possible it appears to realize a world of wisdom and felicity. I cast my eye over the whole of our hemisphere ; I perceive in no place the germ, nor do I foresee the instinctive energy of a happy revolution. All Asia lies buried in profound darkness. The Chinese, degraded by a bamboo-despotism,* blinded by astrological superstition,

* " The Chinese degraded by a bamboo-despotism."—The Jesuits have endeavoured to represent under favorable colors the Chinese government. it is now known to be a pure oriental despotism.

restrained by an immutable code of gestures, by the radical vices of
an ill constructed language, and still more defective writing,* appear
to be in their abortive civilisation, nothing but a people of automatons.
The Indian, borne down by prejudices and enchained in the sacred
fetters of his casts, vegetates in an incurable apathy. The Tartar,
wandering or fixed, always ignorant and ferocious, lives in the savage-
ness of his ancestors. The Arab, endowed with a happy genius,
loses its force and the fruits of his virtue in the anarchy of his tribes
and the jealousy of his families. The African, degraded from the
rank of man, seems irrevocably doomed to servitude. In the north,
I see nothing but vilified serfs, herds of men, with which the land-
lords stock their estates. Ignorance, tyranny and wretchedness have
everywhere stupified the nations; and vicious habits, depraving the
natural senses, have destroyed the very instinct of happiness and of
truth : in some countries of Europe, indeed, reason has begun to dawn,
but even there, do nations partake of the knowledge of individuals ?
are the talents and genius of governors turned to the benefit of the
people ? And those nations which call themselves polished, are they
not the same that for the last three centuries have filled the earth
with their injustice ? Are they not those who, under the pretext of
commerce, have desolated India, dispeopled a new continent, and
subject Africa at present to the most barbarous slavery ? Can liberty be born from the bosom of despots? and shall justice be rendered
by the hands of piracy and extortion ? O Genius ! I have seen the
civilized countries, and the illusion of their wisdom has vanished
from my sight : I saw riches accumulated in the hands of a few, and
the multitude poor and destitute : I have seen all rights, all powers
concentred in certain classes, and the mass of the people passive and
dependent; I have seen families of princes, but no families of the nation; I have seen government interests, but no public interests or
spirit; I have seen that all the science of government was to oppress
prudently; and the refined servitude of polished nations appeared to
me only the more irremediable.

"One obstacle above all has profoundly struck my mind. On
surveying the globe, I have seen it divided into twenty different systems of religion; every nation has received, or formed, opposite

* " By the radical vices of an ill constructed language, and still more
defective writing."—The Chinese people proves to us that in antiquity,
until the discovery of alphabetical writing, the human understanding
found it very difficult to advance, as before Arabian ciphers it was very
difficult to settle accounts. All depends on method : and China can only be changed by an alteration in its language.

opinions; and every one ascribing to itself the exclusive possession of the truth, must believe the other to be wrong. Now if, as must be the fact in this discordance of opinion, the greater part are in an error, and are sincere in it, then it follows that our mind embraces falsehood as it does truth; and if so, how is it to be enlightened? when prejudice has once seized the mind, how is it to be dissipated? How shall we remove the bandage from our eyes, when the first article in every creed, the first dogma in all religion, is the absolute proscription of doubt, the interdiction of examination, and the rejection of our own judgment? How is truth to make herself known? if she resorts to arguments and proofs, the timid man stifles the voice of his own conscience; if she invokes the authority of celestial powers, the prepossessed man opposes it with another authority of the same origin, and calls all innovation blasphemy. Thus man in his blindness has rivetted his own chains, and surrendered himself forever, without defence, to the sport of his ignorance and his passions. To dissolve such fatal chains, a miraculous concurrence of happy circumstances would be necessary; a whole nation, cured of the delirium of superstition, must be inaccessible to the impulse of fanaticism; freed from the yoke of false doctrine, a whole people must impose upon itself that of true morality and reason; this people should be courageous and prudent, wise and docile; each individual, knowing his rights, should not transgress them: the poor should know how to resist seduction, and the rich the allurements of avarice; there should be found leaders disinterested and just; and their tyrants should be seized with a spirit of madness and folly; this people, recovering its rights, should feel its inability to exercise them in person, and should name its representatives; creator of its magistrates, it should know at once to respect and to judge them; in the sudden reform of a whole nation, accustomed to live by abuses, each individual displaced should bear with patience his privations, and submit to a change of habits; this nation should have the courage to conquer its liberty, the power to defend it, the wisdom to establish it, and the generosity to extend it to others: and can we ever expect the union of so many circumstances? But suppose that chance in its infinite combinations should produce them, shall I see those fortunate days! will not my ashes long ere then be cold in the tomb?"

Here, sunk in sorrow, my oppressed heart no longer found utterance.—The Genius answered not, but I heard him say in a low voice : " I must revive the hope of this man ; for if he who loves his fellow creatures be suffered to despair, what will become of nations ? The past is perhaps too discouraging ; I must anticipate futurity, and disclose to the eye of virtue the astonishing age that is ready to begin ; that, on viewing the object she desires, she may be animated with new ardor, and redouble her efforts to attain it."

CHAPTER XV.

THE NEW AGE.

SCARCELY had he finished these words, when a great noise arose m the west ; and turning to that quarter, I perceived at the extremity of the Mediterranean, in one of the nations of Europe, a prodigions movement ; such as when a violent sedition arises in a vast city, a numberless people rushing in all directions, pour through the streets and fluctuate like waves in the public places. My ear, struck with the cries which resounded to the heavens, distinguished these words :

" What is this new prodigy ? what cruel and mysterious scourge is this ? We are a numerous people, and we want hands ? we have an excellent soil, and we are in want of subsistence ! we are active, and laborious, and we live in indigence ! we pay enormous tributes, and we are told they are not sufficient ! we are at peace without, and our persons and property are not safe within ! Who then is the secret enemy that devours us ?"

Some voices from the midst of the multitude, replied : " Raise a discriminating standard, and let all those who maintain and nourish mankind by useful labors gather round it, and you will discover the the enemy that preys upon you."

The standard being raised, this nation divided itself at once into two unequal bodies, of a contrasted appearance : one, innumerable, and almost total, exhibited in the general poverty of its clothing, in its emaciated appearance and sun burnt faces, the marks of misery and labor ; the other, a little group, an imperceptible fraction, pre-

sented in its rich attire bedaubed with gold and silver, and in its
sleek and ruddy faces, the signs of leisure and abundance.

Considering these men more attentively, I found that the great
body was composed of farmers, artificers, merchants, all professions
useful to society, and that the little group was made up of the ministers of worship of every order (monks and priests,) of financiers, nobles and men in livery, of the commanders of troops and other hireling
agents of government.

These two bodies being assembled face to face, and regarding
each other with astonishment, I saw indignation and rage arising in
one side, and a sort of panic in the other; and the larger said to the
smaller body:

" Why are you separated from us? are you not of our number?"

" No," replied the group: "you are the people; we are a privileged
class, who have our laws, customs, and rights, peculiar to ourselves."

PEOPLE.

And what labor do you perform in our society?

PRIVILEGED CLASS.

None, we are not made to work.

PEOPLE.

How then have you acquired these riches?

PRIVILEGED CLASS.

By taking the pains to govern you.

PEOPLE.

What! we toil, and you enjoy! we produce, and you dissipate!
wealth proceeds from us, you absorb it, and you call this governing!
—Privileged class, distinct body not belonging to us, form your nation apart, and we shall see how you will subsist.

Then the smaller group deliberating on this new state of things,
some just and generous men among them said: We must join the
people, and bear our part of the burden, for they are men like us,
and our riches come from them. But others arrogantly exclaimed:
It would be a shame, an infamy for us to mingle with the crowd;
they are born to serve us; are we not the noble and pure descendants

of the conquerors of this empire? this multitude must be reminded of our rights and its own origin.

THE NOBLES.

People! know you not that our ancestors conquered this land, and that your race was spared only on condition of serving us? This is our social compact! this the government constituted by custom and prescribed by time.

PEOPLE.

O conquerors pure of blood! show us your genealogies! we shall then see if what in an individual is robbery and plunder, can be virtuous in a nation.

And forthwith, voices were heard in every quarter calling out the nobles by their names; and relating their origin and parentage, they told how the grandfather, great grandfather or even father, born traders and mechanics, after acquiring wealth in every way, had purchased their nobility for money: so that but very few families were really of the original stock. See, said these voices, see these purse-proud commoners who deny their parents, see these plebeian recruits who look on themselves as illustrious veterans! and peals of laughter were heard.

To stifle them, some astucious men cried out: Mild and faithful people, acknowledge the legitimate authority;* the King wills, the law ordains.

---

* " Acknowledge the legitimate authority."—To ascertain the signification of the word legitimate, it should be considered that it comes from the latin legi-intimus, intrinsic in the law, written in it. If therefore the law is made by the prince alone, the prince alone makes himself legitimate: then he is merely a despot: his will is the law. This is not what is meant; for the same right would be transferred to the power that should overturn him. What is the law (the source of right?) The Latin also informs us: from legere to read, is derived lex, res lecta, thing read; this thing read is an order to do or not to do a particular action, and this on condition of penalty or reward attached to the observance or infringement. This order is read to those concerned, that they might not plead ignorance. it was written that it might be read without any alteration: such is the signification, and such the origin of the word law. Hence the several epithets of which is susceptible; wise law, absurd law, just law, unjust law, according to the effect resulting from it, and it is this effect which characterises the power from whence it proceeds. Now, in the social state, in the government of men, what is just and unjust? Justice consists in preserving or restoring to each individual what belongs to him: consequently, first, life which

PEOPLE.

Privileged class, explain the word legitimate; if it means conformable to intrinsic in the law, say who made the law? Can the law ordain anything else than the preservation of the multitude?

Then the military governors said: The multitude will only submit to force, we must chastise them. Soldiers, strike this rebellious people!

PEOPLE.

Soldiers! you are of our blood! will you strike your brothers, your relations? If the people perish, who will nourish the army?

. And the soldiers, grounding their arms, said: We are likewise the people, show us the enemy!

Then the ecclesiastical governors said: there is but one resource left: the people are superstitious; we must frighten them with the names of God and religion.

Our dear brethren! our children! God has ordained us to govern you.

PEOPLE.

Show us your powers from God?

PRIESTS.

You must have faith; reason leads astray.

PEOPLE.

Do you govern without reason?

he owes to a power above all; 2, the use of the senses and faculties given him by that same power; 3d. the enjoyment of the fruits of his labor; and all this, as long as he injures not these same rights in others; for if he does injure them, there is injustice, that is to say, a breach of equality and equilibrium between man and man. But the greater the number of the injured, the more injustice is committed: consequently, if, as is the fact, what is called the people composes the immense majority of a nation, it is the interest. the happiness of that majority which constitutes Justice: this truth is well expressed by the axiom: salus populi suprema lex esto. The safety of the people, this is the law, this is legitimacy. And observe that salus does not say the will, as some fanatics have imagined; for first the people may be deceived; then how is this collective and abstract will to be expressed? experience proves it Salus populi! the art is to know and to accomplish it.

PRIESTS.

God commands peace : religion prescribes obedience

PEOPLE.

Peace supposes justice ; obedience implies conviction of a duty

PRIESTS.

Suffering is the business of this world.

PEOPLE.

Show us the example.

PRIESTS.

Would you live without gods or kings ?

PEOPLE.

We would live without oppressors.

PRIESTS.

You must have mediators, intercessors.

PEOPLE.

Mediators with God, and with the king ! courtiers and priests, your services are too expensive ; we will henceforth manage our own affairs.

And then the little group said : All is lost, the multitude is enlightened.

And the people answered : All is safe ; since we are enlightened we will commit no violence : we only claim our rights. We feel resentments ; but we forget them ; we were slaves, we might command ; but we only wish to be free, and liberty is but justice.

CHAPTER XVI.

A FREE AND LEGISLATIVE PEOPLE.

CONSIDERING now that all public power was suspended, and that the habitual restraint of the people had suddenly ceased, I shuddered with the apprehension that they would fall into the dissolution of anarchy; but immediately a voice was heard to say :

" It is not enough that we have freed ourselves from tyrants and parasites, we must prevent their return. We are men, and experience has abundantly taught us that every one is fond of power, and wishes to enjoy at the expense of others. It is necessary then to guard against a propensity which is the source of discord ; we must establish certain rules of duty and of right : but the knowledge of our rights and the estimation of our duties are so abstract and difficult as to require all the time and all the faculties of a man. Occupied in our own affairs, we have not leisure for these studies ; nor can we exercise these functions in our own persons. Let us choose then among ourselves such persons as are capable of this employment. To them we will delegate our powers to institute our government and laws ; they shall be the representatives of our wills and of our interests. And in order to attain the fairest representation possible of our wills and our interests, let it be numerous, and composed of men resembling ourselves."

Having made the election of a numerous body of delegates, the people thus addressed them : " We have hitherto lived in a society formed by chance, without fixed agreements, without free conventions, without a stipulation of rights, without reciprocal engagements; and a multitude of disorders and evils have arisen from this precarious state. We are now determined on forming a regular compact ; and we have chosen you to adjust the articles : examine then with care what ought to be its basis and its conditions ; consider what is the end and the principle of every association ; recognise the rights which every member brings, the powers which he gives up, and those which he reserves to himself: point out to us the rules of conduct, and equitable laws ; prepare us a new system of government; for we feel that the one which has hitherto guided us is corrupt. Our fathers have wandered in the paths of ignorance; and habit has taught us to stray after them: everything has been done by fraud, violence and delusion, and the true laws of morality and reason are still obscure; clear up then their chaos; trace out their connexion; publish their code, and we will adopt it."

And the people raised an immense throne, in form of a pyramid, and seating on it the men they had chosen, said to them: "We raise you to day above us, that you may better discover the whole of our relations, and be above the reach of our passions.

"But remember that you are our fellow citizens: that the power we confer on you is our own; that we deposit it with you, not as a property or an inheritance; that you must be the first to obey the laws you make; that to-morrow you redescend among us, and that you will have acquired no other right but that of our esteem and gratitude. And reflect what tribute of glory the world, which reveres so many apostles of error, will bestow on the first assembly of rational men, who shall have solemnly proclaimed the immutable principles of justice, and consecrated in the face of tyrants the rights of nations!"

CHAPTER XVII.

UNIVERSAL BASIS OF ALL RIGHT AND ALL LAW.

THE men chosen by the people to investigate the true principles of morals and of reason, then proceeded in the sacred object of their mission; and after a long examination, having discovered a fundamental and universal principle, a legislator arose and said to the people. "Here is the primordial basis, the physical origin of all justice and of all right.

"Whatever be the active power, the moving cause that governs the universe, since it has given to all men the same organs, the same sensations, and the same wants, it has thereby declared that it has given to all the same right to the use of its treasures, and that all men are equal in the order of nature.

7*

' Secondly, since this power has given to each man the necessary means of preserving his own existence, it is evident that it has constituted them all independent one of another; that it has created them free; that no man is subject to another; that each is absolute proprietor of his own person.

" Equality and Liberty are therefore two essential attributes of man; two laws of the Divinity constitutional and unchangeable like the physical properties of matter.

" Now, every individual being absolute master of his own person it follows that a full and free consent is a condition indispensable to all contracts and all engagements.

" Again, since each individual is equal to another, it follows that the balance of what is received and of what is given, should be strictly in equilibrium: so that the idea of liberty necessarily imports that of justice, the daughter of equality.*

" Equality and Liberty are therefore the physical and unalterable basis of every union of men in society, and consequently the necessary and generating principle of every law and of every system of regular government.

" A disregard of this basis has introduced in your nation and in every other, those disorders which have finally roused you. It is by returning to this rule that you may reform them, and reorganize a happy order of society.

" But observe, this reorganization will occasion a violent commotion in your habits, your fortunes, and your prejudices. Vicious contracts and abusive claims must be dissolved; unjust distinctions, and ill founded property renounced; indeed you must recur for a moment to a state of nature. Consider whether you can consent to so many sacrifices."

Then reflecting on the cupidity inherent in the heart of man, I thought that this people would renounce all ideas of amelioration.

But, in a moment, a great number of generous men of the highest

---

*" The idea of liberty necessarily imports that of justice, the daughter of equality."—The words themselves retrace this connexion: for æquilibrium, æquitas, æqualitas are all of the same family, and the physical idea of equality in the scales of a balance is the archetype of all these abstract ideas. Liberty itself, when rightly analyzed, is only justice, for if a man, because he calls himself free, attacks another, the latter, by the same light of liberty can and ought to repel him; the right of one is equal to the right of the other; force may suspend this equilibrium, but it becomes injustice and tyranny in the lowest democrat as well as in the highest potentate

ank, advancing towards the ,yrai id, made a solemn abjuration of all their distinctions and all their riches. "Establish for us, said they, the laws of equality and liberty; we will henceforth possess nothing but on the sacred title of justice.

"Equality, justice, liberty, these shall be our code and our standard."

And then the people immediately raised a great standard, inscribed with these three words, in three different colors. They displayed it over the pyramid of the legislator, and for the first time the flag of universal justice floated on the face of the earth; and the people raised before the pyramid a new altar, on which they placed golden scales, a sword, and a book with this inscription:

To equal Law, which judges and protects.

And having surrounded the pyramid and the altar with a vast amphitheatre, all the nation took their seats to hear the publication of the law. And millions of men, raising at once their hands to heaven, took the solemn oath to live free and just; to respect their reciprocal properties and rights; to obey the law and its ministers regularly constituted.

A spectacle, so forceful and sublime, so replete with generous emotions, moved me to tears, and addressing myself to the Genius : " Let me now live," said I, " for in future I have everything to hope."

CHAPTER XVIII.

CONSTERNATION AND CONSPIRACY OF TYRANTS.

But scarcely had the solemn voice of liberty and equality resounded through the earth, when a movement of confusion and astonishment arose in different nations; on the one hand the people, warmed with desire, but wavering between hope and fear, between the sentiment of right and the habit of oppression, began to be in motion: the kings, on the other hand, suddenly awakened from the sleep of indolence and despotism, were alarmed for the safety of their thrones;

while on all sides, those clans of civil and religious tyrants, who deceive kings and oppress the people, were seized with rage and consternation; and concerting their perfidious plans : " W'o to us," said they, " if this fatal cry of liberty comes to the ears of the multitude! wo to us if this pernicious spirit of justice be propagated !"—And pointing to the floating banner ; " Conceive," said they, " what a swarm of evils are included in those three words! If all men are equal, where is our exclusive right to honors and to power ? If all men are to be free, what becomes of our slaves, our vassals, our property ? If all are equal in the civil state, where is our prerogative of birth, of inheritance ? what becomes of nobility ? If they are all equal in the sight of God, what need of mediators ? where is the priesthood ? Let us hasten then to destroy a germ so prolific, and so contagious ! We must employ all our cunning against this calamity; we must frighten the kings, that they may join our cause. We must divide the people by national jealousies, and occupy them with commotions, wars and conquests. They must be alarmed at the power of this free nation. Let us form a league against the common enemy, demolish that sacrilegious standard, overturn that throne of rebellion, and stifle the flame of revolution in its birth."

And indeed, the civil and religious tyrants of nations formed a general coalition; and multiplying their followers by force and seduction, they marched in hostile array against the free nation; and surrounding the altar and the pyramid of natural law, they exclaimed; " What is this new and heretical doctrine ? What this impious altar, this sacrilegious worship ?—True believers and loyal subjects ! can you suppose that truth is first disclosed to you to-day; and that hitherto you have been walking in error ? that those rebels, more lucky than you, have the sole privilege of wisdom ? And you, misguided nation, perceive you not that your new leaders are deceiving you, that they pervert the principles of your faith, and overturn the religion of your fathers ? Ah ! tremble ; lest the wrath of heaven should kindle against you, and hasten by speedy repentance, to retrieve your error "

But inaccessible to seduction as well as to fear, the free nation answered not, and rising universally in arms, assumed an imposing attitude.

And the legislator said to the chiefs of nations : " If while we walked with a bandage over our eyes the light guided our steps, why, since we are no longer blindfold, should it escape our search ? If guides who prescribe clearsightedness to man, mislead and deceive him, what can be expected from those who profess to keep him in darkness?

" Leaders of the people! if you possess the truth, show it to us. we will receive it with gratitude; for we seek it with ardor, and have a great interest in finding it: we are men and liable to be deceived; but you are also men, and equally fallible. Aid us then in this labyrinth, where the human race has wandered for so many ages; help us to dissipate the illusion of so many prejudices and vicious habits; amid the shock of so many opinions which dispute for our acceptance, assist us in discovering the proper and distinctive character of truth. Let us terminate this day the long combat of error: let us establish between it and truth a solemn contest: to which we will invite the opinions of men of all nations: let us convoke a general assembly of the nations; let them be judges in their own cause; and in the debate of all systems, let no champion, no argument be wanting either on the side of prejudice or of reason; and let the sentiment of a general and common mass of evidence give birth to an universal concord of opinions and of hearts."

CHAPTER XIX.

GENERAL ASSEMBLY OF THE NATIONS

THUS spoke the legislator; and the multitude, seized with those emotions which a reasonable proposition always inspires, expressed its applause; while the tyrants, left without support, were overwhelmed with confusion.

A scene of a new and astonishing nature then opened to my view all the people and nations inhabiting the globe, men of every race and of every region, converging from their various climates, seemed to assemble in one allotted place; where, forming an immense congress, distinguished in groups by the vast variety of their dresses, features and complexion, the numberless multitude presented a most unusual and affecting sight.

On one side I saw the European, with his short close coat, pointed triangular hat, smooth chin, and powdered hair; on the other
side the Asiatic with a flowing robe, long heard, shaved head, and
round turban. Here stood the nations of Africa with their ebony
skins, their woolly hair, their body girt with white and blue tissues
of bark, adorned with bracelets and necklaces of coral, shells, and
glass: there the tribes of the north, enveloped in their leathern bags;
the Laplander with his pointed bonnet and his snow shoes; the Samoyede, with his feverish body and strong odor; the Tougouse, with
his horned cap, and carrying his idols pendant from his neck; the
Yakoute, with his freckled face; the Calmouk, with his flat nose
and little retorted eyes. Farther distant were the Chinese, attired
in silk, with their hair hanging in tresses; the Japanese of mingled
race; the Malays, with wide-spreading ears, rings in their noses,
and broad hats of the palm-leaf, and the tattooed races of the isles
of the ocean and of the continent of the Antipodes. The view of so
many varieties of the same species, of so many extravagant inventions of the same understanding, and of so many modifications of the
same organization, affected me with a thousand feelings and a thousand thoughts. I contemplated with astonishment this gradation of
color which passing from a bright carnation to a light brown, a
deeper brown, smutty, bronze, olive, leaden, copper, ends in the
black of ebony and jet. And finding the Kachemirian with his rosy
cheek, next to the sun burnt Hindoo, and the Georgian by the side
of the Tartar, I reflected on the effects of climate hot or cold, of
soil high or low, marshy or dry, open or shaded; I compared the
dwarf of the pole with the giant of the temperate zones; the slender
body of the Arab with the clumsy Hollander; the squat stunted figure of the Samoyede with the elegant form of the Greek and the
Sclavonian, the greasy black wool of the Negro with the bright silken
locks of the Dane; the broad face of the Calmouk, his little angular
eyes, and flattened nose, with the oval prominent visage, large blue
eyes, and aquiline nose of the Circassian and the Abazan. I contrasted the brilliant calicoes of the Indian, the well wrought stuffs of
the European, the rich furs of the Siberian, with the tissues of bark,
of osiers, leaves and feathers of savage nations; and the blue figures
of serpents, flowers and stars, with which they painted their bodies.
Sometimes the variegated appearance of this multitude reminded me
of the enamelled meadows of the Nile and of the Euphrates; when, after rains or inundations, millions of flowers are rising on every side;

sometimes their murmurs and their motions called to mind the numberless swarms of locusts which, issuing from the desert, cover in
spring the plains of Hauran.

At the sight of so many rational beings, considering on the one
hand the immensity of ideas and sensations assembled in this place;
and on the other hand, reflecting on the opposition of so many opinions, and the shock of so many passions of men so capricious, I
struggled between astonishment, admiration, and secret dread,—
when the legislator commanded silence, and atracted all my attention.

" Inhabitants of earth, a free and powerful nation addresses you
the words of justice and of peace, and offers you the sure pledges of
her intentions in her own conviction and experience. Long afflicted with the same evils as yourselves, we sought for their source,
and found them all derived from violence and injustice, erected into
law by the inexperience of past ages, and maintained by the prejudices of the present; then abolishing our artificial and arbitrary institutions, and recurring to the origin of all right and all reason, we
have found that there existed in the very order of nature, and in the
physical constitution of man, eternal and immutable laws which only
waited his observance to render him happy. O men! cast your eyes
on the heavens that give you light, and on the earth that gives you
bread! Since they offer the same bounties to you all, since from the
power that gives them motion you have all received the same life,
the same organs, have you not all received the same right to enjoy
its benefits? Has it not hereby declared you all equal and free?
What mortal shall dare refuse to his fellow that which nature gives
him? O nations! let us banish all tyranny and all discord; let us
form but one society, one great family; and, since human nature has
but one constitution, let there exist in future but one law, that of nature; but one code, that of reason; but one throne, that of justice;
but one altar, that of union."

He ceased; and an immense acclamation resounded to the skies:
ten thousand benedictions announced the transports of the multitude;
and they made the earth reecho justice, equality and union. But
different emotions soon succeeded; soon the doctors and the chiefs of
nations exciting a spirit of dispute, there was heard a sullen murmur,
which growing louder, and spreading from group to group, became a
vast disorder, and each nation setting up exclusive pretensions,
claimed a preference for its own code and opinion.

· "You are in error," said the parties, pointing one to the other; "we alone are in possession of reason and truth. We alone have the true law, the real rule of right and justice, the only means of happiness and perfection ; all other men are either blind or rebellious." And great agitation prevailed.

But the legislator having ordered silence: "People," said he, "what is that passionate emotion? Whither will that quarrel conduct you ? What can you expect from this dissension ? The earth has been for ages a field of disputation ; and you have shed torrents of blood for chimerical opinions : what have you gained by so many battles and tears ? When the strong has subjected the weak to his opinion, has he thereby aided the cause of truth ? O nations ! take counsel of your own wisdom ! When among yourselves disputes arise between families and individuals, how do you reconcile them ? Do you not give them arbitrators ? Yes, cried the whole multitude. Do so then to the authors of your present dissensions. Order those who call themselves your instructers, and who force their creeds upon you, to discuss before you their reasons. Since they appeal to your interests, inform yourselves how they support them. And you, chiefs and doctors of the people, before dragging them into the quarrels of your opinions, let the reasons for and against them be discussed. Let us establish one solemn controversy, one public scrutiny of truth, not before the tribunal of a corruptible individual, or a prejudiced party, but in the forum of mankind, presided by all their information and all their interests. Let the natural sense of the whole human race be our arbiter and judge."

CHAPTER XX.

THE SEARCH OF TRUTH.

THE people expressed their applause, and the legislator said: "To proceed with order, and avoid all confusion, let a spacious semicircle be left vacant in front of the altar of peace and union ; let each system of religion, and each particular sect, erect its proper distinctive standard on the line of this semicircle ; let its chiefs and doctors place themselves around the standard, and their followers form a column behind them."

The semicircle being traced, and the order published, there instantly rose an innumerable multitude of standards, of all colors and of every form, like what we see in a great commercial port, when, on a day of rejoicing, a thousand different flags and streamers are floating from a forest of masts. At sight of this prodigious diversity, turning towards the Genius: "I thought," said I, "that the earth was divided only into eight or ten systems of faith, and I then despaired of a reconciliation : now that I behold thousands of different sects, how can I hope for concord?"—"But these," replied the Genius, "are not all; and yet they will be intolerant!—"

Then, as the groups advanced to take their stations, he pointed out to me their distinctive marks, and thus began to explain their characters :

"That first group," said he, "with a green banner, bearing a crescent, a bandage, and a sabre, are the followers of the Arabian prophet. To say there is a God (without knowing what he is;) to believe the words of a man (without understanding his language;) to go into the desert to pray to God (who is everywhere;) to wash the hands with water (and not abstain from blood;) to fast all day (and eat all night;) to give alms of their own goods (and to plunder those of others;) such are the means of perfection instituted by Mahomet, such are the symbols of his followers. Whoever does not adopt them is a reprobate, stricken with anathema, and devoted to the sword. A merciful God, the author of life, has instituted these laws of oppression and murder: he made them for all the world, but has revealed them only to one man; he established them from all eternity, though he made them known but yesterday; they are abundantly sufficient for all purposes, and yet a volume is added to them : this volume was to diffuse light, to exhibit evidence, to lead men to perfection and happiness; and yet every page was so full of obscurities, ambiguities, and contradictions, that commentaries and explanations became necessary, even in the life time of its apostle; and its interpreters, differing in opinion, divided into opposite and hostile sects. One maintains that Ali is the true successor; the other contends for Omar and Aboubekre. This denies the eternity of the Coran; that the necessity of ablutions and prayers; the Carmate forbids pilgrimages and allows the use of wine : the Hakemite preaches the transmigration of souls : thus they make up the number

of seventy-two sects, whose banners are before you.   In this contes-
tation, every one attributing the evidence of truth exclusively to
himself, and taxing all others with heresy and rebellion, turns against
them his sanguinary zeal.   And their religion which celebrates a
mild and merciful God, the common Father of all men, converted to
a torch of discord, a signal for war and murder, has not ceased for
twelve hundred years to deluge the earth in blood,* and to ravage
and desolate the ancient hemisphere from one end to the other.

   " Those men, distinguished by their enormous white turbans
their broad sleeves, and their long rosaries, are the Imams, the Mol-
las, and the Mufties ; and near them are the dervices with pointed
bonnets, and the santons with dishevelled hair.   Behold with what
vehemence they recite their professions of faith !   They are now
beginning a dispute about the greater and lesser impurities ; about
the matter and the manner of ablutions ; about the attributes of God
and his perfections, about the chaitan, and the good and wicked
angels ; about death, the resurrection, the interrogatory in the tomb,
the judgment, the passage of the bridge not broader than a hair, the
balance of works, the pains of hell, and the joys of paradise.

   " Next to these, that second more numerous group, with white
banners intersected with crosses, are the followers of Jesus.   Ac-
knowledging the same God with the Mussulmen, founding their belief on the same books, admitting like them, a first man who damned
the human race by eating an apple, they hold them however in a
holy abhorrence, and out of pure piety, they call each other impious
blasphemers.   The great point of their dissension consists in this,
that after admitting a God one and indivisible, the Christian divides
him into three persons, each of which he believes to be a complete
and entire God, without ceasing to constitute an identical whole, by
the indivisibility of the three.   And he adds, that this being, who
fills the universe, has dwindled into the body of a man, and has assumed material, perishable, and limited organs, without ceasing to
be immaterial, infinite and eternal.   The Mussulman, who does
not comprehend these mysteries, rejects them as follies, and the vis-

----

   * " And this religion (Mahomet's) has not ceased to deluge the earth
in blood."--Read the history of Islamism by its own writers, and you
will be convinced that one of the principal causes of the wars which
have desolated Asia and Africa since the days of Mahomet, has been the
apostolical fanaticism of its doctrine.   Cesar has been supposed to have
destroyed three millions of men : it would be interesting to make a similar calculation respecting every founder of a religious system.

ions of a distempered brain, though he conceives perfectly well the eternity of the Coran and the mission of the prophet; hence their implacable hatreds.

" Again, the Christians, divided among themselves on many points, have formed parties not less violent than the Mussulmen ; and their quarrels are so much the more obstinate, as the objects of them are inaccessible to the senses, and incapable of demonstration : their opinions, therefore, have no other basis but the will and caprice of the parties. Thus, while they agree that God is a being incomprehensible and unknown, they dispute nevertheless about his essence, his mode of acting, and his attributes : while they agree that his pretended transformation into a man, is an enigma above the human understanding, they dispute on the junction or distinction of his two wills and his two natures, on his change of substance, on the real or fictitious presence, on the mode of incarnation, etc. etc.

" Hence those innumerable sects, of which two or three hundred have already perished, and three or four hundred others, which still subsist, display those numberless banners which here distract your sight. The first in order, surrounded by a group in various fantastic dress, that confused mixture of violet, red, white, black and speckled garments : with heads shaved, with tonsures, or with short hair : with red hats, square bonnets, pointed mitres or long beards, is the standard of the Roman pontiff : who, uniting the civil government to the priesthood, has erected the supremacy of his city into a point of religion, and made of his pride an article of faith.

" On his right you see the Greek pontiff, who, proud of the rivalship of his metropolis, sets up equal pretensions, and supports them against the Western church by the priority of that of the East. On the left, are the standards of two recent chiefs,* who shaking off a yoke that had become tyrannical, have raised altar against altar in their reform, and wrested half of Europe from the pope. Behind these are the subaltern sects, subdivided from the principal divisions, the Nestorians, the Eutycheans, the Jacobites, the Iconoclasts, the Anabaptists, the Presbyterians, the Wicliffites, the Osiandrians, the Manicheans, the Pietists, the Adamites, the Contemplatives, the Quakers the Weepers, and a hundred others :† all of distinct parties, persecuting when strong, tolerant when weak, hating each other

* Luther and Calvin.

† "And a hundred others."—Consult upon this subject, Dictionnaire des heresies par l'abbe Pluquet, who has omitted a great number, in 2 vol. 8vo

in the name of a God of peace, forming each an exclusive heaven in
a religion of universal charity, dooming each other to pains without
end in a future state, and realizing in this world the imaginary hell
of the other."

After this group, observing a solitary standard of the color of hy-
acinth, round which were assembled men of all the different dresses
of Europe and Asia; "At least," said I to the Genius, "we shall find
unanimity here:" "Yes," said he, "at first sight, and by a momentary accident: do you not know that system of worship?" Then,
perceiving in Hebrew letters the monogram of the name of God, and
the palms which the rabbins held in their hands: "True," said I,
"these are the children of Moses, dispersed even to this day, abhorring
every nation, and abhorred and persecuted by all."—"Yes," he replied, "and for this reason, that having neither time nor liberty to
dispute, they have the appearance of unanimity, but no sooner will
they come together, compare their principles, and reason on their
opinions, than they will separate, as formerly, at least into two principal sects,* one of which, taking advantage of the silence of their legislator, and adhering to the literal sense of his books, will deny everything that is not clearly expressed therein, and on this principle will
reject as inventions of the circumcised, the immortality of the soul, its
transmigration to places of pain or pleasure, its resurrection, the final
judgment, the good and bad angels, the revolt of the evil Genius,
and all the poetical system of a world to come: and this highly favored people, whose perfection consists in cutting off a little piece
of skin : this atom of a people, which forms but a wave in the Ocean
of mankind, and which insists that God has made nothing but for
them, will by its schism reduce to one half its present trifling weight
in the scale of the universe."

He then showed me a neighbouring group, composed of men
dressed in white robes, wearing a veil over their mouths, and ranged around a banner of the color of the morning sky, on which was
painted a globe cut into two hemispheres, black and white; "The
same thing will happen," said he, "to these children of Zoroaster, the
obscure remnants of a people once so powerful; at present, persecuted like the Jews, and dispersed among other nations, they receive
without discussion the precepts of the representative of their prophet; but as soon as the mobed and the destours shall assemble, they
will renew the controversy about the good and the bad principle; on

* The Sadducees and the Pharisees.

the combats of Ormuzd, god of light, and Ahrimanes, god of darkness; on the direct and allegorical sense; on the good and evil genii;
on the worship of fire and the elements; on impurities and ablutions; on the resurrection of the soul and body or only of the soul;
on the renovation of the present world, and on that which is to take
its place. And the Parses will divide * into sects so much the more
numerous, as during their dispersion their families will have contracted the manners and opinions of foreign nations.

" Next to these, remark those banners of an azure ground, painted with monstrous figures of human bodies, double, triple, quadru-
ple, with heads of lions, boars and elephants, with tails of fishes and
tortoises, etc., these are the ensigns of the sects of India, who find
their gods in various animals, and the souls of their fathers in reptiles and insects. These men endow hospitals for hawks, serpents
and rats; and they abhor their fellow creatures! They purify themselves with the dung and urine of cows; and think themselves defiled
by the touch of a man! They wear a net over the mouth, for fear
of swallowing, in a fly, a soul in a state of penance, and they can see
a paria perish with hunger! They acknowledge the same gods, but
they separate into hostile bands.

" The first standard, retired from the rest, bearing a figure with
four heads, is that of Brahma, who, though the creator of the universe, is without temples or followers; but reduced to serve as a pedestal to the Lingam,† he contents himself with a little water which
the bramin throws every morning on his shoulder, reciting an idle
canticle in his praise.

" The second, bearing a kite with a scarlet body and a white head,
is that of Vichenou, who though preserver of the world, has passed
part of his life in wicked actions. You sometimes see him under
the hideous form of a boar or a lion tearing human entrails, or under
that of a horse, shortly to come armed with a sabre to destroy all
that has life, to extinguish the stars, annihilate the planets, shake
the earth, and force the great serpent to vomit a fire which shall consume the spheres.

* " And the Parses will divide."—The followers of Zoroaster, called
Parses, because they are descended from the Persians, are better known
in Asia by the opprobrious name of Gaures or Guebres, which means infidels; they are in Asia what the Jews are in Europe. The name of
their pope or high-priest is Mobed. See, respecting the rites of this religion, Henry Lord, Hyde and the Zend-Avesta.
† " Brahma—reduced to serve as a pedestal to the Lingam."—See
Sonnerat, Voyage aux Indes, vol. 1

" The third is that of Chiven, god of desolation and destruction, who has however for his emblem the symbol of geneiation ; he is the wickedest of the three, and he has the most followeis. These men proud of his character, express in their devotions to him their contempt for the other gods,* his equals and brothers ; and, in imitation of his inconsistencies, while they profess great modesty and chastity, they publicly crown with flowers and sprinkle with milk and honey the obscene image of the Lingam.

" In the rear of these, approach the smaller standards of a multitude of gods, male, female, and hermaphrodite ; these are friends and relations of the three principal gods, and have passed their lives in wars among themselves : and their followeis imitate them. These gods have need of nothing, and they are constantly receiving presents; they are omnipotent and omnipresent, and a Bramin by muttering a few words shuts them up in an idol or a pitcher, to sell their favors for his own benefit.

" Beyond these, that cloud of standards which, on a yellow ground common to them all, bear various emblems, are those of the same god, who reigns under different names in the nations of the East The Chinese adores him in Fot,† the Japanese, in Budso, the inhabitant of Ceylon in Bedhou and Boudah, of Laos in Chekia, the Peguan in Phta, the Siamese in Sommona-Kodom, the Tibetan in Boudd and in La ; agreeing in some points of his history, they all celebrate his life of penitence, his mortifications, his fastings, his functions of mediator and expiator, the enmity between him and another god his adversary, their battles, and his ascendency. But as they disagree on the means of pleasing him, they dispute about rites and ceremonies, and about the dogmas of interior doctrine and of public doctrine.

---

* When a sectary of Chiven hears the name of Vichenou pronounced, he stops his ears, runs away, and purifies himself.

† " The Chinese adores him in Fot."—The Chinese language having neither B nor D, that people pronounces Fot what the Indians and Persians call Bodd, or Boudd (with short ou.) Fot, in Pegu, changes into Fota and Fta, etc. It is only within a few years that we begin to have exact notions of the doctrine of Boudd and of his various sectaries ; and we are indebted for them to the learned men of England, who, according as their nation subdues the people of India, study their religious and manners in order to make them known. The work entitled Asiatic Researches is a precious collection of the kind : we find in vol. 6, page 163 ; in vol. 7, page 32 and page 399, three instructive memoirs concerning the Boudists of Ceylon and of Birmah or Ava. An anonymous writer, but who appeais to have meditated this subject, has published in the Asiatic Journal of 1816, month of January and following, until May, letters which promise further details of the highest interest. We shall resume this subject in a note to chapter XXI.

That Japanese bonze, with a yellow robe, and naked head, preaches the eternity of souls, and their successive transmigrations into various bodies; near him, the Sintoist denies that souls can exist * separate from the senses, and maintains that they are only the effect of the organs to which they belong, and with which they must perish, as the sound with the musical instrument.—Near him, the Siamese, with his eyebrows shaved, and a talipat screen in his hand,† recommends alms, offerings and expiations, and yet believes in blind necessity and inexorable fate. The Chinese hochang sacrifices to the souls of his ancestors, and next him, the follower of Confucius interrogates his destiny ‡ in the cast of dice and the movement of the stars. That child, surrounded by a swarm of priests in yellow robes and hats, is the Grand Lama,§ in whom the god of Tibet has just become incarnate. But a rival has arisen who partakes this benefit with him; and the Calmouc on the banks of lake Baikal has a God similar to the inhabitant of Lasa; but they agree, however, in one important point, that god can inhabit only a human body; they both laugh at the stupidity of the Indian who pays homage to cowdung, though they themselves consecrate the excrements of their high-priest."

After these, a crowd of other banners which no man could number, came forward into sight: and the Genius exclaimed; " I should never

* " The Sintoist denies that souls can exist."—See in Kempfer the doctrine of the Sintoists, which is a mixture of that of Epicurus and the Stoics.

† " The Siamese, with the talipat screen in his hand."—It is a leaf of the latanier species of the palm tree; hence the Bonzes of Siam take the appellation of Talapoin. The use of this screen is an exclusive privilege.

‡" The follower of Confucius interrogates his destiny."—The sectaries of Confucius are no less addicted to astrology than the Bonzes. It is indeed the moral malady of every Eastern nation.

§ " The Grand-Lama, Dalai-Lama, or immense priest of La."—Is the same person whom we find mentioned in our old books of travels by the name of Prester-John, from a corruption of the Persian word Djehan, which signifies the world. Thus the priest World, and the God World are intimately connected.

In a recent expedition, the English have found certain idols of the Lamas filled in the inside with sacred pastils from the closestool of the high-priest. The fact is attested by Hastings, and colonel Pollier, who perished in the troubles of Avignon. It will be very extraordinary to observe, that this disgusting ceremony is connected with a profound philosophical system, to wit, that of the metempsychosis, admitted by the Lamas. When the Tartars swallow the sacred relics of the pontiff (which they are accustomed to do,) they imitate the laws of the universe, the parts of which are incessantly absorbed and pass into the substance of each other. It is the serpent devouring his tail; and this serpent is Boudd and the world.

finish the detail of all the systems of faith which divide these nations. Here, the hordes of the Tartars adore in the forms of beasts, birds and insects, the good and evil genii ; who, under a principal but indolent god, govern the universe ; in their idolatry they call to mind the ancient paganism of the West.   You observe the fantastical dress of their chamans, who under a robe of leather hung round with bells and rattles, idols of iron, claws of birds, skins of snakes and heads of owls, are agitated by factitious convulsions, and invoke with magical cries the dead to deceive the living.   There, the black tribes of Africa, exhibit the same opinions in the worship of their fetiches. See the inhabitant of Juida worship god in a great snake, which unluckily the swine delight to eat.*   The Teleutean attires his god in a coat of several colors like a Russian soldier :† the Kamchadale, observing that everything goes wrong in his frozen climate, considers him as an old ill natured man, smoking his pipe and hunting foxes and martins in his sledge ; but you may still behold a hundred savage nations who have none of the ideas of civilized people respecting God, the soul, another world, and a future life : who have formed no system of worship, and who nevertheless enjoy the gifts of nature in the irreligion in which she has created them."

* " Worship god in a great snake which the swine delight to eat."— It frequently happens that the swine devour the very species of serpents adored by the negroes, and this occasions great desolation in the country. President de Borsses has given us in his history of the Fetiches, a curious collection of absurdities of this nature

† " The Teleutean attires."—The Teleuteans, a Tartar nation, paint God as wearing a vesture of all colors. particularly red and green , and as these constitute the uniform of the Russian dragoons, they compare him to this description of soldiers.   The Egyptians also dress the God World in a garment of every color Eusebius, Prœp, Evang. p. 115, book 3. The Teleuteans. call God Bou. which is only an alteration of Boudd, the God Egg and World.

CHAPTER XXI.

PROBLEM OF RELIGIOUS CONTRADICTIONS

THE various groups having taken their places, an unbounded silence succeeded to the murmurs of the multitude, and the legislator said: " Chiefs and doctors of mankind! you remark how the nations, living apart, have hitherto followed different paths, each believing its own to be that of truth. If however, truth is one, and opinions are various, it is evident that some are in error. If then such vast numbers of us are in the wrong, who shall dare to say, I am in the right? Begin therefore by being indulgent in your dissensions. Let us all seek truth as if no one possessed it. The opinions which to this day have governed the world, originating from chance, propagated in obscurity, admitted without discussion, accredited by a love of novelty and imitation, have usurped their empire in a clandestine manner. It is time, if they are well founded, to give a solemn stamp to their certainty, and legitimate their existence. Let us summon them this day to a general scrutiny, let each propound his creed, let the whole assembly be the judge, and let that alone be acknowledged true which is so for the whole human race.

Then, by order of position, the first standard on the left was allowed to speak : " You are not permitted to doubt," said their chiefs, " that our doctrine is the only true and infallible one. First it is revealed by God himself.—"

" So is ours," cried all the other standards, " and you are not permitted to doubt it."

" But at least," said the legislator, " you must propose it; for we cannot believe what we do not know."

" Our doctrine is proved," replied the first standard, " by numerous facts; by a multitude of miracles, by resurrections of the dead, by rivers dried up, by mountains removed, etc."

" And we also," cried all the others, " we have numberless miracles :" and each began to recount the most incredible things.

" Their miracles," said the first standard, " are imaginary; or the fictions of the evil spirit, who has deluded them."

" They are yours," said the others, " that are imaginary ;" and

each group, speaking of itself, cried out : " None but ours are true ;
all the others are false."

The legislator asked : " Have you living witnesses ? "

" No," replied they all : " the facts are ancient, the witnesses are
dead, but their writings remain."

" Be it so," replied the legislator ; " but if they contradict each
other, who shall reconcile them ? "

" Just judge ! " cried one of the standards, " the proof that our
witnesses have seen the truth is that they died to confirm it, and our
faith is sealed with the blood of martyrs."

" And ours too," said the other standards : " we have thousands
of martyrs who died in the most excruciating torments, without
ever denying the truth." Then the Christians of every sect, the
Mussulmen, the Indians, the Japanese, recited endless legends of
confessors, martyrs, penitents, etc.

And one of these parties having denied the martyrology of the
others : " Well," said they, " we will then die ourselves to prove
the truth of our belief."

And instantly a crowd of men of every religion and of every sect,
presented themselves to suffer the torments of death. Many even
began to tear their arms, and to beat their heads and breasts, without discovering any symptom of pain.

But the legislator preventing them : " O men ! " said he, " hear
my words with patience : if you die to prove that two and two make
four, will your death render this truth more evident ? "

" No," answered all.

" And if you die to prove that they make five, will that make
them five ? "

Again they all answered, " No."

" What then is your persuasion to prove, if it changes not the existence of things ? Truth is one, your persuasions are various ; many
of you therefore are in error. Now, if man, as is evident, can persuade himself of error, what does his persuasion prove ?

" If error has its martyrs, what is the criterion of truth ?

" If the evil spirit works miracles, what is the distinctive character of God ?

" Besides, why resort forever to incomplete and insufficient miracles ? Instead of changing the course of nature, why not rather
change opinions ? Why murder and terrify men, instead of instruct-
ing and correcting them ?

" O credulous, but opinionated mortals ! none of us know what was done yesterday, what is even doing to day under our eyes, and we swear to what was done two thousand years ago !

" Oh, the weakness, and yet the pride of men ! the laws of nature are immutable and profound, our minds are full of illusion and frivolity, and yet we would comprehend everything, determine everything ! Verily, it is easier for the whole human race to be in an error, than to change the nature of an atom."

" Well then," said one of the doctors, " let us lay aside the evidence of fact, since it is uncertain ; let us come to argument, the proofs inherent in the doctrine."

Then came forward, with a look of confidence, an Imam of the law of Mahomet; and, having advanced into the circle, turned towards Mecca and recited with great fervor his confession of faith : " Praised be God," said he, with a solemn and imposing voice ' ' The light shineth with full evidence, and truth has no need of examination :" then showing the Coran : "'Here," said he, " is the light of truth in its proper essence. There is no doubt in this book; it conducts with safety him who walks in darkness, and who receives without discussion the divine word which descended on the prophet to save the simple, and confound the wise. God has established Mahomet his minister on earth; he has given him the world, that he may subdue with the sword whoever shall refuse to receive his law : infidels dispute and will not believe ; their obduracy comes from God, who has hardened their hearts to deliver them to dreadful punishments.——" *

At these words, a violent murmur arose on all sides, and silenced the speaker. " Who is this man," cried all the groups, " who thus gratuitously insults us ? What right has he to impose his creed on us as conqueror and tyrant ? Has not God endowed us, as well as him, with eyes, understanding and reason ? And have we not an equal right to use them, in choosing what to believe and what to reject ? If he attacks us, shall we not defend ourselves ? If he likes to believe without examination, must we therefore not examine before we believe ?

" And what is this luminous doctrine that fears the light ? What is this apostle of a God of clemency, who preaches nothing but murder and carnage ? What is this God of justice, who punishes blind-

* This passage contains the sense and nearly the very words of the first chapter of the Coran.

ness which he himself has made ? If violence and persecution are
the arguments of truth, must gentleness and charity be looked on
as signs of falsehood ? "

A man then advancing from a neighbouring group, said to the
Imam : " Admitting that Mahomet is the apostle of the best doctrine,
the prophet of the true religion ; have the goodness at least to tell
us, in the practice of his doctrine, whether we are to follow his son-
in-law Ali, or his vicars Omar and Aboubekre ?"*

At the sound of these names a terrible schism arose among the
Mussulmen themselves : the partisans of Omar and of Ali, calling
out heretics and blasphemers, loaded each other with execrations.
The quarrel became so violent, that the neighbouring groups were
obliged to interfere to prevent their coming to blows.

At length, tranquillity being somewhat restored, the legislator said
to the Imams : " See the consequences of your principles ! If you
yourselves were to carry them into practice, you would destroy each
other to the last man ; is it not the first law of God that man should
live ? " Then addressing himself to the other groups : " Doubtless,"
said he, " this intolerant and exclusive spirit shocks every idea of
justice, and overturns the whole foundation of morals and society ;
but before we totally reject this code of doctrine, is it not proper
to hear some of its dogmas, in order not to pronounce on the forms,
without having some knowledge of the substance ? "

The groups having consented, the Imam began to expound how
God, after having sent to the nations, lost in idolatry, twenty-four
thousand prophets, had finally sent the last, the seal and perfection
of all, Mahomet, on whom be the salvation of peace : how, to prevent
the divine word from being any longer perverted by infidels, the supreme bounty had itself written the pages of the Coran : then explaining the particular dogmas of Islamism, the Imam unfolded how
the Coran, partaking of the divine nature, was increate and eternal,
like its author : how it had been sent leaf by leaf in twenty-four
thousand nocturnal apparitions of the angel Gabriel : How the angel
announced himself by a gentle knocking, which threw the prophet
into a cold sweat ; how, in the vision of one night, he had travelled
over ninety heavens, riding on the animal Boraq, half a horse and
half a woman : how, endowed with the gift of miracles, he walked
in the sunshine without a shadow, turned dry trees to green, filled

* These are the two grand parties into which the Mussulmen are divi
ded. The Turks have embraced the second, the Persians the first

y happy, he forbade their tasting a particular fruit which he left within their reach; that these first parents, having yielded to the temptation, all their race (yet unborn) had been condemned to bear the penalty of a fault which they had not committed; that, after having left the human race to damn themselves for four or five thousand years, this God of mercy ordered a dearly beloved son, whom he had engendered without a mother, and who was as old as himself, to go and be put to death on the earth; and this, for the salvation of mankind, of whom much the greater portion, nevertheless, have ever since continued in the way of perdition; that to remedy this new difficulty, this same God, born of a virgin, having died and risen from the dead, assumes a new existence every day, and in the form of a piece of bread, multiplies himself by millions at the voice of one of the vilest of men; then passing on to the doctrine of the sacraments, he was going to treat at large of the power of absolution and reprobation, of the means of purging all sins by a little water and a few words, when, uttering the words indulgence, power of the pope, sufficient or efficacious grace, he was interrupted by a thousand cries. " It is a horrible abuse," exclaimed the Lutherans, " to pretend to remit sins for money." " The notion of the real presence," cried the Calvinists, " is contrary to the text of the gospel." " The pope has no right to decide anything of himself," cried the Jansenists; and thirty other sects, rising up and accusing each other of heresy and error, it was no longer possible to hear anything distinctly.

Silence being at last restored, the Massulmen observed to the legislator ; " since you have rejected our doctrine as containing things incredible, can you admit that of the Christians ? is not theirs still more contrary to common sense and justice ? a God, immaterial and infinite, to become a man ? to have a son as old as himself ! this god-man to become bread, to be eaten and digested ! have we anything equal to that ? Have the Christians an exclusive right to exact implicit faith ? and will you grant them privileges of belief to our detriment ? "

Some savage tribes then advanced : " What ! " said they, " because a man and woman ate an apple six thousand years ago, all the human race are damned ? and you call God just ! What tyrant ever rendered children responsible for the faults of their fathers ! What man can answer for another's actions : Is not this subversive of every idea of justice and of reason ? "

Others exclaimed : " Where are the proofs, the witnesses of these pretended facts ? Can we receive them without examining the evidence ? The least action in a court of justice requires two witnesses ; and we are ordered to believe all this on mere tradition and hearsay ! ''

A Jewish rabbin then addressing the assembly, said ; '' As to the fundamental facts we are sureties ; but with regard to their form and application, the case is different, and the Christians are here condemned by their own arguments ; for they cannot deny that we are the original source from which they are derived, the primitive stock on which they are grafted ; and hence the reasoning is very short : either our law is from God, and then theirs is a heresy, since it differs from ours ; or our law is not from God, and then theirs falls at the same time.''

'' But you must make this distinction,'' replied the Christian: ''your law is from God, as typical and preparative, but not as final and absolute ; you are the image of which we are the substance.''

'' We know,'' replied the rabbin, '' that such are your pretensions ; but they are absolutely gratuitous and false. Your system turns altogether on mystical meanings, on visionary and allegorical interpretations : * with violent distortions on the letter of our books, you substitute the most chimerical ideas to the true ones, and find in them whatever pleases you, as a wild imagination will find figures in the clouds. Thus you have made a spiritual Messiah of that which, in the spirit of our prophets, is only a temporal king : you have made a redemption of the human race out of the simple reestablishment of our nation ; your conception of the virgin is founded on a single phrase, which you have misunderstood. Thus you make from our scriptures whatever your fancy dictates, you even find there your trinity, though there is not the most distant allusion to it, and it is an invention of profane writers, admitted into your system with a host of other opinions of every religion and of every sect, during the anarchy of the three first centuries of your era.''

At these words, the Christian doctors crying sacrilege and blasphemy, sprang forward in a transport of fury to fall upon the Jew.

---

* '' Your system turns altogether on allegorical interpretations.''— When we read the Fathers of the church, and see upon what arguments they have built the edifice of religion, we are inexpressibly astonished with their credulity or their knavery ; but allegory was the rage of that period : the pagans employed it to explain the actions of their gods, and the Christians acted in the same spirit when they employed it in another manner. It would be interesting to publish now such books, or only extracts from them

And a troop of monks in motley dresses of black and white, advanced with a standard, on which were painted pincers, gridirons, lighted fagots and the words justice, charity, mercy: " We must," said they, "make an example of these impious wretches, and burn them for the glory of God." They began even to prepare the pile, when a Musulman answered in a strain of irony: " This then is your religion of peace, that meek and beneficent system which you so much extol ! This is that evangelical charity which combats infidelity with persuasive mildness, and repays injuries with patience ! Ye hypocrites ! it is thus that you deceive mankind ; thus that you propagate your ac cursed errors ! When you were weak, you preached liberty, tolera- .ion, peace ; when you are strong, you practise persecution and vio- lence."——And he was going to begin the history of the wars and slaughters of Christianity, when the legislator demanding silence, suspended this scene of discord.

The monks, affecting a tone of meekness and humility, exclaimed, " It is not ourselves that we avenge, it is the cause of God, it is his glory that we defend."

" And what right have you, more than we," said the Imams, " to constitute yourselves the representatives of God ? Have you privileges that we have not ? Are you not men like us ?"

" To defend God," said another group, " to pretend to avenge him, is to insult his wisdom and his power. Does he not know better than men what befits his dignity ?"

" Yes," replied the monks, " but his ways are secret."

" And it remains for you to prove," said the rabbins, " that you have the exclusive privilege of understanding them." Then, proud of finding supporters to their cause, the Jews thought that their law would be triumphant, when the mobed (high priest) of the Parses obtained leave to speak :

" We have heard," said he, " the account of the Jews and Christians of the origin of the world ; and, though greatly mutilated, we find in it some facts which we admit ; but we deny that they are to be attributed to their prophet Moses, first because it cannot be shown that the books which bear his name were really his ; we can prove on the contrary, by twenty positive passages, that they were written at least six centuries later, and proceed evidently from the connivance of a high priest and a king, both well known ; * next if

* See on this subject the 1st vol. of New Researches on ancient History, where this question is fundamentally investigated after chapter V

you examine attentively the laws, the ceremonies, the precepts established by Moses in those books, you will not find the slightest indication, either expressed or understood, of what constitutes the bases
of the present theological doctrine of the Jews and of their children
the Christians. You nowhere find the least trace of the immortality of the soul, or of a future life, or of heaven or of hell, or of the
revolt of the principal angel, author of the evils of the human race, etc.

"These ideas were not known to Moses, and the reason is very
obvious, since it was not till two centuries afterwards that our prophet
Zerdoust, named Zoroaster, first evangelized them in Asia. Thus,
added the mobed, turning to the rabbins, it is not till after that epoch,
that is to say, in the time of your first kings, that these ideas begin
to appear in your writers; and then their appearance is obscure and
gradual, according to the progress of the political relations between
your ancestors and ours. It was especially when, having been conquered by the kings of Nineveh and Babylon, and transported to the
banks of the Tygris and Euphrates, they resided there for three successive generations, that they imbibed manners and opinions which
had been rejected as contrary to their law. When our king Cyrus
had delivered them from slavery, they became our disciples and imitators;* the most distinguished families, whom the kings of Babylon
had got instructed in the Chaldean sciences, carried back to Jerusalem new ideas and foreign tenets.

"At first the mass of the people, who had not emigrated, pleaded
the text of the law and the absolute silence of the prophet; but the
Pharisean or Parsee doctrine prevailed; and, being modified according to the ideas and genius of your nation, gave rise to a new sect.
You expected a king to restore your political independence; we
announced a God to regenerate and save mankind: from this combination of ideas, your Essenians laid the foundation of Christianity:
and whatever your pretensions may be, Jews, Christians, Mussulmen,
you are, in your systems of spiritual beings, only the blundering followers of Zoroaster!"

The mobed, then passing on to the details of his religion, quoting
from the Sadder and the Zend-Avesta, recounted, in the same order

* "They became our disciples and imitators."—See on this subject the
1st. vol. of New Researches on ancient History, where it is proved that
the Pentateuch is not the work of Moses: this opinion prevailed in the
first ages of Christianity, as may be seen in the Clementines, homily 11,
§ 51, and homily 8, § 42; but no one had proved that the true author was
the high-priest Hilkiah, in the year 621 before J C.

as Genesis, the creation of the world in six gahans; the formation
of a first man and a first woman in a divine place, under the reign of
good; the introduction of evil into the world by the great snake, emblem of Ahrimanes: the revolt and battles of the Genius of evil and
darkness against Ormuzd, God of good and light: the division of the
angels into white and black, or good and bad; their hierarchal orders,
cherubim, seraphim, thrones, dominions, etc.; the end of the world
at the close of six thousand years; the coming of the lamb the regen-
erator of nature; the new world; the future life, and the regions of
happiness and misery; the passage of souls over the bridge of the
bottomless pit; the celebration of the mysteries of Mythras; the un-
leavened bread which the initiated eat; the baptism of new born
children; the unction of the dead, the confession of sins; and in a
word, he recited so many things analogous to the three religions before mentioned,* that it seemed like a commentary or a continuation
of the Coran and the Apocalypse.

But the Jewish, Christian and Mahometan doctors, crying out
against this recital, and treating the Parses as idolaters and worshippers of fire, charged them with falsehood, interpolations, falsification
of facts; and there arose a violent dispute as to the dates of the events,
their order and succession, the origin of the doctrines, their transmission from nation to nation, the authenticity of the books that established them, the epoch of their composition, the character of their
compilers, and the validity of their testimony: and the various parties,
pointing out reciprocal contradictions, improbabilities and forgeries,
accused each other of having established this belief on popular rumors,

---

* "So many things analogous to the three religions."—The modern
Parses and the ancient Mithriacs, who are the same sect, observe all the
Christian sacraments, even the laying on of hands in confirmation.
'The priest of Mithra,' says Tertullian, de Præscriptione, c. 40, 'promises
absolution from sin on confession and baptism; and, if I rightly remember, Mithra marks his soldiers in the forehead (with the chrism, the
Egyptian Kouphi;) he celebrates the sacrifice of bread, which is the resurrection, and presents the crown to his followers, menacing them at
the same time with the sword, etc.'

In these mysteries they tried the courage of the initiated with a thousand terrors, presenting fire to his face, a sword to his breast, etc.; they
also offered him a crown which he refused, saying: God is my crown,
and this crown is to be seen in the celestial sphere by the side of Bootes.
The personages in these mysteries were distinguished by the names
of the annual constellations. The ceremony of mass is nothing more
than an imitation of these mysteries and of those of Eleusis. The bene-
diction, the Lord be with you, is a literal translation of the formule
of admission chn-k. am, p.ak. See Beausobre, histoire du Manicheisme, vol. II

vague traditions and absurd fables, invented without discernment, and admitted without examination by unknown, ignorant or partial writers, and at false or uncertain epochs.

A great murmur now arose from under the standards of the various Indian sects; and the Bramins, protesting against the pretensions of the Jews and Parses, said; " What are these new and almost unheard of nations, who arrogantly set themselves up as the sources of the human race, and the depositaries of its archives? To hear their calculations of five or six thousand years, it would seem that the world was of yesterday, whereas our monuments prove a duration of many thousands of centuries. And for what reason are their books to be preferred to ours? Are then the Vedas,* Chastras, and Pourans inferior to the Bibles, Zend-avestas, and Sad-ders? And is not the testimony of our fathers and our Gods as valid as that of the fathers and the Gods of the Occidentals? Ah! if it were permitted to reveal our mysteries to profane men! if a sacred veil did not justly conceal them from every eye!—"

The Bramins stopping short at these words: " How can we admit your doctrine," said the legislator, " if you will not make it known? And how did its first authors propagate it, when being alone possessed of it, their own people were to them profane? Did heaven reveal it to be kept a secret?"

But the Bramins persisting in their silence: " Let them have the honor of the secret," said an European. " Their doctrine is now divulged: we possess their books; and I can give you the substance of them."

Then beginning with an abstract of the four Vedas, the eighteen Pourans and the five or six Chastras, he recounted how a being, infi-

---

* The Vedas or Vedams are the sacred volumes of the Hindoos, as the Bibles with us. They are three in number. the Itiek Veda, the Yadjour Veda, and the Sama Veda: they are so scarce in India, that the English could with great difficulty find an original one, of which a copy is deposited in the British Museum; they who reckon four Vedas, include among them the Attar Veda, concerning ceremonies, but which is lost. There are besides commentaries named Upanishada, one of which was published by Anquetil du Peron, and entitled Oupnekhat, a curious work. The date of these books is more than twenty five centuries prior to our era; their contents prove that all the reveries of the Greek metaphysicians come from India and Egypt.—Since the year 1788, the learned men of England are working in India a mine of literature totally unknown in Europe, and which proves that the civilisation of India ascends to a very remote antiquity. After the Vedas come the Chastras amounting to six. They treat of theology and the sciences. Afterwards 18 Pouranas, treating of Mythology and History: see the Bahgenet-guita, the Baga Vadam, and the Ezour-Vedam, etc

nite, eternal, immaterial and round, after having passed an eternity
in self-contemplation, and determining at last to manifest himself,
separated the male and female faculties which were in him, and performed an act of generation, of which the Lingam remains an emblem ;
how that first act gave birth to three divine powers, Brahma, Bichen
or Vichenou, and Chib or Chiven, whose functions were, the first to
create, the second to preserve, and the third to destroy or change the
form of the universe : then, detailing the history of their operations
and adventures, he explained how Brahma, proud of having created
the world and the eight spheres of purifications, thought himself superior to Chib, his equal ; how this pride brought on a battle between
them, in which the celestial globes, or orbits, were crushed like a
basket of eggs ; how Brahma, vanquished in this conflict, was reduced to serve as a pedestal to Chib, metamorphosed into a Lingam ;
how Vichenou, the God mediator, has assumed at different times, to
preserve the world, nine mortal forms of animals ; how first, in shape
of a fish, he saved from the universal deluge a family who repeopled
the earth ; how afterwards, in form of a tortoise, he drew from the
milky sea the mountain Mandreguiri (the pole :) then, becoming a
boar, he tore the belly of the giant Erenniachessen, who was drown-
ing the earth in the abyss of Djole, and saved it on his tusks ; how
becoming incarnate in a black shepherd, and under the name of Chris-
en, he delivered the world of the venomous serpent Calengam, and
then crushed his head, after having been wounded by him in the heel

Then passing on to the history of the secondary genii, he related
how the Eternal, to manifest his glory, created various orders of angels, who were to sing his praises and to direct the universe ; how a
part of these angels revolted under the guidance of an ambitious chief,
who strove to usurp the power of God, and to govern all ; how God
plunged them into a world of darkness, there to undergo the punishment of their crimes ; how at last, touched with compassion, he
consented to release them, and receive them into favor, after they
should undergo a long series of probations; how, after creating for
this purpose, fifteen orbits or regions of planets, and peopling them
with bodies, he ordered these rebel angels to undergo in them eighty-
seven transmigrations ; he then explained how souls, thus purified,
returned to the first source, to the ocean of life and animation from
which they had proceeded ; and since all living creatures contain
portions of this universal soul, he taught how criminal it was to deprive them of it. He was finally proceeding to explain the rites and

ceremonies, when speaking of offerings and libations of milk and butter to gods of copper and wood, and then of purifications by the dung and urine of cows, there arose an universal murmur, mixed with peals of laughter, which interrupted the orator.

Each of the different groups began to reason on that religion : " They are idolaters," said the Mussulmen, " and should be exterminated." ' They are deranged in their intellect," said the followers of Confucius, " we should try to cure them." " What ridiculous gods," said others, " are these puppets, besmeared with grease and smoke, that must be washed like dirty children, and from whom you must brush away the flies, attracted by honey, and fouling them with their excrements !"

But a Bramin exclaimed with indignation : " These are profound mysteries, emblems of truth which you are not worthy to hear."

" And in what respect are you more worthy than we," exclaimed a lama of Tibet. " Is it because you pretend to be issued from the head of Brama,* and the rest of the human race from the less noble parts of his body ? But to support the pride of your distinctions of origin and casts, prove to us in the first place that you are different from other men. Establish in the next place, as historical facts, the allegories which you relate, show us indeed that you are the authors of all this doctrine ; for we will demonstrate, if necessary, that you have only stolen and disfigured it ; that you are only the imitators of the ancient paganism of the Occidental ; to which, by an ill assorted mixture, you have allied the pure and spiritual doctrine of our God ; a doctrine totally detached from the senses, and entirely unknown on earth, till Boudh taught it to the nations."

A number of groups having inquired what was this doctrine, and

---

* All this cosmogony of the Lamas, the Bonzes, and even the bramins, as Henry Lord asserts, is literally that of the ancient Egyptians. ' The Egyptians,' says Porphyry, 'call Kneph, the intelligence or efficient cause (of the universe.) They relate that this God vomited an egg, from which was produced another God, named Phtha or Vulcan (igneous principle or the sun,) and they add, that this egg is the world.' Euseb Prœp. Evang. p. 115.

' They represent,' says the same author in another place, 'the god Kneph, or efficient cause, under the form of a man in deep blue (the color of the sky,) having in his hand a sceptre, a belt round his body, and a small bonnet royal of light feathers on his head, to denote how very subtle and fugacious the idea of that being is.' Upon which I shall observe that Kneph in Hebrew signifies a wing, a feather, and that this color of sky blue is to be found in the majority of the Indian gods, and is, under the name of narayan, one of their most distinguished epithets

who was this God, whose name the greater part of them had never heard, the lama resumed and said :

" In the beginning, a sole and self-existent God, having passed an eternity in the contemplation of his own being, resolved to manifest his perfections out of himself, and created the matter of the world; the four elements being produced, but still in a state of confusion, he breathed on the face of the waters, which swelled like an immense bubble in form of an egg, which unfolding, became the vault or orb of heaven enclosing the world; having made the earth, and the bodies of animals, this God, essence of motion, imparted to them a portion of his own being to animate them ; for this reason, the soul of everything that breathes being a fraction of the universal soul, no one of them can perish, they only change their form and mould in passing successively into different bodies : of all these forms, the one most pleasing to God is that of man, as most resembling his own perfections ; when a man, by an absolute disengagement from his senses, is wholly absorbed in self-contemplation, he then discovers the divinity and becomes himself god : of all the incarnations of this kind that God has hitherto taken, the greatest and most solemn was that in which he appeared twenty-eight centuries ago in Kachemire, under the name of Fot or Boudh, to preach the doctrine of self-deni-al, and self-annihilation." Then, pursuing the history of Fot, the lama said ; " He was born from the right flank of a virgin of royal blood, who did not cease to be a virgin for having become a mother; that the king of the country, alarmed at his birth, wished to destroy him, and for this purpose ordered a massacre of all the males born at that period; that being saved by shepherds, Boudh lived in the desert till the age of thirty, when he began his mission, to enlighten men and cast out devils; that he performed a multitude of the most astonishing miracles; that he spent his life in fasting and severe penitence, and at his death, bequeathed to his disciples a book which contained his doctrines;" and the lama began to read....

" ' He that leaveth his father and mother to follow me,' says Fot, ' becomes a perfect samanean (heavenly man;)

" ' He that practises my precepts to the fourth degree of perfec-tion, acquires the faculty of flying in the air, of moving heaven and earth, of prolonging and shortening life (rising from the dead.)

" ' The samenean despises riches, and uses only what is strictly necessary ; he mortifies his body; silences his passions ; desires nothing ; forms no attachments ; meditates my doctrines without ceasing ; endures injuries with patience, and bears no malice to his neighbour.

" ' Heaven and earth shall perish,' says Fot : ' despise therefore your bodies composed of the four perishable elements, and think only of your immortal soul.

" ' Listen not to the flesh : fear and sorrow spring from the passions : stifle the passions, and you destroy fear and sorrow.

" ' Whoever dies without having embraced my religion,' says Fot, 'returns among men until he embraces it.' "

The lama was proceeding, when the Christians, interrupting him, exclaimed that this was their own religion adulterated ; that Fot was no other than Jesus himself disfigured, and that the lamas were the Nestorians and Manicheans disguised and bastardized.*

But the lama, supported by the chamans, bonzes, gonnis, talapoins of Siam, of Ceylon, of Japan, and of China, proved to the Christians, even from their own authors, that the doctrine of the Samaneans was diffused through the East more than a thousand years before the Christian era ; that their name was cited before the time of Al-

* " The Lamas were Manicheans disguised."—See the History of Manicheism, by Beausobre, who proves that these sectaries were pure Zoroastrians ; which makes the existence of their opinions to precede J. C. by 1200 years. It follows from hence that Boudd Chaucasam was still more ancient, since the Boudite doctrine is found in the oldest Indian books, that preceded our era by 3,000 years (such as Bahgouet Guita.) Observe moreover that Boudd is the 9th avatar or incarnation of Vicheneu which places him at the origin of this theology. Further, among the Indians, Chinese, Tibetans, etc. Boudd is the name of the planet we call Mercury, and of the day of the week consecrated to that planet (Wednesday ;) this carries him back to the origin of the calendar ; at the same time that it shows him to have been primitively identical with Hermes : his existence therefore extended to Egypt : now observe that the Egyptian priests make Hermes at his death to say : ' I have hitherto lived banished from my true country ; I now go back there : do not weep for me : I return to the celestial country whither every one goes in his turn ; there dwells God ; this life is but death.' See Chalcidius in Timœum. Now, this doctrine is precisely that of the ancient Bouditos, or Samaneans, of the Pythagoricuns and of the Orphies : in the doctrine of Orpheus, the god world is represented by an egg : in the Hebrew and Arabian idioms, the egg is called baidh, analogous to Boudd (God,) and to Boud, in Persian, existence, what is (the world.) Boudd is also analogous to bed vad, signifying amongst the Indians, science. Hermes was its god : he was the author of the sacred books or Egyptian Vedas. What ramifications, and what a remote antiquity does not all this suppose : now the Boudite priest of Ava adds : ' It is an article of faith that from time to time heaven sends upon earth some Bouddas to reclaim men, to save them from vice, and show them the ways of salvation.' With such a dogma extending over India, Persia, Egypt and Judea, it is no wonder that men's minds should be prepared long before hand for what latter ages offer to our view.

exander, and that Boutta or Boudh was known long before Jesus.*
Then, retorting the pretensions of the Christians against themselves.
"Prove to us now," said the lama, "that you are not yourselves
degenerate Samaneans : and that the man whom you make the author of your sect is not Fot himself disfigured. Prove to us by historical facts that he even existed at the epoch you pretend; for it
being destitute of authentic testimony,† we absolutely deny it; and

* " Long before Iesous."—According to the English Orientalists, the
doctrine of Boudda is very ancient in India. The anonymous writer
mentioned page 228, line 51, cites a Treatise written a few years ago by
the chief of the Boudite priests of Ava, at the request of the catholic
bishop of that city, stating : 'That the Gods, who have appeared in
this world until the present day, are four in number, to wit: Boudda
Chaucasam, Boudda Gonagom, Boudda Gaspa, and Boudda Gautama,
whose law is now in vigor ; he obtained divinity at the age of 35, and
spent in immortality 2362 years (before the date of the writing, about the
year 1805.) ' Consequently Gautama died about 557 years before the
Christian era, at the time when Cyrus reigned in Persia, and when
Pythagoras flourished.
2dly. On the other hand, Arabian and Persian writers, cited in the
history of the Huns, vol. II. by de Guignes ; in the Hist. of China, vol
5. in 4to. note to page 50, and in the preface to the Ezour-Vedam (Yad-
jour-Veda,) place the apparition of another Boudda in the year 1027
before our era (it must be Gaspa.)
3dly. The statistical Table of the Mogul emperor Akbar ; entitled Ain
Akberi, translated by Gladwin, says, page 4 3, vol. II. that Boudd disappeared 2962 years before the 40th of that emperor, that is to say 1366
years before J. C. (This must be Gonagom.)

† " Being destitute of authentic testimony."—'All the world knows,'
says Faustus, who though a manichean, was one of the most learned
men of the third century, 'all the world knows that the gospels were
neither written by Jesus Christ, nor his apostles, but a long time after,
by unknown persons, who rightly judging that they should not obtain
belief respecting things which they had not seen, placed at the head of
their recitals the names of contemporary apostles.' Consult upon this
question, Histoire des Apologistes de la Religion chretienne, attributed
to Freret, but which was written by Burigny, member of the academy
of Inscriptions. See also Mosheim, de Rebus christianorum ; Correspon-
dence of Atterbury, archbishop, 5 vols. in 8vo., 1798. Toland Nazare-
nus ; and Beausobre, Histoire du Manicheisme, vol. I. From all that
has been written for and against it results that the precise origin of
Christianity is unknown ; that the pretended testimonies of Josephus
(Antiq. Jud. lib. xviii, c. 3) and of Tacitus (Annals, b. xv. c. 44,) have
been interpolated about the time of the council of Nice, and that nobody
could ever demonstrate the radical fact, that is to say, the real existence
of the personage who gave rise to the system. Without that existence
however, it would be difficult to conceive the appearance of the system
at its known epoch, although history offers many examples of gratuitous and absolute suppositions. To resolve this truly curious and important problem, some man of sagacity, instruction, and above all
impartiality, benefiting by the researches already made, should form a
comparative table of the doctrine of the Boudites, and specially of the
sect of Samana Gautama, contemporary with Cyrus ; he should examine
what was the facility of communication of India with Persia and Syria,
particularly after the reign of Darius Hystaspes, who, according to

we maintain that your very gospels are only the book of some M h-
riacs of Persia, and Essenians of Syria who were a branch of re-
formed Samaneans."

At these words, the Christians set up a general cry, and a new
dispute was going to begin, when a number of Chinese chamans and
talapoins of Siam, came forward, and said that they would settle the
whole controversy. And one of them speaking for the whole : " **It**
is time," said he, " to put an end to these frivolous contests by
drawing aside the veil from the interior doctrine* that Fot himself
revealed to his disciples on his death-bed."

" All these theological opinions," said he, " are but chimeras; all
the stories of the nature of the gods, of their actions and lives, are
but allegories and mythological emblems, under which are enveloped
ingenious ideas of morals, and the knowledge of the operations of
nature in the action of the elements and the movement of the planets.

" The truth is that all is reduced to nothing ; that all is illusion,

Agathius and Ammianus, consulted the wise men of India, and introduced several of their ideas among the magi : further, what facility there
was after Alexander's time, under the Seleucidœ, who kept up diplo-
matical relations with the Indian kings ; he would see that, through
these communications, the system of the Samaneans might have gradually extended as far as Egypt ; that it might have been the determining
cause of the corporation of the Essenians in Judea, etc. ; the only question then would be if, when all was thus prepared, the general exaltation of men's minds might not have prompted an individual to fill the
allotted part ; either because he declared and believed himself to be the
personage announced, or because the multitude, enchanted with his
conduct, doctrine and preaching, attributed to him that character. In
either case, it is extremely probable that popular disturbances excited
the suspicions and vigilance of the Roman government, and that at
length some remarkable incident, such as the entrance into Jerusalem,
forced the prefect to adopt a measure of rigor, an act of severity, that
suddenly put an end to the drama (nearly as related,) but which only
augmented the interest which the regretted personage inspired, and, by
that means, gave rise to narrations and associations the result of which
would perfectly agree with the state of things afterwards seen in history.
Doubtless where her positive testimony is wanting there no moral certainty can exist ; but by the concatenation of causes and effects, a degree
of probability producing the same effect may be attained ; since even
with the most positive testimonies, history can only pretend to a greater
or lesser degree of probability.

* " The interior doctrine."—The Bouddites have two doctrines, the
one public and ostensible, the other interior and secret, precisely like
the Egyptian priests. It may be asked, why this distinction ? Because,
as the public doctrine recommends offerings, expiations, endowments,
etc., the priests find their profit in preaching it to the people ; whereas
the other, teaching the vanity of worldly things and being attended
with no lucre, it is thought proper to make it known only to adepts
Thus are men divided into the two evidently distinct classes of knaves
and dupes !

appearance, dream; that the moral metempsychosis is only the figurative sense of the physical metempsychosis, or the successive movement by which the elements of the same body perish not, but at its dissolution, pass into other mediums and form other combinations. The soul is but the vital principle which results from the properties of matter and from the action of the elements in those bodies where they create a spontaneous movement. To suppose that this product of the play of the organs, born with them, matured with them, and which sleeps with them, can subsist when they cease, is the romance of a wandering imagination, perhaps agreeable but absolutely chimerical. God itself is nothing more than the moving principle, the occult force inherent in all beings; the sum of their laws and properties; the animating principle, in a word, the soul of the universe; which on account of the infinite variety of its connexions and operations, sometimes simple, sometimes multiple, sometimes active, sometimes passive, has always presented to the human mind an insolvable enigma. All that man can comprehend with certainty is, that matter does not perish; that it possesses essentially those properties by which the world is held together like a living and organized being; that the knowledge of these laws, with respect to man, is what constitutes wisdom; that virtue and merit consist in their observance; and evil, sin, and vice, in the ignorance and violation of them; that happiness and misery result from these by the same necessity which makes heavy bodies descend, and light ones rise by a fatality of causes and effects, whose chain extends from the smallest atom to the greatest of the heavenly bodies. All this was revealed on his death-bed by our Boudah Somona Goutama."*

At these words, a crowd of theologians of every sect cried out that this doctrine was materialism; and those who profess it were unpious atheists, enemies to God and man, who must be exterminated.—" Very well!" replied the Chamans, " suppose we are in an error, which is not impossible, since the first attribute of the human mind is to be subject to illusion; but what right have you to take away from men like yourselves, the life which heaven has given them? If heaven holds us guilty, and in abhorrence, why does it

* " This was revealed by our Boudah."—These are the very expressions of La Loubere, in his description of the kingdom of Siam and of the theology of the Bonzes. Their dogmas, compared with those of the ancient philosophers of Greece and Italy, give a complete representation of the whole system of the Stoics and Epicureans, mixed with astrological superstitions and some traits of Pythagorism.

impart to us the same blessings as to you? And if it tolerates us, what right have you to be less indulgent? Pious men! who speak of God with so much certainty and confidence, please to tell us what it is; give us to comprehend what these abstract metaphysical beings are, which you call God and soul, substance without matter, existence without body, life without organs or sensation. If you know those beings by your senses or their reflections, render them in like manner perceptible to us · or if you speak of them on testimony and tradition, show us an uniform account, and give a determinate basis to our creed." There now arose among the theologians a great controversy respecting God and his nature : his manner of acting and of manifesting himself; on the nature of the soul and its union with the body; whether it exists before the organs, or only after they are formed : on the future life and the other world : and every sect, every school, every individual, differing on all these points, and each assigning plausible reasons, and respectable though opposite authorities, for his opinion, they fell into an inextricable labyrinth of contradictions.

Then the legislator having commanded silence and recalled the dispute to its true object, said : " Chiefs and instructers of the people, you came together in search of truth; at first, every one of you, thinking he possessed it, demanded of the others an implicit faith ; but receiving the contrariety of your opinions, you found it necessary to submit them to a common rule of evidence, and to bring them to one general term of comparison ; and you agreed that each should exhibit the proofs of his doctrine. You began by alleging facts ; but each religion and every sect, being equally furnished with miracles and martyrs, each producing an equal cloud of witnesses, and offering to support them by a voluntary death, the balance on this first point, by right of parity, remained equal.

" You then passed to the trial of reasoning ; but the same arguments applying equally to contrary positions ; the same assertions, equally gratuitous, being advanced and repelled with equal force, and all having an equal right to refuse assent, nothing was demonstrated What is more, the confrontation of your systems has brought up new and extraordinary difficulties ; for amidst the apparent or adventitious diversities, you have discovered a fundamental resemblance, a common groundwork ; and each of you pretending to be the inventor, and first depositary, you have taxed each other with adulterations and plagiarisms ; and thence arises a difficult question concerning the transmission of religious ideas from people to people.

" Finally to repeat the embarrassment, when you endeavoured to explain your doctrines to each other, they appeared confused and foreign, even to their adherents; they were founded on ideas inaccessible to your senses; of consequence you had no means of judging of them, and you confessed yourselves in this respect to be only the echoes of your fathers : hence follows this other question, how came they to the knowledge of your fathers, who themselves had no other means than you to concieve them : so that, on the one hand, the succession of these ideas being unknown, and on the other, their origin and existence being a mystery, all the edifice of your religious opinions becomes a complicated problem of metaphysics and history.—

" Since however these opinions, extraordinary as they may be, must have had some origin; since even the most abstract and fantastical ideas have some physical model, it may be useful to recur to this origin, and discover this model; in a word, to find out from what source the human understanding has drawn these ideas, at present so obscure of the divinity, the soul, and all immaterial beings which make the basis of so many systems; to unfold the filiation which they have followed and the alterations which they have undergone in their transmissions and ramifications. If then there are any persons present who have made a study of these objects, let them come forward, and endeavour, in the face of nations, to dissipate the obscurity in which their opinions have so long strayed."

CHAPTER XXII.

ORIGIN AND FILIATION OF RELIGIOUS IDEAS.

AT these words, a new group, formed in an instant by men from various standards, but not distinguished by any, came forward in the circle; and one of them spoke in the name of the whole.

" Legislator, friend of evidence and truth ! it is not astonishing that the subject in question should be enveloped in so many clouds, since, besides its inherent difficulties, thought itself has always been encumbered with superadded obstacles peculiar to this study, where all free enquiry and discussion have been interdicted by the intolerance of every system; but now that our views are permitted to expand, we will expose to open day, and submit to the judgment of nations, that which unprejudiced minds after long researches have found to be the most reasonable; and we do this, not with the pretension of imposing a new creed, but with the hope of provoking new lights, and obtaining better information.

"Doctors and instructers of nations! You know what thick darkness covers the nature, the origin, the history of the dogmas which you teach: imposed by force and authority, inculcated by education, and maintained by example, they pass from age to age, and strengthen their empire from habit and inattention. But if man, enlightened by reflection and experience, brings to mature examination the prejudices of his childhood, he soon discovers a multitude of incongruities and contradictions which awaken his sagacity and excite his reasoning powers.

"At first, remarking the diversity and opposition of the creeds which divide the nations, he rejects the infallibility which each of them claims; and arming himself with their reciprocal pretensions, he conceives that his senses and his reason derived immediately from God, are a law not less holy, a guide not less sure than the mediate and contradictory codes of the prophets

"If he then examines the texture of these codes themselves, he observes that their laws, pretended to be divine, that is, immutable and eternal, have arisen from circumstances of times, places and persons; that they have issued, one from the other, in a kind of genealogical order, borrowing from each other reciprocally a common and similar fund of ideas, which every lawgiver modifies according to his fancy.

"If he ascends to the source of these ideas, he finds it involved in the night of time, in the infancy of nations, even in the origin of the world, to which they claim alliance; and there, placed in the darkness of chaos, in the empire of fables and traditions, they present themselves accompanied with a state of things so full of prodigies, that it seems to forbid all access to the judgment; but this state itself excites a first effort of reason, which resolves the difficulty; for if the prodigies, found in the theological systems, have really existed. if, for instance, the metamorphosis, the apparitions, the conversations with one or many gods recorded in the sacred books of the Indians, the Hebrews, the Parses, are historical events, he must agree that nature in those times was totally different from what it is at present; that the present race of men are quite another species from those who then existed, and, therefore, he ought not to trouble his head about them

" If, on the contrary, these miraculous events have really not existed in the physical order of things, then he readily conceives that they are creatures of the human intellect; and this faculty being still capable of the most fantastical combinations, explains at once the phenomenon of these monsters in history; it only remains then to find how and wherefore they have been formed in the imagination: now, if we examine with care the subjects of these intellectual creations, analyze the ideas which they combine and associate, and attentively weigh all the circumstances which they allege, we shall find that this first obscure and incredible state of things is explained by the laws of nature; we find that these stories of a fabulous kind have a figurative sense different from the apparent one; that these events, pretended to be marvellous, are simple and physical facts, which being misconceived or misrepresented, have been disfigured by accidental causes dependent on the human mind; by the confusion of signs employed to paint the ideas; the want of precision in words, permanence in language, and perfection in writing; we find that these gods, for instance, who display such singular characters in every system, are only the physical agents of nature, the elements, the winds, the stars and the meteors, which have been personified by the necessary mechanism of language and of the human understanding; that their lives, their manners, their actions, are only their mechanical operations and connexions; and that all their pretended history is only the description of these phenomena, formed by the first naturalists who observed them. and misconceived by the vulgar who did not understand them, or by succeeding generations, who forgot them. In a word, all the theological dogmas on the origin of the world, the nature of God, the revelation of his laws, the manifestation of his person, are known to be only the recital of astronomical facts, only figurative and emblematical accounts of the motion of the heavenly bodies; we are convinced that the very idea of a God, that idea at present so obscure, is, in its first origin, nothing but that of the physical powers of the universe, considered sometimes as a plurality by reason of their agencies and phenomena, sometimes as one simple and only being by reason of the universality of the machine and the connexion of its parts; so that the being called God has been sometimes the wind, the fire, the water, all the elements; sometimes the sun, the stars, the planets, and their influence; sometimes the matter of the visible world, the totality of the universe; sometimes abstract and metaphysical qualities, such as space, duration, motion and intelligence; and we everywhere see this conclusion, that the idea of God has not been a miraculous revelation of invisible beings, but a natural offspring of the human intellect, an operation of the mind, whose progress it has followed and whose revolutions it has undergone, in all the knowledge it has acquired of the physical world and its agents.

" It is then in vain that nations attribute their religion to heavenly inspirations, it is in vain that their dogmas pretend to a primeval state of supernatural events: the original barbarity of the human race,* attested by their own monuments, belies these assertions at once, but there is one constant and indubitable fact which refutes beyond contradiction all these doubtful accounts of past ages. From this position, that man acquires and receives no ideas but through the medium of his senses,† it follows with certainty that every notion which pretends to any other origin than that of sensation and experience, is the erroneous supposition of a posterior reasoning; now, it is sufficient to cast an eye upon the sacred systems of the origin of the world, and of the actions of the gods, to discover in every idea, in every word, the anticipation of an order of things which could not exist till a long time after. Reason, strengthened by these contradictions, rejecting everything that is not in the order of nature, and admitting no historical facts but those founded on probabilities, lays open its own system, and pronounces itself with assurance:

" Before one nation had received from another nation dogmas already invented; before one generation had inherited ideas acquired by a preceding generation, none of these complicated systems could have existed in the world. The first men, being children of nature, anterior to all events, ignorant of all science, were born without any

---

* " The original barbarity of the human race."—It is the unanimous testimony of history and even of legends, that the first human beings were everywhere savages, and that it was to civilize them and teach them to make bread, that the gods manifested themselves.

† " Receives no ideas but through the medium of his senses."—The rock on which the ancients split, and which has occasioned all their errors, has been the supposing the idea of God innate, and co-eternal with the soul: and hence all the reveries developed in Plato and Jamblicus. See the Timœus, the Phedon, and de Mysteriis Ægyptiorum, sect 1, c. 2.

idea of the dogmas arising from scholastic disputes ; of rights founded on the practice of arts not then known ; of precepts framed after the developement of passions ; of laws which suppose a language, a state of society not then in being, of God, whose attributes all refer to physical objects, and his actions to a despotic state of government ; or of the soul, or of any of those metaphysical beings, which we are told, are not the objects of sense, and for which however, there can be no other means of access to the understanding. To arrive at so many results, the necessary circle of preceding facts must have been observed; slow experience and repeated trials must have taught the rude man the use of his organs ; the accumulated observations of successive generations must have invented and improved the means of living ; and the mind, freed from the cares of the first wants of nature, must have raised itself to the complicated art of comparing ideas, of digesting argument, and seizing abstract similitudes."

Origin of the Idea of God : Worship of the Elements and of the Physical Powers of Nature.

" It was not till after having overcome these obstacles, and gone through a long career in the night of history, that man, reflecting on his condition, began to perceive that he was subjected to forces superior to his own and independent of his will. The sun enlightened and warmed him, fire burned him, thunder terrified him, the wind beat upon him, and water drowned him ; all beings acted upon him powerfully and irresistibly. He sustained this action for a long time, like a machine, without inquiring the cause ; but the moment he began his inquiries, he fell into astonishment ; and passing from the surprise of his first reflections to the revery of curiosity, he began a chain of reasoning.

" First, considering the action of the elements on him, he conceived an idea of weakness and subjection on his part, and of power and domination on theirs ; and this idea of power was the primitive and fundamental type of every idea of the Divinity.

" Secondly, the action of these natural existences excited in him sensations of pleasure or pain, of good or evil; and by a natural effect of his organization, he conceived for them love or aversion ; he desired or dreaded their presence ; and fear or hope gave rise to the first idea of religion.

" Then, judging everything by comparison, and remarking in these beings a spontaneous movement like his own, he supposed this move-

ment directed by a will, an intelligence, of the nature of his own ·
and hence by induction, he formed a new reasoning.—Having experienced that certain practices towards his fellow creatures had the
effect to modify their affections and direct their conduct, he resorted
to the same practices towards these powerful beings of the universe:
he reasoned thus, ' When my fellow creature, stronger than I, is disposed to do me injury, I demean myself before him, and by prayers
succeed in appeasing him.   I will pray to these powerful beings who
strike me; I will implore the intelligences of the winds, the stars
and the waters, and they will hear me.   I will conjure them to avert
the evil and give me the good that is at their disposal ; I will move
them by my tears, I will soften them by offerings, and will enjoy happiness.'

" Thus simple man, in the infancy of his reason, spoke to the sun
and moon ; he animated with his own understanding and passions,
the great agents of nature ; he thought by vain sounds, and vain
practices, to change their inflexible laws : fatal error ! he prayed the
stone to ascend, the water to rise above its level, the mountains to
remove, and substituting a fantastical world to the real one, he peopled it with imaginary beings, to the terror of his mind and the torment of his race.

" In this manner the ideas of God and religion have sprung, like
all others, from physical objects, and were produced in the mind of
man by his sensations, his wants, the circumstances of his life and
the progressive state of his knowledge.

" Now, as the ideas of the Divinity had their first models in physical agents, it followed that the Divinity was at first varied and
manifold, like the form under which he appeared to act : every being
was a power, a genius ; and the first men conceived the universe filled
with innumerable gods.

" Again, the ideas of the Divinity have been created by the affections of the human heart ; they became necessarily divided into two
classes, according to the sensations of pleasure or pain, love or
hatred : the powers of nature, the gods, the genii were divided into
beneficent and malignant, good and evil; and hence the universality
of these two characters in all the systems of religion.

" These ideas, analogous to the condition of their inventors, were
for a long time confused and ill digested.   Savage men, wandering
in the woods, beset with wants, and destitute of resources, had not
the leisure to combine principles and draw conclusions ; affected with

more evils than they found pleasures, their most habitual sentiment was that of fear, their theology terror; their worship was confined to a few salutations and offerings to beings whom they conceived as ferocious and as greedy as themselves. In their state of equality and independence, no man offered himself as a mediator between men and gods as insubordinate and poor as himself. No man having super-fluities to g᾽ e, there existed no parasite by the name of priest, no tribute by t᾽᾽᾽᾽ me of victim, no empire by the name of altar; their dogmas and their morals were the same thing, it was only self-pre-servation; and religion, that arbitrary idea, without influence on the mutual relations of men, was a vain homage rendered to the visible powers of nature.

"Such was the necessary and original idea of the divinity."

And the orator addressing himself to the savage nations :—" We appeal to you, men who have received no foreign and factitious ideas; say, have you ever gone beyond what I have described? And you, doctors, we call you to witness; is not this the unanimous testimony of all ancient monuments?" *

* "Testimony of all ancient monuments."—' It clearly results,' says Plutarch, ' from the verses of Orpheus and the sacred books of the Ægyp-tians and Phrygians, that the ancient theology, not only of the Greeks, but of all nations, was nothing more than a system of physics, a picture of the operations of nature, wrapped up in mysterious allegories and enigmatical symbols, so that the ignorant multitude attended rather to their apparent than to their hidden meaning, and even in what they un-derstood of the latter, supposed something more deep than what they perceived.' Fragment of a work of Plutarch now lost, quoted by Eu-sebius Præpar. Evang. lib. 3, c. 1, p. 85.
The majority of philosophers, says Porphyry, and among others Obœ-remon (who lived in Egypt in the first age of Christianity,) imagine there never existed any other world than the one we see, and acknow-ledged no other gods, of all those recognised by the Egyptians, than such as are commonly called planets, signs of the Zodiac, and constellations; whose aspects (risings and settings,) are supposed to influence the for-tunes of men! to which they add their divisions of the signs into decans or rulers of time, whom they style lords of the ascendant, whose names, virtues in healing distempers, rising, setting, and presages of future events, are the subjects of almanacs (and the Egyptian priests had almanacs the exact counterpart of Matthew Laensberg's;) for when the priests affirmed that the sun was the architect of the universe, Chœre-mon presently concludes that all their narratives respecting Isis and Osiris, together with their other sacred fables, referred in part to the planets, the phases of the moon, and the revolution of the sun, and in part to the stars of the daily and nightly hemispheres and the river Nile; in a word, to physical and natural existences, and never to such as might be immaterial and incorporeal.—All these philosophers believe that the acts of our will and the motion of our bodies depend upon those of the stars to which they are subjected, and they refer everything to the laws of (physical) necessity, which they call destiny or fate, sup-posing a chain of causes and effects which binds, by I know not what

II. *Second System.   Worship of the Stars or Sabeism.*

" But those same monuments present us likewise a more methodical
and complicated system, that of the worship of all the stars, adored
sometimes in their proper forms, sometimes under figurative emblems
and symbols ; and this worship was the effect of the knowledge men
had acquired in physics, and was derived immediately from the first
causes of the social state, that is, from the necessities and arts of the
first degree which are among the elements of society.

" Indeed, as soon as men began to unite in society, it became necessary for them to multiply the means of subsistence, and consequently
to attend to agriculture : agriculture, to be carried on with success,
requires the observation and knowledge of the heavens.*   It was necessary to know the periodical return of the same operations of nature,
and the same phenomena in the skies ; indeed, to go so far as to ascertain the duration and succession of the seasons and the months of
the year.   It was indispensable to know in the first place, the course
of the sun, who, in his zodiacal revolutions, shows himself the first
and supreme agent of the whole creation ; then, of the moon, who,
by her phases and periods, regulates and distributes time ; then of
the stars, and even planets, which by their appearance and disappearance on the horizon and nocturnal hemisphere, marked the minutest
divisions ; finally, it was necessary to form a whole system of astronomy, or a calendar ; and from these works there naturally followed·
a new manner of considering these predominant and governing powers.
Having observed that the productions of the earth had a regular and
constant relation with the heavenly bodies ; that the rise, growth and
decline of each plant kept pace with the appearance, elevation, and

connexion, all beings together, from the atom, to the supreme power
and primary influence of the gods ; so that, whether in their temples
or in their images and idols, the only subject of worship is the power
of destiny. (Porphyr. Epist. ad Janebonem.)

* " Requires the knowledge of the heavens."—It continues to be repeated every day, on the indirect authority of the book of Genesis, that
astronomy was the invention of the children of Noah.   It has been
gravely said, that while wandering as shepherds in the plains of Shinar,
they employed their leisure in composing a planetary system ; as if
shepherds were under the necessity of knowing more than the polar
star ; and as if necessity was not the sole motive of every invention !
If the ancient shepherds were so studious and sagacious, how does it
happen that the modern ones are so ignorant and inattentive?   Now it
is a fact, that the Arabs of the desert do not know six constellations,
and do not understand a word of astronomy

declination of the same star, or group of stars; in short, that the languor or activity of vegetation seemed to depend on celestial influences, men drew from thence an idea of action, of power in those beings, superior to earthly bodies; and the stars dispensing plenty or scarcity, became powers, genii, gods, authors of good and evil.*

"As the state of society had already introduced a regular hierarchy of ranks, employments and conditions, men, continuing to reason by comparison, carried their new notions into their theology, and formed a complicated system of gradual divinities, in which the sun, as first god, was a military chief, a political king; the moon was his wife, and queen; the planets were servants, bearers of commands, messengers; and the multitude of stars were a nation, an army of heroes, genii whose office was to govern the world under the orders of their chiefs; and all the individuals had names, functions, attributes drawn from their relations and influences; and even sexes, from the gender of their appellations.†

"And as the social state had introduced certain usages and ceremonies, religion also adopted similar ones; these ceremonies, at first simple and private, became public and solemn; the offerings became rich and more numerous, and the rites more methodical; they assigned certain places for the assemblies, and began to have chapels and temples; they instituted officers to administer them, and these became priests and pontiffs; they established liturgies, and sanctified certain days, and religion became a civil act, a political tie. But in this arrangement, religion did not change its first principles, and the idea of God was always that of physical beings, operating good or evil, that is, impressing sensations of pleasure or pain; the dogma was the

* "Genii, gods, authors of good and evil."—It appears that by the word genius, the ancients denoted a productive quality, a generative power, for the following words, which are all of one family, convey this meaning: generare, genos, genesis, genius, gens.
'The ancient and modern Sabeans, says Mammonides, acknowledge a principal God, the maker and inhabitant of heaven; but on account of his great distance they conceive him to be inaccessible; and in imitation of the conduct of people towards their kings, they employ as mediators with him the planets and their angels, whom they call princes and potentates, and whom they suppose to reside in those luminous bodies, as in palaces or tabernacles, etc.' (More Nebuchim, pars III c. 29.)

† "Sexes, from the gender of their appellations."—According as the gender of the object was in the language of the nation masculine or feminine, the divinity who bore its name was male or female. Thus the Cappadocians called the moon god, and the sun goddess; a circumstance which gives to the same beings a perpetual variety in ancient mythology.

knowledge of their laws cr manner of acting; virtue and sin, the observance or infraction of these laws; and morality, in its native simplicity, was the judicious practice of whatever contributes to the
preservation of existence, the wellbeing of one's self and his fellow
creatures.*

"Should it be asked at what epoch this system took its birth, we
shall answer, on the testimony of the monuments of astronomy itself,
that its principles appear incontestably to have been established more
than fifteen thousand years ago :† and if it be asked to what people
it is to be attributed, we shall answer that the same monuments, supported by unanimous traditions, attribute it to the first tribes of Egypt;
and when reason finds in that country all the circumstances which
could lead to such a system; when it finds there a zone of sky, bor-
dering on the tropic, equally free from the rains of the equator and

* " Whatever contributes to the preservation of one's self and his fellow creatures."—To this Plutarch adds that these (Egyptian) priests
always regarded the preservation of health as a point of first importance.
—and as indispensably necessary to the practice of piety and the service
of the gods, etc. (See Isis and Osiris, towards the end.)

† " More than fifteen thousand years ago."—The historical orator
follows here the opinion of the learned Dupuis, who first in his Memoir
concerning the origin of the Constellations, and afterwards in his great
work concerning the origin of all Worship, has collected a great many
arguments to prove that formerly Libra was the sign of the vernal, and
Aries of the autumnal equinox; that is, that the precession of the equinoxes has produced a change of more than seven signs. The action of
this phenomenon cannot be denied: the most recent calculations value
it at 50 seconds, 12 or 15 thirds a year: therefore every degree of the
zodiacal signs is removed and put back, in 71 years 8 or 9 months:
therefore an entire sign in 2152 or 53 years. But if, as is the fact, the
equinoct of spring was exactly in the 1st degree of Aries, in the
year 388 oefore J. C; that is, if at that period, the sun had gone through
and put back whole sign, to enter into Pisces, which he has left in our
own time, it follows that if he had left Taurus 2153 years before, that
is about the year 2540 before J. C. and had entered it about the year
4692 before J. C. Thus ascending from sign to sign, the 1st degree of
Aries was the autumnal equinoctial point, about 12,912 years before the
year 388, that is to say 13,300 years before the Christian era: add our
eighteen centuries, you will find fifteen thousand one hundred years,
and moreover, the quantity of time and of ages necessary to bring astronomical knowledge to such a degree of perfection. Now it is to be
observed, that the worship of the Bull is the principal article in the
theological creed of the Egyptians, Persians, Japanese, etc., which
clearly indicates at that epoch some common system of ideas among
these nations. The five or six thousand years of Genesis can be object
ed only by those who believe in it from education. (See on this subject
the analysis of Genesis, in the 1st. vol. of New Researches on ancient
History; see also Origin of Constellations, by Dupuis, 1781; the Origin
of Worship, in 3 vol. 1794, and the Chronological Zodiac, in 4to. 1806)

the fogs of the north ; when it finds there a central point of the sphere of the ancients, a salubrious climate, a great, but manageable river, a soil fertile without labor or art, inundated without morbid exhalations, and placed between two seas which communicate with the richest countries, it conceives that the inhabitant of the Nile, addicted to agriculture from the nature of his soil, to geometry from the annual necessity of measuring his lands, to commerce from the facility of communications, to astronomy from the state of his sky always open to observation, must have been the first to pass from the savage to the social state, and consequently to attain the physical and moral sciences necessary to civilized life.

" It was then on the borders of the upper Nile among a black race of men, that was organized the complicated system of the worship of the stars considered in relation to the productions of the earth and the labors of agriculture ; and this first worship, characterised by their adoration under their own forms and natural attributes, was a simple proceeding of the human mind ; but in a short time, the multiplicity of the objects, of their relations, and their reciprocal influence, having complicated the ideas, and the signs that represented them, there followed a confusion as singular in its cause as pernicious in its effects."

III. *Third System. Worship of Symbols, or Idolatry*

" As soon as this agricultural people began to observe the stars with attention, they found it necessary to individualize or group them, and to assign to each a proper name, in order to understand each other in their designation : but to this there was a great obstacle ; for, on the one hand, the heavenly bodies, similar in form, offered no distinguishing characteristics by which to denominate them ; and on the other, language in its infancy and poverty, had no expressions for so many new and metaphysical ideas. Necessity, the usual stimulus of genius, surmounted everything. Having remarked that in the annual revolution, the renewal, and periodical appearance of terrestrial productions were constantly associated with the rising and setting of certain stars, and to their position as relative to the sun, the fundamental term of all comparison, the mind, by a natural operation, connected in thought these terrestrial and celestial objects, which were connected in fact ; and applying to them a common sign,

it gave to the stars, and their groups, the names of the terrestrial objects to which they answered. *

"Thus the Ethiopian of Thebes named stars of inundation, or
Aquarius, those under which the Nile began to overflow; stars of the
ox or bull, those under which he began to plough; stars of the lion,
those under which that animal, driven from the desert by thirst, appeared on the banks of the Nile; stars of the sheaf or of the harvest
virgin, those of the reaping season; stars of the lamb, stars of the
kids, those under which these precious animals were brought forth:
and thus was resolved the first part of the difficulty.

"Moreover, man having remarked in the beings which surrounded him, certain qualities distinctive and peculiar to each species;
and having thence derived a name by which to designate them; he
found in the same source an ingenious mode of generalizing his ideas;
and, transferring the name already invented to everything which
bore any resemblance or analogy, he enriched his language with a
perpetual round of metaphors.

"Thus, the same Ethiopian having observed that the return of the
inundation always corresponded with the rising of a beautiful star
which appeared towards the source of the Nile, and seemed to warn
the husbandman against the coming waters, he compared this action
to that of the animal who, by his barking, gives notice of danger,
and he called this star the dog, the barker (Syrius;) in the same
manner he named the stars of the crab, those where the sun, having
arrived at the tropic, retreated by a slow retrograde motion like the
crab or cancer; he named stars of the wild goat, or capricorn, those
where the sun, having reached the highest point in his annuary tract,
rests at the summit of the horary gnomon, and imitates the goat, who
delights to climb the summit of the rocks; he named stars of the
balance or libra, those where the days and nights, being equal,
seemed in equilibrium like that instrument: and stars of the scorpion, those where certain periodical winds bring vapors, burning like
the venom of the scorpion. In the same manner he called by the
name of rings and serpents the figured traces of the orbits of the stars
and planets: and such was the general mode of naming † all the

* " The names of the terrestrial objects to which they answered."—
" The ancients, says Maimonides, directing all their attention to agriculture, gave to the stars names derived from their occupation during
the year." (More Neb——, pars 5.)

† " Such was the general mode of naming."—The ancients had verbs
from the substantives crab, goat, tortoise, as the French have at present

stars, and even the planets, taken by groups or as individuals, according to their relations with husbandry and terrestrial objects, and according to the analogies which each nation found between them and the objects of its particular soil and climate.

" From this it appeared that abject and terrestrial beings became associated with the superior and powerful inhabitants of heaven; and this association became stronger every day by the mechanism of language and the constitution of the human mind. Men would say, by a natural metaphor; ' The bull spreads over the earth the germs of fecundity (in spring:) he restores vegetation and plenty; the lamb (or ram) delivers the skies from the malevolent genii of winter; he saves the world from the serpent (emblem of the humid season,) and restores the empire of goodness (summer, joyful season.) The scorpion pours out his poison on the earth, and scatters diseases and death, etc.; the same of all similar effects.'

" This language, understood by every one, was attended at first with no inconvenience; but in the course of time, when the calendar had been regulated, the people, who had no longer any need of observing the heavens, lost sight of the original meaning of these expressions; and the allegories remaining in common use, became a fatal stumbling-block to the understanding and to reason. Habituated to associate to the symbols the ideas of their archetypes, the mind at last confounded them: then the same animals, whom fancy had transported to the skies, turned again to the earth; but being thus returned, clothed in the livery of the stars, they claimed the stellary attributes, and imposed on their own authors. Then it was that the people, believing that they saw their gods among them, could pray to them with more convenience; they demanded from the ram of their flock the influences which might be expected from the heavenly ram; they prayed the scorpion not to pour out his venom upon nature; they revered the crab of the sea, the scarab of the mire, the fish of the river; and by a series of corrupt but inseparable analogies, they lost themselves in a labyrinth of well connected absurdities.

" Such was the origin of that ancient whimsical worship of the animals; such is the train of ideas by which the character of the divinity became common to the vilest of brutes, and by which was formed that theological system, extremely comprehensive, complicated and learned, which, rising on the borders of the Nile, propagated

the verbs serpenter, coqueter; the mechanism of all languages is nearly the same.

11*

from country to country, by commerce, war and conquest, overspread the whole of the ancient world; and which modified by time, circumstances and prejudices, is still seen entire among a hundred nations, and remains as the essential and secret basis of the theology of those even who despise and reject it."

Some murmurs at these words being heard from various groups: "Yes," continued the orator, "hence arose, for instance, among you, nations of Africa, the adoration of your fetiches, plants, animals, pebbles, pieces of wood, before which your ancestors would not have had the folly to bow, if they had not seen in them talismans endowed with the virtue of the stars.* Here, ye nations of Tartary! is the origin of your marmosets, and of all that train of animals with which your chamans ornament their magical robes. This is the origin of those figures of birds and of snakes which savage nations imprint upon their skins with sacred and mysterious ceremonies. Ye inhabitants of India! in vain you cover yourselves with the veil of mystery: the hawk of your god Vichenou is but one of the thousand emblems of the sun in Egypt; and your incarnations of a god in the fish, the boar, the lion, the tortoise, and all his monstrous adventures, are only the metamorphoses of the sun, who, passing through the signs of the twelve animals, was supposed to assume their figures, and perform their astronomical functions.† People of Japan! your

* "Endowed with the virtue of the stars."—The ancient astrologers, says the most learned of the Jews (Maimonides,) having consecrated to each planet a color, an animal, a tree, a metal, a fruit, a plant, formed from them all a figure or representation of the star, taking care to select for the purpose a proper moment, a fortunate day, such as the conjunction or some other favorable aspect; they conceived that by their (magic) ceremonies they could introduce into those figures or idols the influences of the superior beings after which they were modelled. These were the idols that the Kaldean Sabeans adored; and in the performance of their worship they were obliged to be dressed in the proper color——. Thus, the astrologers, by their practices, introduced idolatry, desirous of being regarded as the dispensers of the favors of heaven: and as agriculture was the sole employment of the ancients, they succeeded in persuading them that the rain and other blessings of the seasons were at their disposal; thus, the whole art of agriculture was exercised by rules of astrology, and the priests made talismans or charms, which were to drive away locusts, flies, etc. See Maimonides, More Nebuchim, pars III, c. 9
'The priests of Egypt, Persia, India, etc., pretended to bind the Gods to their idols, and to make them descend from heaven at their pleasure; they threatened the sun and moon to reveal the secret mysteries, to shake the heavens, etc.' (Euseb. Præpar. Evang. page. 198 and Jamblicus, de Mysteriis Ægypt.)
† "And perform their astronomical functions."—These are the very words of Jamblicus, de symbolis Ægyptiorum, c. 2, sect. 7. The sun was the grand Proteus, the universal metamorphist.

bull, which breaks the mundane egg, is only the bull of the zodiac, which in former times opened the seasons, the age of creation, the vernal equinox. It is the same bull Apis which Egypt adored, and which your ancestors, O Jewish rabbins! worshipped in the golden calf. This is still your bull, followers of Zoroaster! which, sacrificed in the symbolic mysteries of Mithra, poured out his blood which fertilized the earth : and, ye Christians! your Bull of the apocalypse, with his wings, symbol of the air, has no other origin ; and your lamb of God, sacrificed, like the bull of Mithra, for the salvation of the world, is only the same sun, in the sign of the celestial ram, which, in a later age, opening the equinox in his turn, was supposed to deliver the world from evil, that is to say, from the constellation of the serpent, from that great snake, the parent of winter, the emblem of the Ahrimanes or Satan of the Persians, your instructers. Yes, in vain does your imprudent zeal consign idolaters to the torments of Tartarus which they invented : the whole basis of your system is only the worship of the sun, with whose attributes you have decorated your principal personage. It is the sun which, under the name of Orus, was born, like your god, at the winter solstice, in the arms of the celestial virgin, and who passed a childhood of obscurity, indigence, and want, answering to the season of cold and frost. It is he that, under the name of Osiris, persecuted by Typhon and by the tyrants of the air, was put to death, shut up in a dark tomb, emblem of the hemisphere of winter ; and afterwards, ascending from the inferior zone towards the zenith of heaven arose again from the dead triumphant over the giants and the angels of destruction.

" Ye priests ! who murmur at this relation, you wear his emblems all over your bodies ; your tonsure is the disk of the sun,* your stole is his zodiac, your rosaries are symbols of the stars and planets. Ye

* " Your tonsure is the disk of the sun."—' The Arabs, says Herodotus, b III, shave their heads in a circle and about their temples, in imitation, as they pretend, of Bacchus (who is the sun.) Jeremiah speaks also of this custom, c. 25, v. 23. The tuft of hair which the Mussulmen preserve, is taken also from the sun, who was painted by the Egyptians at the winter solstice, as having but a single hair on his head. (Your stole is his zodiac.) The robes of the goddess of Syria and of Diana of Ephesus, from whence are borrowed the dress of the priests, have the twelve animals of the Zodiac painted on them. The rosaries are found upon all the Indian idols, erected more than four thousand five hundred years ago, and their use in the East has been universal from time immemorial. The crosier is precisely the staff of Bootes of Osiris. (See plate 3.) All the lamas wear the mitre or cap in the shape of a cone, which was an emblem of the sun.

pontiffs and prelates! your mitre, your crosier, your mantle, are
those of Osiris: and that cross, whose mystery you extol without
comprehending it, is the cross of Serapis, traced by the hands of
Egyptian priests on the plan of the figurative world; which, passing
through the equinoxes and tropics, became the emblem of the future
life, and of the resurrection, because it touched the gates of ivory
and of horn, through which the soul passed to heaven."

At these words, the doctors of all the groups began to look at each
other with astonishment, but no one breaking silence, the orator
proceeded:

"Three principal causes concur to produce this confusion of ideas.
First the figurative expressions under which an infant language was
obliged to describe the relations of objects; which expressions passing afterwards from a limited to a general sense, and from a physical
to a moral one, caused by their ambiguities and synonymes, a great
number of mistakes.

"Thus, it being first said that the sun had surmounted, or finished
twelve animals, it was thought afterwards that he had killed, fought,
conquered them; and this gave rise to the historical life of Hercules.*

"It being said that he regulated the periods of rural labor, the
seed time, and the harvest; that he distributed the seasons, and oc-
cupations; that he ran through the climates and ruled the earth, etc.,
he was taken for a legislative king, a conquering warrior; and they
framed from this the history of Osiris, of Bacchus, and others of that
description.

"Having said that a planet entered into a sign, they made of this
conjunction a marriage, an adultery, an incest. Having said that·
the planet was hid or buried, when it came back to light and ascended to its exaltation, they said it had died, risen again, ascended into
heaven, etc.

"A second cause of confusion was the material figures themselves
by which men first painted thoughts, and which, under the name of
hieroglyphics or sacred characters, were the first invention of the
mind. Thus, to give warning of the inundation and of the necessity
to guard against it, they painted a boat, the ship Argo; to express
the wind, they painted the wing of a bird; to designate the season
or the month, they painted the bird of passage, the insect, or the animal which made its appearance at that epoch; to describe the win-

---

* "This gave rise to the historical life of Hercules."—See Dupuis'
work, Origin of Constellations and Origin of all Worship.

ter, they painted a hog or serpent, which delight in humid places; and the combination of these figures carried the known sense of words and phrases.* But as this sense could not be fixed with pre-

* " The combination of these figures carried the known sense."—The reader will doubtless see with pleasure some examples of ancient hieroglyphics.

'The Egyptians, says Hor-Apollo, represent eternity by the figures of the sun and moon. They designate the world by a blue serpent with yellow scales (stars ; it is the Chinese Dragon.) If they had to express the year, they painted Isis, who is also in their language called Sothis, or dog-star, the first of the constellations, by the rising of which the year commences ; its inscription at Sais was, it is I that rise in the constellation of the Dog.

' They also represent the year by a palm tree, and the month by one of its branches ; because it is the nature of this tree, to produce a branch every month.

' They further represent it by a quarter of an acre. (The acre, divided into four, denotes the bissextile period of four years , the abbreviation of this figure of a field in four divisions is manifestly the letter ha or heth, the seventh in the Samaritan alphabet ; in general the letters of the alphabet are merely astronomical hieroglyphics ; and it is for this reason that the mode of writing is from right to left, like the march of the stars.) They denote a prophet by the image of a dog, because the dog star (Anoubis) by its rising gives notice of the inundation.

' They represent inundation by a lion, because it takes place under that sign ; and hence, says Plutarch, the custom of placing at the gates of temples figures of lions spouting water from their mouths.

' They express God and destiny by a star. They also represent God, says Porphyry, by a black stone, because his nature is dark and obscure. All white things express the celestial and luminous gods ; all circular ones the world, the moon, the sun, the orbits, all bows and crescents, the moon.—Fire and the gods of Olympus, they represent by pyramids and obelisks (the name of the sun, Baal, is found in this latter word ;) the sun by a cone (the mitre of Osiris ;) the earth by a cylinder (which rolls ;) the generative power (of the air) by the phallus, and that of the earth by a triangle, emblem of the female organ. Eusch., Præpar. Evang. p. 98.)

'Clay, says Jamblicus, de symbolis, sect. 7, c. 2, denotes matter, the generative and nutritive power ; everything which receives the warmth and fermentation of life.

' A man sitting upon the lotos or nenuphar, represents the moving spirit (the sun) which, in like manner as that plant lives in the water without any communication with clay, exists equally distinct from matter, swimming in space, resting on itself ; round in all its parts like the fruit, leaves and flowers of the Lotos. (Brahma has lotos-eyes, says the Chaster Neardisen, to denote his intelligence, his eye, swimming over everything, like the flower of the lotos on the waters.) A man at the helm of a ship, adds Jamblicus, is descriptive of the sun which governs all. And Porphyry tell us that the sun is also represented by a man in a ship resting on a crocodile (the amphibious emblem of air and water.)

' At Elephantina they worshipped the figure of a man sitting, of a blue color, with a ram's head, and a goat's horns encompassing the disk ; all which represented the sun and moon's conjunction in the ram ; the blue color denoting the power of the moon, at the period of junction, to raise water into clouds (apud Euseb. Præpar. Evang. p. 116.)

' The hawk is an emblem of the sun and light, on account of his rap-

cision; as the number of these figures and their combinations became excessive, and overburdened the memory, the immediate consequence was confusion and false interpretations. Genius afterwards having invented the more simple art of applying signs to sounds, of which the number is limited, and painting words, instead of thoughts, alphabetical writing threw into disuse hieroglyphical painting; and its signification, falling daily into oblivion, gave rise to a multitude of illusions, ambiguities and errors.

"Finally, a third cause of confusion was the civil organization of ancient states. When the people began to apply themselves to agriculture, the formation of a rural calendar requiring a continued series of astronomical observations, it became necessary to appoint certain' individuals charged with the functions of watching the appearance and disappearance of certain stars: to foretell the return of the inundation, of certain winds, of the rainy season, the proper time to sow every kind of grain: these men, on account of their service, were exempt from common labor, and the society provided for their maintenance. With this provision, and wholly employed in their

id flight and his soaring into the highest regions of the air where light abounds.

'A fish is the emblem of aversion, and the hippopotamus of violence, because it is said to kill its father and ravish its mother. Hence, says Plutarch, the hieroglyphical inscription of the temple of Sais, where we see painted on the vestibule, 1stly. a child ; 2dly. an old man ; 3dly. a hawk ; 4thly. a fish ; and 5thly. a hippopotamus ; which signify, 1stly. entrance into life, 2dly. departure, 3dly. god, 4thly. hates, 5thly. injustice. (See Isis and Osiris.)

'The Egyptians, adds he, represent the world by a scarab, because this insect pushes in a direction contrary to that in which it proceeds, a ball containing its eggs, just as the heaven of the fixed stars causes the revolution of the sun (the yolk of an egg) in an opposite direction to its own.

'They represent the world also by the number five, being that of the elements, which, says Diodorus, are earth, water, air, fire and ether or spiritus (they are the same amongst the Indians ;) and according to the mystics, in Macrobius, they are the supreme God or primum mobile, the intelligence or meus born of him, the soul of the world which proceeds from him, the celestial spheres and all things terrestrial. Hence, adds Plutarch, the analogy between the Greek petite, five, and Pan, all.

'The ass,' says he again, ' is the emblem of Typhon, because he is of a ruddy color like that animal ; now Typhon signifies whatever is of a miry or clayey nature, and in Hebrew I find the three words clay, ruddy and ass to be formed from the same root, hamr.) Jamblicus has farther told us that clay denoted matter, and he elsewhere adds that all evil and corruption proceeded from matter ; which compared with the phrase of Macrobius, all is perishable, liable to change in the celestial sphere, gives us the theory, first physical, then moral, of the system of good and evil of the ancients.' (See also the Memoir concerning the Zodiac of Dendera, which the learned Dupuis has inserted in the journal entitled Revue Philosophique, year 1801.)

observation, they soon became acquainted with the great phenomena of nature, and even learned to penetrate the secret of many of
her operations. They discovered the movement of the stars and
planets : the coincidence of their phases and returns with the productions of the earth and the action of vegetation ; the medicinal
and nutritive properties of plants and fruits ; the action of the elements and their reciprocal affinities. Now, as there was no other
method of communicating the knowledge of these discoveries but the
laborious one of oral instruction, they transmitted it only to their relations and friends ; it followed that all science and instruction were
confined to a few families, who arrogating it to themselves as an exclusive privilege, assumed a professional distinction, a corporation
spirit, fatal to the public welfare. This continued succession of the
same researches and the same labors, hastened, it is true, the progress of knowledge ; but by the mystery which accompanied it, the
people were daily plunged in deeper shades, and became more superstitious and more enslaved. Seeing their fellow mortals produce
certain phenomena, announce, as at will, eclipses and comets, heal
diseases, and handle serpents, they thought them in alliance with
celestial powers ; and to obtain the blessings and avert the evils
which they expected from above, they took them for mediators and
interpreters : and thus became established in the bosom of every state
sacrilegious corporations of hypocritical and deceitful men, who en-
grossed all the authority ; and the priests, being at once astronomers,
theologians, naturalists, physicians, magicians, interpreters of the
gods, oracles of men, and rivals of kings or their accomplices, established under the name of religion, an empire of mystery and a monopoly of instruction, which to this day have ruined every nation."—
Here the priests of all the groups interrupted the orator ; and with
loud cries accused him of impiety, irreligion, blasphemy, and endeavoured to cut short his discourse ; but the legislator observing that this
was only an exposition of historical facts, which if false or forged,
would be easily refuted ; that hitherto the declaration of every opinion had been free, and without this it would be impossible to discover
the truth, the orator proceeded ·
" Now, from all these causes and from the continual association of
ill-assorted ideas, arose a mass of disorders in theology, in morals
and in traditions : first, because the animals represented the stars,
the characters of the animals, their appetites, their sympathies, their
aversions, passed over to the gods, and were supposed to be their

actions : thus, the god ichneumon made war against the god crocodile ; the god wolf liked to eat the god sheep ; the god ibis devoured
the god serpent ; and the deity became a strange, capricious and
ferocious being, whose idea deranged the judgment of man, and corrupted his morals and his reason.

" Again, because in the spirit of their worship every family, every
nation, took for its special patron a star or constellation, the affections
or antipathies of the symbolic-animal were transferred to its sectaries ;
and the partisans of the god dog were enemies to those of the god
wolf; those who adored the god ox abhorred those who eat him ; and
religion became the senseless cause of frenzy and superstition.*

" Besides, the names of those animal-stars having, for this same
reason of patronage, been conferred on nations, countries, mountains
and rivers, these objects were taken for gods, and hence followed a
mixture of geographical, historical, and mythological beings, which
confounded all traditions

" Finally, by the analogy of the actions which were ascribed to
them, the god-stars having been taken for men, for heroes, for kings,
kings and heroes took in their turn the actions of gods for models,
and by imitation became warriors, conquerors, proud, lascivious, indolent, sanguinary ; and religion consecrated the crimes of despots,
and perverted the principles of government."

IV. *Fourth System.   Worship of two Principles, or Dualism.*

" In the meantime, the astronomical priests, enjoying peace and
abundance in their temples, made every day new progress in the
sciences; and the system of the world unfolding gradually to their
view, they raised successively various hypotheses, as to its agents and
effects, which became so many theologica systems.

" The voyages of the maritime nations and the caravans of the
Nomads of Asia and Africa, having given them a knowledge of the
earth from the Fortunate-islands to Serica, and from the Baltic to the
sources of the Nile, the comparison of the phenomena of various
zones taught them the rotundity of the earth, and gave birth to a new,
theory.   Having remarked that all the operations of nature, during

* " The senseless cause of superstition."—These are Plutarch's own
words, who relates that those various worships were given by a king
of Egypt to the different towns, to disunite and enslave them, (and
these kings had been chosen from the cast of priests.) See Isis and
Osiris

the annual period, were reducible to two principal ones, that of producing and that of destroying; that on the greater part of the globe, these two operations were performed in the intervals of the two equinoxes, that is to say, during the six months of summer everything was procreating and multiplying, and that during winter everything languished and almost died; they supposed in NATURE two contrary powers, which were in a continual state of contention and exertion; and considering the celestial sphere in this view, they divided the images which they figured upon it into two halves or hemispheres, so that the constellations which were on the summer heaven, formed a direct and superior empire, and those which were on the winter heaven composed an antipode and inferior empire. Therefore, as the constellations of summer accompanied the season of long, warm and unclouded days, and that of fruits, and harvests, they were considered as the powers of light, fecundity and creation, and, by a transition from a physical to a moral sense, they became genii, angels of science, or beneficence, of purity and virtue: and as the constellations of winter were connected with long nights and polar fogs, they were the genii of darkness, of destruction, of death, and, by transition, angels of ignorance, of wickedness, of sin and vice. By this arrangement the heaven was divided into two domains, two factions: and the analogy of human ideas already opened a vast field to the errors of imagination; but the mistake and the illusion were determined, if not occasioned by a particular circumstance. (*Observe plate* III.)

" In the projection of the celestial sphere, as traced by the astronomical priests,* the zodiac and the constellations, disposed in circular

* " In the projection of the sphere as traced by the astronomical priests."—The ancient priests had three kinds of spheres, which it may be useful to make known to the reader.

'We read in Eubulus,' says Porphyry, 'that Zoroaster was the first who, having fixed upon a cavern pleasantly situated in the mountains adjacent to Persia, formed the idea of consecrating it to Mithra (the sun,) creator and father of all things; that is to say, having made in this cavern several geometrical divisions, representing the seasons and the elements, he imitated on a small scale the order and disposition of the universe by Mithra. After Zoroaster, it became a custom to consecrate caverns for the celebration of mysteries! so that in like manner as temples were dedicated to celestial gods, rural altars to heroes and terrestrial deities, subterraneous abodes to infernal (inferior) deities, so caverns and grottoes were consecrated to the world, the universe, and the nymphs; and from hence Pythagoras and Plato borrowed the idea of calling the world a cavern, a cave. (Porphyry, antro Nympharum.)

'Such was the first projection of the sphere in relief; and though the Persians give the honor of the invention to Zoroaster, it is doubtless due to the Egyptians; for we may suppose from this projection being the most simple that it was the most ancient: the caverns of Thebes, full of similar pictures, tend to strengthen this opinion.'

order, presented their halves in diametrical opposition : the hemisphere of winter, antipode of that of summer, was adverse, contrary,
opposed to it.* By a continual metaphor, these words acquired a
moral sense ; and the adverse genii, or angels, became revolted enemies. From that moment all the astronomical history of the constellations was changed into a political history ; the heavens became a
human state, where things happened as on the earth. Now, as the
earthly states, the greater part despotic, had already their monarchs,
and as the sun was apparently the monarch of the skies, the summer
hemisphere, empire of light, and its constellations, a people of white
angels, had for king an enlightened God, a creator intelligent and
good. And as every rebel faction must have its chief, the heaven of
winter, the subterranean empire of darkness and wo, and its stars,
a people of black angels, giants or demons, had for their chief a malignant Genius, whose character was applied by different people to
the constellation which to them was the most remarkable. In Egypt,
it was primitively the scorpion, first zodiacal sign after Libra, and

The following was the second projection : ' the prophets or hierophants
of the Egyptians,' says bishop Synnesius, 'who had been initiated in the
mysteries, do not permit the common workmen to form idols or images
of the gods ; but they descend themselves into the sacred caves, where
they have concealed coffers containing certain spheres upon which they
construct those images secretly and without the knowledge of the people,
who despise simple and natural things, and wish for prodigies and fables.' (Syn., in Calvit.) That is, the ancient priests had armillary
spheres like ours ; and this passage, which so well agrees with that of
Chœremon, gives us the key to all their theological astrology.
Lastly, they had fiat models of the nature of plate III , with this difference, that they were of a very complicated nature, having every
fictitious division of decan and subdecan, with the hieroglyphic indica-
tions of their influence. Kirker has given us a copy of one of them in
his Egyptian Ædipus, and Gebelin a figured fragment in his book of the
calendar (under the name of Egyptian Zodiac.) The ancient Egyptians
says the astrologer Julius Firmicus, Astron., lib. II, c. 4, and lib. IV, c.
16, divide each sign of the zodiac into three sections ; and each section
was under the direction of an imaginary being whom they called Decan
or chief of ten : so that there were three decans in a month, and thirty-six
in a year. Now, these decans, who were also called gods (Theoi,) regulated the destinies of mankind—and they were placed particularly in certain
stars.—They afterwards imagined in every ten three other gods, whom
they called arbiters, so that there were nine for every month, and these
were farther divided into an infinite number of powers. (The Persians
and Indians made their spheres on a similar plan ; and if a picture thereof
were to be drawn from the description given by Scaliger at the end of
Manilius, we should find in it a precise definition of their hieroglyphics,
for every article forms one.)

* " The hemisphere of winter was antipode to it."—It was for this
reason the Persians always wrote the name of Ahrimanes inverted
thus, ˙uɐɯᴉɹɥ∀

for a long time chief of the winter signs; then it was the bear, or polar ass, called Typhon, that is to say deluge, on account of the rains* which deluge the earth during the dominion of that constellation. At a later period in Persia,† it was the serpent who, under the name of Ahrimanes, formed the basis of the system of Zoroaster : and it is the same, O Christians and Jews! that has become your serpent of Eve (the celestial virgin) and that of the cross, in both cases, emblem of Satan, the enemy and great adversary of the ancient of days, sung by Daniel.

" In Syria, it was the hog or wild boar, enemy of Adonis, because, in that country, the functions of the northern bear were performed by the animal whose inclination for mire and dirt was emblematic of winter : and this is the reason, followers of Moses and of Mahomet! that you hold him in horror, in imitation of the priests of Memphis and Baalbek who detested him as the murderer of their God the sun. This likewise O Indians! is the type of your Chib-en, who was formerly the Pluto of your brethren the Romans and Greeks: in like manner, your Brahma, God the creator, is only the Persian Ormuzd and the Egyptian Osiris, whose very name expresses creative power, producer of forms. And these Gods received a worship analogous to their attributes real or imaginary, which worship was divided into two branches, according to their characters. The good God receives a worship of love and joy, from which are derived all

* " Typhon, that is to say deluge, on account of the rains."—Typhon, pronounced touphon by the Greeks, is precisely the touphan of the Arabs, which signifies deluge: and all these deluges in mythology are nothing more than winter and the rains, or the overflowing of the Nile ; as the pretended conflagrations that are to destroy the world, are simply the summer season. And it is for this reason that Aristotle, de Meteoris, lib 1, c. 14, says, that the winter of the great cyclic year is a deluge, and its summer a conflagration. ' The Egyptians,' says Porphyry, 'employ every year a talisman in remembrance of the world ; at the summer solstice, they mark their houses, flocks, and trees with red, supposing that on that day the whole world had been set on fire. It was also at the same period that they celebrated the pyrrhic or fire dance.' (And this illustrates the origin of purification by fire and water; for having denominated the tropic of Cancer, gate of heaven and of heat or celestial fire, and that of Capricorn, gate of deluge or of water, it was imagined that the spirits or souls who passed through these gates in their way to and from heaven, were scorched or bathed ; hence the baptism of Mithra, and the passage through the flames, observed throughout the East long before Moses.)

† " At a later period in Persia."—That is when the ram became the equinoctial sign, or rather when the alteration of the skies showed that it was no longer the bull.

religious acts of gaiety,* such as festivals, dances, banquets, offerings of flowers, milk, honey, perfumes, in a word, everything grateful to the senses and to the soul. The evil God, on the contrary, received a worship of fear and pain, whence originated all religious acts of the gloomy sort,† tears, desolation, mourning, abstinence, bloody offerings and cruel sacrifices.

"Hence arose that distinction of terrestrial beings into pure and impure, sacred and abominable, according as their species were of the number of the constellations of one of these two Gods, and made part of his domain; and this produced on the one hand the superstitions concerning pollutions and purifications, and on the other the pretended efficacious virtues of amulets and talismans.

"You conceive now," continued the orator, addressing himself to the Indians, Persians, Jews, Christians, and Mussulmen, "you conceive the origin of those ideas of battles and rebellions, which equally abound in all your mythologies. You see what is meant by white and black angels; your cherubim and seraphim with heads of eagles, of lions and of bulls; your deus, devils or demons with horns of goats and tails of serpents; your thrones and dominions ranged in seven orders or gradations like the seven spheres of the planets; all beings acting the same parts, and endowed with the same attributes in the vedas, bibles or zend-avestas, whether they have for chiefs Ormuzd or Brahma, Typhon or Chiven, Michael or Satan; whether they appear under the form of giants with a hundred arms and feet of serpents, or that of Gods metamorphosed into lions, storks,

---

* "All religious acts of gaiety."—All the ancient festivals respecting the return and exaltation of the sun, were of this description; hence the hilaria of the Roman calendar at the passage (pascha) of the vernal equinox. The dances were imitations of the march of the planets. Those of the Dervises still represent it to this day.

† "All religious acts of the gloomy sort."—'Sacrifices of blood,' says Porphyry, 'were only offered to demons and evil genii to avert their wrath.—Demons are fond of blood, humidity, stench.' (Apud Euseb., Præp. Evang., p. 1. 73.)
'The Egyptians,' says Plutarch, 'only offer bloody victims to Typhon They sacrifice to him a red ox; and the victim is held in abhorrence, and loaded with all the sins of the people (the goat of Moses.)' See de Iside et Osiride.
"That distinction of terrestrial beings into sacred and abominable."—Strabo says, speaking of Moses and the Jews; 'Circumcision and the prohibition of certain kinds of meat sprung from superstition. And I observe, respecting the ceremony of circumcision, that its object was to take from the symbol of Osiris (phallus) the pretended obstacle to fecundity; an obstacle which bore the seal of Typhon, 'whose nature,' says Plutarch, 'is made up of all that hinders, opposes or obstructs '

oulls or cats, as in the sacred fables of the Greeks and Egyptians; you perceive the successive filiation of these ideas, and how, in proportion to their remoteness from their source, and as the minds of men became refined, their gross forms have been polished, and rendered less disgusting.

" But, in the same manner as you have seen the system of two opposite principles or Gods arise from that of symbols, and interwoven into its texture, your attention shall now be called to a new system which has grown out of this, and to which this has served in its turn as a basis and support."

V. *Moral and mystical Worship, or System of a future State.*

" Indeed, when the vulgar heard speak of a new heaven and another world, they soon gave a body to these fictions; they erected therein a real theatre of action, and their notions of astronomy and geography served to strengthen, if not to originate this illusion.

" On the one hand, the Phenician navigators who passed the pillars of Hercules to fetch the tin of Thule, and the amber of the Baltic, related that at the extremity of the world, the end of the Ocean (the Mediterranean,) where the sun sets for the countries of Asia, were the fortunate islands, the abode of eternal spring, and beyond were the Hyperborean regions, placed under the earth (relatively to the tropics,) where reigned an eternal night.* From these stories misunderstood, and no doubt confusedly related, the imagination of the people composed the Elysian fields,† regions of delight placed in a world below, having their heaven, their sun and their stars, and Tartarus, a place of darkness, humidity, mire and frost. Now, as man, inquisitive of that which he knows not, and desirous of protracting his existence, had already interrogated himself concerning what was to become of him after his death, as he had early reasoned on the principle of life which animates his body, and which leaves it without deforming it, and as he had imagined airy substances, phantoms, and shades, he fondly believed that he should continue, in the subterranean world, that life which it was too painful for him to lose;

* Nights of six months.

† Ahz, in the Phenician or Hebrew language, signifies dancing and rejoicing

12*

and these lowe˙˙ regions seemed commodious for the reception of the
beloved objects which he could not willingly resign.

. " On the other hand, the astrological and geological priests told
such stories and made such descriptions of their heavens, as accorded
perfectly well with these fictions. Having, in their metaphorical
language, called the equinoxes and solstices, the gates of heaven, the
entrance of the seasons, they explained the terrestrial phenomena
by saying, ' that through the gate of horn (first the bull, afterwards
the ram) and through the gate of cancer, descended the vivifying
fires which give life to vegetation in the spring, and the aqueous
spirits which bring, at the solstice, the inundation of the Nile ; that
through the gate of ivory (libra, formerly sagittarius or the bow) and
by that of capricorn or the urn, the emanations or influences of the
heavens returned to their source, and reascended to their origin ; and
the milky way, which passed through these gates of the solstices,
seemed to be placed there to serve them as a road or vehicle ; besides, in their atlas, the celestial scene presented a river (the Nile,
designated by the windings of the hydra,) a boat (the ship Argo) and
the dog Syrius, both relative to this river, whose inundation they
foretold.   These circumstances, added to the preceding and still farther explaining them, increased their probability, and to arrive at
Tartarus or Elysium, souls were obliged to cross the rivers Styx and
Acheron in the boat of the ferryman Caron, and to pass through the
gates of horn or ivory, guarded by the dog Cerberus.   Finally, these
inventions were applied to a civil use, and thence received a further
consistency.

" Having remarked that in their burning climate, the putrefaction
of dead bodies was a cause of pestilential diseases, the Egyptians in
many of their towns had adopted the practice of burying their dead
beyond the limits of the inhabited country, in the desert of the West.
To go there, it was necessary to pass the channels of the river, and
consequently to be received into a boat, and pay something to the
ferryman, without which, the body deprived of sepulture, must have
been the prey of wild beasts.   This custom suggested to the civil and
religious legislators the means of a powerful influence on manners ;
and, addressing uncultivated and ferocious men with the motives of
filial piety and a reverence for the dead, they established as a necessary condition, their undergoing a previous trial, which should decide
whether the deceased merited to be admitted to the rank of the fami-

ly in the black city. Such an idea accorded too well with all the others not to be incorporated with them; the people soon adopted it, and hell had its Minos and its Rhadamanthus, with the wand, the bench, the ushers and the urn, as in the earthly and civil state. It was then that god became a moral and political being, a social legislator so much the more formidable, as this supreme legislator, th's final judge was inaccessible and invisible : then it was that this fabulous and mythological world, composed of such odd materials and disjointed members, became a place of punishments and of rewards, where divine justice was supposed to correct what was vicious and erroneous in the judgment of men ; and this spiritual and mystical system acquired the more credit, as it took possession of man by all his natural inclinations : the oppressed found in it the hope of indemnity, and the consolation of future vengeance, the oppressor, expecting by rich offerings to purchase his impunity, formed out of the errors of the vulgar an additional weapon of oppression ; the chiefs of nations, the kings and priests found in this a new instrument of domination, by the privilege which they reserved to themselves of distributing the favors and punishments of the great judge, according to the merit or demerit of actions, which they took care to characterize as best suited their system.

" This then is the manner in which an invisible and imaginary world has been introduced into the real and visible one ; this is the origin of those regions of pleasure and pain, of which you Persians have made your regenerated earth, your city of resurrection placed under the equator, with this singular attribute, that in it the blessed cast no shade.* Of these materials, Jews and Christians, disciples

* " The blessed cast no shade."—There is on this subject a passage in Plutarch so interesting and explanatory of the whole of this system, that we shall cite it entire ; having observed that the theory of good and evil had at all times occupied the attention of naturalists and theologians, he adds : ' Many suppose there are two gods of opposite inclinations, one delighting in good, the other in evil ; the first of these is called particularly by the name of God, the second by that of Genius or Demon. Zoroaster has denominated them Oromaze and Ahrimanes, and has said that of whatever falls under the cognizance of our senses, light is the best representative of the one, and darkness and ignorance of the other. He adds that Mithra is an intermediate being, and it is for this reason that the Persians call Mithra the Mediator or intercessor. Each of these gods has distinct plants and animals consecrated to him ; for instance, dogs, birds, and hedgehogs belong to the good Genius ; and all aquatic animals to the evil one.
.' The Persians also say that Oromaze was born or formed out of the purest light ; Ahrimanes, on the contrary, out of the thickest darkness ; that Oromaze made six gods as good as himself, and Ahrimanes opposed

of the Persians, have you formed your Jerusalem of the apocalypse, your paradise, your heaven, copied in all its parts from the astrological heaven of Hermes : and your hell, ye Mussulmen ! your bottomless pit, surmounted by a bridge; your balance for weighing souls and their works, your last judgment by the angels Monkir and Nekir, are likewise modelled from the mysterious ceremonies of the cave of Mithra ; * and your heaven differs not in the least from that of Osiris, of Ormuzd and of Brahma."

to them six wicked ones. That afterwards Oromaze trebled himself (Hermes tris-megistus,) and removed to a distance as remote from the earth ; that he there formed stars, and among others, Syrius, which he placed in the heavens as a guard and sentinel. He made also twenty-four other gods whom he inclosed in an egg ; but Ahrimanes created an equal number who cracked the egg, and from that moment good and evil were mixed (in the universe.) But Ahrimanes is one day to be conquered, and the earth to be made equal and smooth, that all men may live happy.

'Theopompus adds, from the books of the magi, that one of these gods reigns in turn every three thousand years, during which the other is kept in subjection : that they afterwards contend with equal weapons during the same space of time. but that in the end the evil Genius will fall (never to rise again.) Then men will become happy, and shall have no shadow. But the god who meditates all these things reclines at present in repose, waiting to meet them.' (De Iside et Osiride.) The allegory is evident through the whole of this passage. The egg is the sphere of fixed stars, the world : the six gods of Oromaze are the six signs of summer ; those of Ahrimanes the six signs of winter. The forty-eight other gods are the forty-eight constellations of the ancient sphere, divided equally between Ahrimanes and Oromaze. The office of Syrius as guard and sentinel, tells us that the origin of these ideas was Egyptian ; finally, the expression that the earth is to become equal and smooth and that the bodies of the happy shall cast no shadow, proves that the equator was considered as their true paradise.

* "The ceremonies of the cave of Mithra."—In the factitious caves which priests everywhere constructed, they celebrated mysteries which consisted, says Origen against Celsus, in imitating the motion of the stars, the planets and the heavens. The initiated took the name of constellations, and assumed the figure of animals. One was a lion, another a raven, and a third a ram. Hence the use of masks in the first representation of the drama. See Antiq. devoilee, vol. II. p. 244. In the mysteries of Ceres, the chief in the procession called himself the creator ; the torch-bearer was denominated the Sun, the person nearest to the altar, the Moon ; the herald or deacon, Mercury. In Egypt, there was a festival in which men and women represented the year, the century, the seasons, the divisions of the day, and they followed the procession of Bacchus. Athen. lib. v. c. 7. In the cave of Mithra was a ladder with seven steps, representing the seven spheres of the planets, by means of which souls ascended and descended : this is precisely the ladder in Jacob's vision ; which shows that at that epoch, the whole system was formed. There is in the royal library a superb volume of pictures of the Indian gods, in which the ladder is represented with the souls of men ascending it, last plate.

See Bailly's ancient astronomy, where our assertions respecting the knowledge of the priests are fully proved.

VI. *Sixth System.* *The Animated World or Worship of the Universe under diverse Emblems.*

" While the nations were wandering in the dark labyrinth of mythology and fables, the physical priests, pursuing their studies and inquiries into the order and disposition of the universe, came to new conclusions, and formed new systems concerning powers and first causes.

" Long confined to simple appearances, they saw nothing in the movement of the stars but an unknown play of luminous bodies rolling round the earth, which they believed the central point of all the spheres; but as soon as they discovered the rotundity of our planet, the consequences of this first fact led them to new considerations; and from induction to induction, they rose to the highest conceptions in astronomy and physics.

" Indeed, after having conceived this luminious idea, that the terrestrial globe is a little circle inscribed in the greater circle of the heavens, the theory of concentric circles served naturally in their hypothesis, to determine the unknown circle of the terrestrial globe by certain known points of the celestial circle; and the measurement of one or more degrees of the meridian gave with precision the whole circumference. Then, taking for a compass the known diameter of the earth, some fortunate genius applied it with a bold hand to the boundless orbits of the heavens; and man, the inhabitant of a grain of sand, embracing the infinite distances of the stars, launched into the immensity of space and the eternity of time : there he is presented with a new order of the universe; of which the atom-globe which he inhabited appeared no longer to be the centre : this important post was reserved to the enormous mass of the sun ; and that body became the flaming pivot of eight surrounding spheres, whose movements were henceforth subjected to precise calculation.

" It was already a great effort of the human mind to have undertaken to determine the disposition and order of the great engines of nature; but not stopping there, it still endeavoured to develope the mechanism, and discover the origin and the instinctive principle; hence, engaged in the abstract and metaphysical nature of motion and its first cause, of the inherent or incidental properties of matter, its successive forms and its extension, that is to say, of time and space unbounded, the physical theologians lost themselves in a chaos of subtle reasoning and scholastic controversy.

" In the first place, the action of the sun on terrestrial bodies teaching them to regard his substance as a pure and elementary fire, they
made it the focus and reservoir of an ocean of igneous and luminous
fluid, which, under the name of ether, filled the universe and nourished all beings. Afterwards, having discovered by a physical and
attentive analysis, this same fire, or another perfectly resembling it,
in the composition of all bodies, and having perceived it to be the essential agent of that spontaneous movement which is called life in
animals, and vegetation in plants, they conceived the mechanism and
harmony of the universe as of a homogeneous whole, of one identical
body, whose parts, though distant, had nevertheless an intimate relation ;* and the world was a living being, animated by the organic
circulation of an igneous and even electrical fluid,† which by a
term of comparison borrowed first from men and animals, had the sun
for a heart or focus. ‡

" From this time the physical theologians seem to have divided
into several classes ; one class, grounding itself on these principles
resulting from observation, ' that nothing can be annihilated in the
world : that the elements are indestructible ; that they change their
combinations but not their nature ; that the life and death of beings
are but the different modifications of the same atoms ; that matter
itself possesses properties which give rise to all its modes of existence;
that the world is eternal, or unlimited in space and duration ;' said,
' that the whole universe was God ;' and according to them, God was
a being, effect and cause, agent and patient, moving principle and
thing moved, having for laws the invariable properties that consti-

* " Whose parts had an intimate relation."—These are the very
words of Jamblicus. De Myst. Ægypt.

† " An igneous and electrical fluid."—The more I consider what the
ancients understood by ether and spirit, and what the Indians call
akache, the stronger do I find the analogy between it and the electrical
fluid. A luminous fluid, principle of warmth and motion, pervading
the universe, forming the matter of the stars, having small round parti-
cles, which insinuating themselves into bodies fill them by dilating itself, be their extent what it may : what can more strongly resemble
electricity ?

‡ " Heart or focus."—Natural philosophers, says Macrobius, call the
sun the heart of the world, c. 20, som. Scip. The Egyptians, says Plutarch, call the East the face, the North the right side, and the South the
left of the world, ' because there the heart is placed ;' they continually
compare the universe to a man, and hence the celebrated Microcosm of
the alchymists. We observe, by the by, that the alchymists, cabalists,
freemasons, magnetizers, martinists and all other such visionaries, are
but the errong disciples of this ancient school. Consult likewise the
Pythagorean Ocellus Lucanus, and the Ædipus Ægyptiacus of Kirker
t. II, p. 205.

tute fatality; and this class conveyed their idea by the emblem of Pan (the Great Whole,) or of Jupiter with a forehead of stars, body of planets, and feet of animals, or of the orphic egg, whose yolk, suspended in the centre of a liquid surrounded by a vault, represented the globe of the sun, swimming in ether in the midst of the vault of heaven; * sometimes by a great round serpent, representing the heavens where they placed the moving principle, and for that reason of an azure color, studded with golden spots (the stars,) devouring his tail, that is, folding and unfolding himself eternally like the revolutions of the spheres; sometimes by that of a man, having his feet joined together and tied, to signify immutable existence; wrapped in a cloak of all colors, like the face of nature, and bearing on his head a golden sphere,† emblem of the sphere of the stars; or by that of another man, sometimes seated on the flower of the lotos borne on the abyss of waters, sometimes lying on a pile of twelve cushions, denoting the twelve celestial signs. And here, Indians, Japanese, Siamese, Tibetans, and Chinese, is the theology which, founded by the Egyptians and transmitted to you, is preserved in the pictures which you compose of Brahma, of Beddou, of Sommonacodom, of Omito; this, ye Hebrews and Christians, is likewise the opinion of which you have preserved a part in your God, moving on the face of the waters, by an allusion to the wind, which, at the beginning of the world, that is, the departure of the spheres from the sign of cancer, announced the inundation of the Nile, and seemed to prepare the creation."

* " In ether in the midst of the vault of heaven."—This comparison with the yolk of an egg refers, 1st. to its round and yellow figure: 2d. to its central situation; 3d. to the germ or principle of life contained in the yolk. May not the oval form allude to the ellipsis of the orbits? I am inclined to this opinion. The word orphic offers a farther observation. Macrobius says (Som. Scip., c. 14, and c. 20) that the sun is the brain of the universe, and that it is from analogy that the human skull is round, like the planet, the seat of intelligence: now, the word œrph (by ain) signifies in Hebrew the brain and its seat (cervix;) Orpheus, then, is the same as Bedou or Baites; and the Bonzes are those very Orphics represented by Plutarch as quacks, who eat no meat, sold talismans, stones, etc., and deceived not only individuals but the governments. See a learned Memoir of Freret, sur les Orphiques, Acad. des Inscrip., tom. xxiii. in 4to.

† " On his head a golden sphere."—See Porphyry, in Eusebius, Præpar. Evang., lib. iii, p. 115.

VII. *Seventh System.* *Worship of the* Soul *of the* World, *that is to say, the Element of Fire, vital Principle of the Universe.*

" But others, disgusted at the idea of a being at once effect and cause, agent and patient, and uniting contrary natures in the same nature, distinguished the moving principle from the thing moved; and premising that matter in itself was inert, they pretended that its properties were communicated to it by a distinct agent, of which it was itself only the cover or the case. This agent was called by some the igneous principle, known to be the author of all motion ; by others it was supposed to be the fluid called ether, which was thought more active and subtile ; and, as in animals the vital and moving principle was called a soul, a spirit, and as they reasoned constantly by comparisons, especially those drawn from human beings, they gave to the moving principle of the universe the name of soul, intelligence, spirit ; and God was the vital spirit which extended through all beings and animated the vast body of the world. And this class conveyed their idea sometimes by You-piter, essence of motion and animation, principle of existence, or rather existence itself; sometimes by Vulcan or Phtha, elementary principle of fire, or by the altar of Vesta, placed in the centre of her temple, like the sun amidst the spheres ; sometimes by Kneph, a human figure dressed in dark blue, having in one hand a sceptre and a girdle (the Zodiac,) with a cap of feathers, to express the fugacity of thought, and producing from his mouth the great egg.

" Now, as a consequence of this system, every being containing in itself a portion of the igneous and etherial fluid, common and universal mover ; and this fluid, soul of the world, being the Divinity, it followed that the souls of all beings were a portion of God himself, partaking of all his attributes, that is, being a substance indivisible, simple and immortal ; and hence the whole system of the immortality of the soul,* which at first was eternity. Hence also its transmigra-

---

* " Hence the whole system of the immortality of the soul."—In the system of the first spiritualists, the soul was not created with, or at the same time as the body, in order to be inserted in it : it existed anteriorly and from all eternity. Such, in a few words, is the doctrine of Macrobius on this head. Om. Scip. Spassim.

‘ There exists a luminous, igneous, subtile fluid, which under the name of ether and spiritus, fills the universe ; it is the essential principle and agent of motion and life ; it is the deity. When an earthly body is to be animated, a small round particle of this fluid gravitates through the milky way towards the lunar sphere, where, when it arrives, it

tions, known by the name of metempsychosis, that is, the passage of the vital principle from one body to another; an idea which arose from the real transmigration of the material elements. And behold, ye Indians, Boudhists, Christians, and Mussulmen! whence are derived all your opinions on the spirituality of the soul; behold what was the source of the dreams of Pythagoras and Plato, your masters, who were themselves but the echoes of another, the last sect of visionary philosophers, which we will proceed to examine.'

VIII. *Eighth System. The* WORLD-MACHINE: *Worship of the Demi-Ourgos or grand Artificer.*

'Hitherto the theologians, employing themselves in examining the fine and subtile substances of ether or the generating fire, had not

unites with a grosser air, and becomes fit to associate with matter: it then enters and entirely fills the body, animates it, suffers, grows, increases and diminishes with it; lastly, when the body dies, and its gross elements dissolve, this incorruptible particle quits it, and returns to the grand ocean of ether, if not retained by its union with the lunar air; it is this air (or gas) which, retaining the shape of the body, becomes a phantom or shade, the perfect image of the deceased. The Greeks called this shade the image or idol of the soul, the Pythagoreans, its chariot, its mould: and the rabbinical school, its vehicle, or boat. When a man had conducted himself well in this world, this entire soul, that is its chariot and ether, ascended to the moon, where a separation took place; the chariot lived in the lunar elysium, and the ether returned to the fixed stars, that is to God; for, says Macrobius, the heaven of the fixed stars was by many called God.' (c. 14.)
If a man had not lived virtuously, the soul remained on earth to be purified, and wandered to and fro, like the shades of Homer, to whom this doctrine must have been known in Asia, three centuries before Pherecides and Pythagoras had revived it in Greece. Herodotus upon this occasion says, that the whole romance of the soul and its transmigrations was invented by the Egyptians, and propagated in Greece by men, who pretended to be its authors. I know their names, adds he, but shall not mention them. (lib 11.) Cicero, however, has positively informed us, that it was Pherecides, master of Pythagoras. (Tuscul. lib. 1. § 16.) In Syria and in Judea, we find a palpable proof of its existence, five centuries before Pythagoras, in this phrase of Solomon, where he says: 'Who knoweth the spirit of a man that it goeth upwards? I said in my heart concerning the estate of the sons of men, that God might manifest them and that they might see that they themselves are beasts. For that which befalleth the sons of men, befalleth beasts; even one thing befalleth them; as the one dieth, so dieth the other; yea they have all one breath, so that a man hath no preeminence above a beast: for all is vanity.' Eccles. c. iii. v. 11.
And such had been the opinion of Moses, as has been justly observed by the translator of Herodotus (Larcher, in his first edition, note 389 of book 11,) where he says also that the immortality of the soul was not introduced among the Hebrews till their intercourse with the Assyrians. In other respects, the whole Pythagorean system, properly analysed, appears to be merely a system of physics misunderstood.

however ceased to treat of beings palpable and perceptible to the senses, and theology continued to be the theory of physical powers, placed sometimes exclusively in the stars, and sometimes disseminated through the universe; but at this period, certain superficial minds, losing the chain of ideas which had directed them in their profound studies, or ignorant of the facts on which they were founded, distorted all the conclusions tuat flowed from them by the introduction of a strange and novel chimera. They pretended that this universe, these heavens, these stars, this sun, were only a machine of an ordinary kind; and applying to this first hypothesis a comparison drawn from the works of art, they raised an edifice of the most whimsical sophisms. 'A machine,' said they, ' does not make itself; it has had an anterior workman, its very existence proves it. The world is a machine: therefore it had an artificer.'

" Here then is the demi-ourgos or grand artificer, constituted god autocratical and supreme. In vain the ancient philosophy objected to this by saying that the artificer himself must have had parents and progenitors, and that they only added another link to the chain by taking eternity from the world and giving it to its supposed author The innovators, not content with this first paradox, passed on to a second; and, applying to their artificer the theory of the human understanding, they pretended that the demi-ourgos had framed his machine on a plan preexisting in his understanding. Now, as their masters, the naturalists, had placed in the regions of the fixed stars the great primum mobile, under the name of intelligence and reason, so their mimics, the spiritualists, seizing this idea, applied it to their demi-ourges, and making it a substance distinct and self-existent, they called it mens or logos (reason or word.) And as they likewise admitted the existence of the soul of the world, or solar principle, they found themselves obliged to compose three ranks or gradations of divine beings, which were, 1st. the demi-ourgos, or working god; 2dly. the logos, word or reason, and 3dly. the spirit or soul (of the world.) And here, Christians! is the romance on which you have founded your Trinity; here is the system which, born a heretic in the temples of Egypt, transported a pagan into the schools of Italy and Greece, is now found to be catholic and orthodox, by the conversion of its partisans, the disciples of Pythagoras and Plato, to Christianity.

" It is thus that the Divinity, after having been first the visible and various action of the meteors and elements;

" Afterwards, the combined powers of the stars considered in their relations to terrestrial beings;

" After, these terrestrial beings themselves, by confounding the symbols with their archetypes;

" Next, the double power of nature in its two principal operations of producing and destroying;

"Again, the animated world, without distinction of agent and patient, of effect and cause;

" Finally, the solar principle, or the element of fire considered as the only mover;

" It is thus that the Divinity is become, in the last resort, a chimerical and abstract being; a scholastic subtilty, of substance without form, a body without a figure; a very delirium of the mind, beyond the power of reason to comprehend. But vainly does it seek in this last transformation to illude the senses; the seal of its origin is too deeply imprinted on it to be effaced; and its attributes, all borrowed from the physical attributes of the universe. such as immensity, eternity, indivisibility, incomprehensibility; or on the moral affections of man, such as goodness, justice, majesty, etc.; its names* even, all derived from the physical beings which were its types, and

---

* " Its names even, all derived."—When analyzed, all the names of the deity seem to be derived from some material object in which it was supposed to reside. We have given many instances; let us add one more relative to our word God. This is the deas of the Latins, which is but the theos of the Greeks. Now, by the confession of Plato (in Cratylo,) of Macrobius, (Saturn., lib. 1, c. 24,) and of Plutarch (Isis et Osiris,) its root is them, which signifies to wander, like planein: that is to say, it is synonymous with planets, because, add our authors, both the ancient Greeks and Barbarians particularly worshipped the planets. I know that such inquiries into etymologies have been much decried; but if, as is the case, words are the representative signs of ideas, the genealogy of the one becomes that of the other, and a good etymological dictionary would be the most perfect history of the human understanding. It would only be necessary to observe certain precautions in this inquiry, which have hitherto been neglected, and particularly to make an exact comparison of the value of the letters of the different alphabets. But, to continue our subject, we shall add that in the Phenician language, the word thah (with am) signifies also to wander, and from it them seems to be derived: if we suppose deus to be derived from the Greek Zeus, a proper name of Youpiter, having Zaw, I live, for its root, its sense will be precisely that of you, and will mean soul of the world, igneous principle. Div-us, which only signifies Genius, God of the second order, appears to me to come from the oriental word div for dib, wolf and Jackal, one of the emblems of the sun. At Thebes, says Macrobius, the sun was painted under the form of a wolf or Jackal (for there are no wolves in Egypt.) The reason of this emblem, doubtless, is that the jackal, like the cock, announces by its cries the rising of the sun, and this reason is confirmed by the analogy of the words lykos, wolf, and lyke, light of the morning, whence comes lux.

especially from the sun, the planets and the world, constant y bring to mind, in spite of its corrupters, indelible marks of its real nature.

" Such is the chain of ideas which the human mind had already run through at an epoch provious to the records of history : and since their continuity proves that they were the produce of the same series of studies and labors, we have every reason to place their origin in Egypt, the cradle of their first elements : and their progress there may have been rapid ; because the idle curiosity of the physical priests had no other food, in the retirement of the temples, but the enigma of the universe always present to their minds ; and because in the political districts into which that country was for a long time divided, every State had its college of priests, who, being by turns auxiliaries or rivals, hastened by their disputes, the progress of science and discovery.*

Dius, which is to be understood also of the sun, must be derived from dih, a hawk. 'The Egyptians,' says Porphyry (Easeb. Præp. Evang. p. 92,) 'represent the sun under the emblem of a hawk, because this bird soars to the highest regions of air where light abounds.' And in reality we continually see at Cairo thousands of these birds, hovering in the air, from whence they descend only to stun us with their shrieks, which are like the monosyllable dih : and here, as in the preceding example, we find an analogy between the word dies, day, light, and dius, god, sun.

* " Hastened by their disputes the progress of science and discovery."— A most plausible proof that all these systems were invented in Egypt, is that this is the only country where we see a complete body of doctrine formed from the remotest antiquity.

Clemens Alexandrinus has transmitted to us (Stromat. lib. vi) a curious detail of the 42 volumes which were borne in the procession of Isis. 'The leader,' said he, 'or chanter, carries one of the symbolic instruments of music, and two of the books of Mercury, one containing hymns of the gods, the other the list of kings. Next to him the horoscope (calculator of time) carries a palm and a dial, symbols of astrology ; he must know by heart the four books of Mercury which treat of astrology, the first on the order of the planets, the second on the risings of the sun and moon, and the two last on the rising and aspect of the stars. Then comes the sacred writer, with feathers on his head (like Kneph) and a nook in his hand, together with ink and a reed to write with (as is still the practice among the Arabs,) He must be versed in Hieroglyphics, must understand the description of the universe, the course of the sun, moon, and planets , be acquainted with the division of Egypt (into 36 names,) with the course of the Nile, with instruments, measures, sacred ornaments and holy places, etc. Next comes the Stole-hearer, carrying the cubit of justice or measure of the Nile, and a chalice for the libations · ten volumes treat of the sacrifices, hymns. prayers, offerings, ceremonies, festivals. Lastly arrives the prophet, hearing in his bosom and exposed to view a pitcher ; he is followed by persons carrying loaves of bread (as at the marriage of Cana.) This prophet, as president of the mysteries, learns ten (other) sacred volumes concerning the laws, the gods, and the discipline of the priests, etc. Now there are in all forty-two volumes, thirty-six of which are learned by these personages, and

"There happened already on the borders of the Nile, what has since been repeated in every country; as soon as a new system was formed, its novelty excited quarrels and schisms. then, gaining credit by persecution itself, sometimes it effaced antecedent ideas, sometimes it modified and incorporated them; then by the intervention of political revolutions, the aggregation of States and the mixture of nations confused all opinions: and the filiation of ideas being lost, theology fell into a chaos, and became a mere logogriphe of old traditions no longer understood. Religion, having strayed from its object, was now nothing more than a political engine to conduct the credulous vulgar, and it was used for this purpose, sometimes, by men, credulous themselves and dupes of their own visions, and sometimes by bold and energetic spirits in pursuit of great objects of ambition."

IX. *Religion of Moses, or Worship of the Soul of the World* (*You-piter.*)

"Such was the legislator of the Hebrews, who, wishing to separate his nation from all others, and to form a distinct and solitary empire, conceived the design of establishing its basis on religious prejudices, and of raising around it a sacred rampart of opinions and of rites. But in vain did he prescribe the worship of the symbols which prevailed in lower Egypt and Phœnicia; his god was nevertheless an Egyptian god,* invented by those priests of whom Moses

the remaining six are reserved for the pastophores; they treat of medicine, the construction of the human body (anatomy,) diseases, remedies, instruments, etc.'

We leave the reader to deduce all the consequences of such an encyclopedia. It was ascribed to Mercury; but Jamblichus tells us that all books composed by the priests were dedicated to that God, who, being a Genius or decan opening the zodiac, presided over enterprise; he is the Janus of the Romans, the Guianese of the Indians, and it is remarkable that Yanus and Guianes are synonymous. In short, it appears that these books are the source of all that has been transmitted to us by the Greeks and Latins in every science, even in alchymy, necromancy, etc. What is most to be regretted in their loss is that part which related to the principles of medicine and diet, in which the Egyptians appear to have made a considerable progress and useful observations.

* "His god was nevertheless an Egyptian god."—'At a certain period,' says Plutarch, [de Iside] 'all the Egyptians have their animal gods painted. The Thebans are the only people who do not employ painters, because they worship a god whose form comes not under the senses and cannot be represented.' And this is the god whom Moses, educated at Heliopolis, adopted, but the idea was not of his invention.

13*

had been the disciple; and Yahouh, betrayed by its very name,* essence (of beings,) and by its symbol, the burning bush, is only the
soul of the world, the moving principle which the Greeks soon after

* "And Yahouh betrayed by its very name."—Such is the true pronun-
ciation of the Jehovah of the moderns, who violate, in this respect, every
rule of criticism, since it is evident that the ancients, particularly the
eastern Syrians and Phenicians were acquainted neither with the J. nor
the V. borrowed from the Tartars. The subsisting usage of the Arabs,
which we have reestablished here, is confirmed by Diodorus, who calls
the God of Moses law [lib. 1.:] and Iaw and Iahouh are manifestly the
same word: the identity continues in that of Joupiter; but in order to
render it more complete, we shall demonstrate the signification to be
the same.

In Hebrew, that is to say, in one of the dialects of the common language of lower Asia, the word Yahouh is equivalent to our periphrasis
he who is, the being that exists, in other words, the principle of life,
the mover or even motion [the universal soul of beings.] Now what
is Jupiter? Let us hear the Greeks and Latins explain their theology:
'The Egyptians, says Diodorus, after Manetho, priest of Memphis, the
Egyptians, assigning names to the live elements, called spirit [or ether]
Youpiter, on account of the true meaning of that word; for spirit is the
source of life, author of the vital principle in animals, and for this reason they considered him as the father, the generator of beings.' For
the same reason, Homer says, father and king of men and gods. [Diod
lib. I. sect. 1.]

Theologians, says Macrobius, consider Youpiter as the soul of the
world, hence the words of Virgil. Muses, let us begin with Youpiter:
the world is full of Youpiter [Bonin. Scip c. 17;] and in the Saturnalia,
he says: Jupiter is the sun himself: It was this also which made Virgil
say: 'The spirit nourishes the life [of beings,] and the soul diffused
through the vast members [of the universe] agitates the whole mass and
forms but one immense body.'

'Joupiter,' say the very ancient verses of the Orphic sect, which
originated in Egypt, verses collected by Onomacritus, in the days of Pis-
istratus, 'Joupiter, represented with the thunder in his hand, is the beginning, origin, end and middle of all things: a single and universal
power, he governs all, heaven, earth, the, water, the elements, day
and night. These are what constitute his immense body; his eyes are
the sun and moon; he is space and eternity: in fine, adds Porphyry, Jupiter is the world, the universe. that which constitutes the existence and
life of all beings. Now, continues the same author, as philosophers differed in opinion respecting the nature and constituent parts of this God,
and as they could invent no figure that could represent all his attributes,
they painted him in the form of a man. He is in a sitting posture, in
allusion to his immutable essence; the upper part of his body is uncov-
ered, because it is in the upper regions of the universe [the stars,] that
he is most conspicuous. He is covered from the waist downwards, because respecting terrestrial things he is more mysterious. He holds a
sceptic in his left hand because it is the side of the heart, and the heart
is the seat of the understanding, which, [in human beings] regulates
every action.' [Euseb. Præpar. Evang. p. 100.]

The following passage of the geographer and philosopher, Strabo, re-
moves every doubt as to the identity of the ideas of Moses and those of
the heathen theologians.

'Moses, who was one of the Egyptian Priests, taught that it was a
monstrous error to represent the deity under the form of animals, as the
Egyptians did, or in the shape of men, as was the practice of the Greeks

adopted under the same denomination in their You-pi&er, generating being ; and under that of Ei,* existence, which the Thebeans consecrated by the name of Kneph ; which Sais worshipped under the emblem of Isis veiled, with this inscription : I am all that has been, that is, and that shall be, and no mortal has raised my veil; which Pythagoras honored under the name of Vesta, and which the stoic philosophy defined precisely by calling it the principle of fire. In vain did Moses wish to blot from his religion everything which had relation to the stars; many traits call them to mind in spite of all he has done ; the seven luminaries or planets of the great candlestick, the twelve stones or signs in the urim of the high priest, the feast of the two equinoxes, entrances and gates of the two hemispheres, the ceremony of the lamb or celestial ram ; lastly the name even of Osirist† preserved in his canticle, and the ark or coffer, an imitation of the tomb in which that god was laid, all remain as so many witnesses of the filiation of his ideas, and of their derivation from the common source."

X. *Religion of Zoroaster.*

" Such also was Zoroaster, who, two centuries after Moses, revived and moralised among the Medes and Battrians the whole Egyp-

and Africans ; that alone is the deity, said he, which constitutes heaven, earth and being ; that which we call the world, the sum of all things, nature ; and no reasonable person will think of representing such a being by the image of any one of the objects around us; it is for this reason, that, rejecting every species of images [idols,] Moses wished the Deity to be worshipped without emblems, and according to his proper nature ; and he accordingly ordered a temple worthy of him to be erected, etc.' Geograph. lib. xvi, page 1104, edit. of 1707.

The theology of Moses has therefore differed in no respect from that of the worshippers of the soul of the world, that is, from the Stoics and Epicureans.

As to the history of Moses, Diodorus properly represents it when he says, lib. xxxiv and xl, ' that the Jews were driven out of Egypt during a famine, when the country was full of foreigners, and that Moses, a man of extraordinary prudence and courage, seized this opportunity of establishing his nation in the mountains of Judea.' As to 600,000 armed men, whom Exodus gives him, it is an error of the transcribers, the proof of which, taken from the books themselves, is to be found in the 1st vol. of New Researches on ancient History, page 162, and following.

* "Under that of Ei."—This was the monosyllable written on the gate of the temple of Delphos. Plutarch has made it the subject of a dissertation.

† " The name even of Osiris."—It is expressly mentioned in Deuteronomy, chap. 32. ' The works of Tsour are perfect.' Now Tsour has been translated by the word creator ; its proper signification is to give forms ; and this is one of the definitions of Osiris in Plutarch.

tian system of Osiris and Typhon, under the names of Ormuzd and
Ahrimanes; who, to explain the system of nature, supposed two
great gods or powers, one occupied in creating and producing, in an
empire of light and genial heat (represented by summer,) and therefore, god of science, beneficence and virtue; the other occupied in
destroying, in an empire of darkness and cold (represented by the
pole of winter,) and therefore god of ignorance, malevolence and
sin: who, by figurative expressions, afterwards misunderstood, called creation of the world the renewal of nature in spring; called resurrection the renewal of the periods of the stars in their conjunc-
tions; future life, hell and paradise, what was only the Tartarus
and Elysium of the astrologers and geographers; in a word, he did
nothing but consecrate the preexisting dreams of the mystical system."

XI. *Brahmism, or Indian System.*

" And such too was the Indian legislator, who under the name of
Menou, preceded Zoroaster and Moses, and consecrated, on the
banks of the Ganges, the doctrine of the three principles or gods
known to the Greeks, one of whom, named Brahma, or Joupiter
was author of all production or creation (the sun in spring;) the sec
ond, named Chiven or Pluto, was the god of all destruction (the sun
in winter;) and the third, named Vichenou or Neptune, was god the
preserver of the stationary state (the sun in the solstices, stator;) all
three distinct, and yet forming all three only one god or power, who,
sung in the vedas, as in the orphic hymns, is no other than the three
eyed Joupiter,* or sun with three modes of action, in the three ri-
tous or seasons; this is the origin of all the trinitary system subtilized
by Pythagoras and Plato, and totally disfigured by their interpreters."

XII. *Boudhism, or Mystical Systems.*

" Such in fine were the moralist reformers revered after Menou,
under the names of Boudah, Gaspa, Chekia, Goutama, etc., who
from the principles of the metempsychosis, variously modified, deduc-
ed mystical doctrines useful at first because they inspired their sectaries with a horror of murder, compassion for every feeling being,
fear of the punishments and hope of the rewards reserved for virtue

---

* Eye and sun are expressed by the same word in most of the ancient
languages of Asia.

and vice, in another life, and under a new form; but which afterwards became pernicious by the abuse of a visionary system of metaphysics, that endeavoured to oppose the natural order, and pretended
that the palpable and material world was a fantastical illusion; that
the existence of man was a dream from which he awoke only at his
death; that his body was an impure prison which he ought to quit
as soon as possible, or else a coarse covering which to be pervaded
by the internal light should be attenuated, and rendered diaphanous
by fasting, macerations, contemplations, and a number of anchoritic
practices so strange, that the astonished vulgar could only explain
the character of their authors by considering them as supernatural
beings, and were only embarrassed to know if they were god huma-
ized or man deified.

"These are the materials which existed in a scattered state for
many centuries in Asia, when a fortuitous concourse of events and
circumstances, on the borders of the Euphrates and the Mediterranean, served to form them into new combinations."

XIII. *Christianity, or the Allegorical Worship of the Sun
under the cabalistical names of Chris-en or Christ, and Yesus
or Jesus.*

"In constituting a separate nation, Moses strove in vain to defend
it against the invasion of foreign ideas: an invincible inclination,
founded on the affinity of their origin, had constantly brought back
the Hebrews towards the worship of the neighbouring nations; and
the commercial and political relations which necessarily existed between them, strengthened this propensity from day to day. As long
as the constitution of the state remained entire, the coercive force of
the government and laws opposed these innovations, and retarded
their progress; nevertheless the high places were full of idols, and
the god Sun had his chariot and horses painted in the palaces of the
kings and even in the temples of Yahouh: but when the conquests
of the sultans of Nineveh and Babylon had dissolved the bands of
civil power, the people, left to themselves, and solicited by their
conquerors, restrained no longer their inclination for profane opinions,
and they were publicly professed in Judea. First the Assyrian colonies, which came and occupied the lands of the tribes, filled the
kingdom of Samaria with dogmas of the Magi, which very soon
penetrated into the kingdom of Judah: afterwards Jerusalem being

subjugated the Egyptians, Syrians and Arabs, entering this defenceless country, introduced their opinions, and the religion of Moses was doubly mutilated. Besides, the priests and great men, being transported to Babylon and educated in the sciences of the Kaldeans imbibed, during a residence of fifty years, the whole of their theology; and from that moment the dogmas of the hostile genius (Satan,) the archangel Michael,* the ancient of days (Ormuzd,) the rebel angels, the battles in heaven, the immortality of the soul, and the resurrection, all unknown to Moses, or rejected by his total silence respecting them, were introduced and naturalized among the Jews.

"The emigrants returned to their country with these ideas; and their innovation at first excited disputes between their partisans the Pharisees, and their opponents the Sadducees, who maintained the ancient national worship. But the former, aided by the propensities of the people, and their habits already contracted, and supported by the Persians their deliverers and masters, gained the ascendant over the latter, and the sons of Moses consecrated the theology of Zoroaster.†

"A fortuitous analogy between two leading ideas was highly favorable to this coalition, and became the basis of a last system, not less surprising in the fortune it has had in the world than in the causes of its formation.

"After the Assyrians had destroyed the kingdom of Samaria, some judicious men foresaw the same destiny for Jerusalem, which they did not fail to predict and publish; and their predictions had the particular turn of being terminated by prayers for a reestablishment and regeneration, uttered in the form of prophecies: the hierophants, in their enthusiasm, had painted a king as a deliverer who was to reestablish the nation in its ancient glory: the Hebrews

* "Satan, the archangel Michael."—'The names of the angels and of the months, such as Gabriel, Michael, Yar, Nisan, etc. came from Babylon with the Jews,' says expressly the Talmud of Jerusalem. See Beausobre, Histoire du Manich. vol. 11, p. 624, where he proves that the saints of the calendar are an imitation of the 365 angels of the Persians; and Iamblicus, in his Egyptian mysteries, sect. 2, c. 3, speaks of angels, archangels, seraphims, etc. like a true Christian.

† "Consecrated the theology of Zoroaster."—'The whole philosophy of the gymnosophists,' says Diogenes Laertius, on the authority of an ancient writer, 'is derived from that of the Magi, and many assert that of the Jews to have the same origin,' [lib. 1, c. 9.] Megasthenes, an historian of repute in the days of Seleucus Nicanor, and who wrote particularly upon India, speaking of the philosophy of the ancients respecting natural things, puts the Brahmans and the Jews precisely on the same footing.

were to become once more a powerful, a conquering nation, and Jerusalem the capital of an empire extended over the whole earth.

"Events having realized the first part of these predictions, the ruin of Jerusalem, the people adhered to the second with a firmness of belief in proportion to their misfortunes; and the afflicted Jews expected with the impatience of want and desire, this victorious king and deliverer who was to come and save the nation of Moses, and restore the empire of David.

"On the other hand, the sacred and mythological traditions of preceding times had spread through all Asia a dogma perfectly analogous. The cry there was a great mediator, a final judge, a future saviour, a king, god, conqueror and legislator, who was to restore the golden age upon earth,* to deliver it from the dominion of evil, and bring men back to the empire of good, peace, and happiness. The people seized and cherished these ideas with so much the more avidity, as they found in them a consolation under that deplorable state of suffering into which they had been plunged by the devastations of successive conquests, and the barbarous despotism of their governments. This conformity between the oracles of nations and those of the prophets, excited the attention of the Jews; and doubtless the prophets had the art to compose their descriptions after the style and genius of the sacred books employed in the pagan mysteries; there was therefore a general expectation in Judea of a great ambassador, a final Saviour, when a singular circumstance determined the epoch of his coming.

"It is found in the sacred books of the Persians and Kaldeans, that the world, composed of a total revolution of twelve thousand, was divided into two partial revolutions, one of which, the age and reign of good, terminated in six thousand, and the other, the age and reign of evil, was to terminate in six thousand more.

"By these records, the first authors had understood the annual revolution of the great celestial orb, called the world, (a revolution composed of twelve months or signs, divided each into a thousand parts;) and the two systematic periods of winter and summer, composed each of six thousand. These expressions, wholly equivocal and badly explained, having received an absolute and moral, instead of a physical and astrological sense, it happened that the annual

* "To restore the golden age upon earth."—This is the reason of the application of the many pagan oracles to Jesus, and particularly the fourth eclogue of Virgil and the sibylline verses so celebrated among the ancients

world was taken for the secular world, the thousand of the zodiacal divisions for a thousand of years; and supposing, from the state of things, that they lived in the age of evil, they inferred that it would end with the six thousand pretended years.*

" Now, according to calculations admitted by the Jews, they began to reckon near six thousand years since the (supposed) creation of the world. This coincidence caused a fermentation in the public mind. Nothing was thought of but the approaching end; they consulted the hierophants and the mystical books, which differed as to the term, the great restorer was expected and desired; he was so much spoken of, that some person finally was said to have seen him, or some one of a heated imagination fancied himself such and acquired proselytes, who, deprived of their leader by an incident true no doubt, but obscurely recorded, gave rise by their reports to a rumor which was gradually converted into an historical fact; upon this first basis, all the circumstances of mythological traditions took their stand, and produced an authentic and entire system, which it was no longer permitted to call in question.

" These mythological traditions recounted: 'that in the beginning, a woman and a man had, by their fall, introduced into the world sin and misery.' (Consult plate III.)

"By this was denoted the astronomical fact that the celestial virgin and the herdsman (Bootes,) by setting heliacally at the autumnal equinox, delivered the world to the wintry constellations, and seemed, on falling below the horizon, to introduce into the world the genius of evil, Ahrimanes, represented by the constellation of the serpent.†

---

* " End with the six thousand pretended years."—Read upon this subject the 17th chapter of the 1st volume of New Researches on ancient history, where the Mythology of the creation is explained. The septuagint reckoned five thousand and nearly six hundred years; and this calculation was generally adopted; it is well known how much, in the first ages of the Church, this opinion of the end of the world agitated the minds of men. In the sequel, the general councils, taking courage, pronounced the expectation that prevailed heretical and its believers were called millenarians; a circumstance curious enough, since it is evident from the history of the gospels that Jesus was a millenarian, and of consequence an heretic.

† " Represented by the constellation of the serpent."—' The Persians,' says Ghardin, 'call the constellation of the serpent Ophiucus, serpent of Eve,' and this serpent Ophiucus or Ophioneus plays a similar part in the theology of the Phenicians; for Pherecydes, their disciple and the master of Pythagoras, said: ' that Ophioneus Serpentinus had been chief of the rebels against Jupiter.' See Mars. Ficin. Apol. Socrat., p. m. 797, col. 2. I shall add that æphah [with ain] signifies in Hebrew viper serpent.

"These traditions related : that the woman had decoyed and seduced the man.

"And in fact, the virgin setting first seems to draw the herdsman after her.

"That the woman tempted him by offering him fruit fair to the sight and good to eat, which gave the knowledge of good and evil.

"And in fact, the virgin holds in her hand a branch of fruit which she seems to offer to the herdsman; and the branch, emblem of autumn, placed in the picture of Mithra between winter and summer, seems to open the door and give knowledge, the key of good and evil.

"That this couple had been driven from the celestial garden, and that a cherub with a flaming sword had been placed at the gate to guard it.

"And in fact, when the virgin and the herdsman fall beneath the western horizon, Perseus rises on the other side,* and this genius with a sword in his hand, seems to drive them from the summer heaven, the garden and dominion of fruits and flowers.

"That of this virgin should be born, spring up, an offspring, a child, who should bruise the head of the serpent, and deliver the world from sin.

"This denotes the sun, which, at the moment of the winter solstice, precisely when the Persian magi drew the horoscope of the new year, was placed on the bosom of the virgin, rising heliacally in the eastern horizon; on this account he was figured in their astrological pictures under the form of a child suckled by a chaste virgin,† and

In a physical sense to seduce, seducere, means only to attract, to draw after one.
See this picture of Mithra in Hyde, p. 111, edit. of 1760, de religione veterum Persarum.

* " Perseus rises on the other side."—Rather the head of Medusa, that head of a woman once so beautiful, which Perseus cut off, and which he holds in his hand, is only that of the Virgin, whose head sinks below the horizon at the very moment that Perseus rises; and the serpents which surround it are Ophiucus and the polar dragon, who then occupy the zenith. This shows us in what manner the ancient astrologers composed all their figures and fables; they took such constellations as they found at the same time on the circle of the horizon, and collecting the different parts, they formed groups which served them as an almanack in hieroglyphic characters: such is the secret of all their pictures, and the solution of all their mythological monsters. The Virgin is also Andromeda, delivered by Perseus from the whale that pursues her [prosequitur.]

†" Suckled by a chaste virgin."—Such was the picture of the Persian sphere cited by Aben-Ezra, in the Cœlum poeticum of Blaeu, page 71. 'The division of the first decan of the virgin,' says that writer, 'repre-

Fecame afterwards, at the vernal equinox, the ram or lamb, triumphant over the constellation of the serpent, which disappeared from the skies.

" That in his infancy, this restorer of divine and celestial nature would live abased, humble,* obscure and indigent.

"And this, because the winter sun is abased below the horizon, and that this first period of his four ages or seasons, is a time of obscurity, scarcity, fasting and want.

" That, being put to death by the wicked, he had risen gloriously; that he had reascended from hell to heaven, where he would reign forever.

" This is a sketch of the life of the sun, who, finishing his career at the winter solstice, when Typhon and the rebel angels gain the dominion, seems to be put to death by them; but who soon after is born again and rises into the vault of heaven where he reigns.†

sents a beautiful virgin with flowing hair, sitting in a chair, with two ears of corn in her hand, and suckling an infant called Iesus by some nations and Christ in Greek.'

There is to be found in the French king's library an Arabian manuscript, no 1165, in which is a picture of the twelve signs; and that of the virgin represents a young girl with an infant by her side, the whole scene indeed of the birth of Jesus is to be found in the adjacent part of the heavens. The stable is the constellation of the charioteer and the goat, formerly capricorn; a constellation called præsepe Jovis Heniochi, stable of Iou, and the word Iou is found in the name of Iou-seph [Joseph] At no great distance is the ass of Typhon [the great bear,] and the ox or bull, the ancient attendants of the manger. Peter, the porter, is Janus with his keys and bald forehead, the twelve apostles are the genii of the twelve months, etc. This virgin has acted very different parts in the various systems of mythology: she has been the Isis of the Egyptians, who said of her in one of their inscriptions cited by Julian the fruit I brought forth is the sun. Most of the traits mentioned b Plutarch apply to her, in the same manner as those of Osiris apply to Bootes. Also the seven principal stars of the bear, called David's chariot, were called the chariot of Osiris [See Kirker,] and the crown that is situated behind, formed of ivy, was called Chen-Osiris, Osiris' tree. The Virgin has likewise been Ceres, whose mysteries were the same with those of Isis and Mithra; she has been the Diana of Ephesus, the great goddess of Syria, Cybele drawn by lions: Minerva, the mother of Bacchus; Astrea, a chaste virgin taken up into heaven at the end of the golden age; Themis, at whose feet is the balance that was put in her hands; the Sybil of Virgil, who descends into hell, or sinks below the hemisphere with a branch in her hand, etc.

* " Live abased, humble."—This word humble comes from the Latin humilis, humi-jacens, lying on or inclined towards the ground; and the physical signification is always found to be the root of the abstract and moral sense.

† " Born again and rises into the vault of heaven."—Resurgere, to rise a second time, cannot signify to return to life, but in a bold metaphorical sense; and we see continually mistakes of this kind result from the ambiguous meaning of the words made use of in ancient tradition

" Finally, these traditions went so far as to mention even his astrological and mysterious names, and inform us that he was called sometimes Chris, that is to say preserver;* and from that ye Indians, have made your God Chris-en or Chris-na; and ye Greek and Western Christians, your Chris-tos, son of Mary is the same; sometimes he is called Yes, by the union of three letters, which by their numerical value form the number 608, one of the solar periods;† and this, Europeans, is the name which, with the Latin termination, is become your Iesus or Jesus, the ancient and cabalistic name attributed to young Bacchus, the clandestine (nocturnal) son of the virgin Minerva, who, in the history of his whole life, and even of his death, brings to mind the history of the God of the Christians, that is, of the star of day, of which they are each of them the emblems."

Here a great murmur having arisen among all the Christian

*" Chris, that is to say preserver."—The Greeks used to express by χ or the Spanish Jota, the aspirated ha of the Orientals, who said haris: in Hebrew, heres signifies the sun: but in Arabic, the radical word means to guard, to preserve, and haris, guardian, preserver. It is the proper epithet of Vichenou, which demonstrates at once the identity of the Indian and Christian trinities, and their common origin. It is manifestly but one system, which divided into two branches, one in the east, and the other in the west, assumed two different forms; its principal trunk is the Pythagorean system of the soul of the world, or Jupiter. The epithet piter or father having been applied to the Demi-ourgos of the Platonicians, gave rise to an ambiguity which caused an inquiry to be made after the son. In the opinion of the philosophers it was the understanding, nous and logos, from which the Latins made their verbum; and thus we clearly perceive the origin of the eternal father and of the verb his son, proceeding from him [meus ex Deo nata, says Macrobius;] the anima or spiritus mundi was the holy Ghost; and it is for this reason that Manes, Basilides, Valentinus, and other pretended heretics of the first ages, who traced things to their source, said that God the father was the supreme inaccessible light of heaven [the first circle, or the aplanes;] the son, the secondary light resident in the sun, and the Holy Ghost the atmosphere of the earth. [See Beausob. vol. 11, pag. 586.] Hence among the Syrians, his emblem of a dove, the bird of Venus Urania, that is of the air. 'The Syrians [says Nigidius in Germanico,] assert that a dove sat several days in the Euphrates on the egg of a fish, whence Venus was born.' Sextus Empiricus also observes, Inst. Pyrrh., lib. 111, c. 23, that the Syrians abstain from eating doves; this intimates to us a period commencing in the sign of Pisces [in the winter solstice.] We may farther observe, that if Chris comes from Harisch by a chin, it will signify artificer, an epithet belonging to the sun. These variations, which must have embarrassed the ancients, prove it to be the real type of Jesus, as had been already remarked in the time of Tertullian. ' Many,' says this writer, 'suppose with greater probability that the sun is our God, and they refer us to the religion of the Persians.' (Apologet. c. 16.)

† " One of the solar periods."—See a curious ode to the sun by Martianus Capella, translated by Gebelin, volume of the Calendar, pages, 547 and 548.

groups, the Mussulmen, the Lamas, the Indians called them to order, and the orator went on to finish his discourse :

" You know at present :" said he, " how the rest of this system was composed in the chaos and anarchy of the three first centuries ; what a multitude of singular opinions divided the minds of men, and armed them with an enthusiasm and a reciprocal obstinacy, because being equally founded on ancient tradition, they were equally sacred. You know how the government, after three centuries, having embraced one of these sects, made it the orthodox, that is to say, the predominant religion to the exclusion of the rest : which being inferior in number, became heretical, you know how and by what means of violence and seduction this religion was propagated, extended, divided, and enfeebled ; how, six hundred years after the Christian innovation, another system was formed from it, and from that of the Jews : and how Mahomet found the means of composing a political and theological empire at the expense of those of Moses and the vicars of Jesus.——

" Now, if you take a review of the whole history of the spirit of religion, you will see that in its origin it has had no other author than the sensations and wants of man, that the idea of God has had no other type and model than those of physical powers, material beings producing either good or evil, by impressions of pleasure or pain on sensitive beings ; that in the formation of all these systems, the spirit of religion has always followed the same course, and been uniform in its proceedings ; that in all of them the dogma has never failed to represent, under the name of gods, the operations of nature, the passions and prejudices of men ; that the moral of them all has had for its object the desire of happiness and aversion to pain : but that the people and the greater part of legislators, not knowing the route to be pursued, have formed false, and therefore discordant ideas, of virtue and vice, of good and evil, that is to say, of what renders man happy or miserable : that in every instance, the means and the causes of propagating and establishing systems have exhibited the same scenes of passion and the same events ; everywhere disputes about words, pretexts for zeal, revolutions and wars excited by the ambition of princes, the knavery of apostles, the credulity of proselytes, the ignorance of the vulgar, the exclusive cupidity and intolerant arrogance of all : in fine, you will see that the whole history of the spirit of religion is only the history of the errors of the human mind, which, placed in a world that it does not comprehend, endeavours nevertheless to solve the enigma ; and which, beholding with astonishment this mysterious and visible prodigy, imagines causes, supposes reasons, builds systems ; then, finding one defective, destroys it for another not less so ; hates the error that it quits, misconceives the one it embraces, rejects the truth it is seeking, composes chimeras of discordant beings, and always dreaming of wisdom and happiness, wanders in the labyrinth of illusion and of pain."

CHAPTER XXIII.

THE OBJECT OF ALL RELIGIONS IDENTICAL.

THUS spoke the orator in the name of those men who had studied the origin and succession of religious ideas.—

The theologians of various systems, reasoning on this discourse : " It is an impious representation," said some ; " whose tendency is nothing less than to overturn all belief, to destroy subordination in the minds of men, and annihilate our ministry and power : " It is a romance," said others, " a tissue of conjectures, composed with art, but without foundation." The moderate and the prudent men added : " Supposing all this to be true, why reveal these mysteries? Doubtless our opinions are full of errors : but these errors are a necessary restraint on the multitude. The world has gone thus for two thousand years, why change it now ?"

A murmur of disapprobation, which never fails to rise at every innovation, now began to increase, when a numerous group of the common classes of people and of untaught men of all countries and of every nation, without prophets, without doctors, and without doctrine, advancing in the circle, drew the attention of the whole assembly ; and one of them, in the name of all, thus addressed the legislator :

" Mediator and arbiter of nations ! the strange relations which have occupied the present debate were unknown to us until this day ; our understanding, confounded and amazed at so many things, some of them learned, others absurd, and all incomprehensible, remains in uncertainty and doubt. One only reflection has struck us; on reviewing so many prodigious facts, so many contradictory assertions, we ask ourselves ; what are all these discussions to us ? What need have we to know what happened five or six thousand years ago, in countries we never heard of, and among men who will ever be unknown to us ? True or false, what interest have we in knowing whether the world has existed six thousand, or twenty thousand years, whether it was made of nothing or of something, by itself or by a maker, who in his turn would require another maker ? What ! we are not sure of what happens near us, and we shall answer for what happens in the sun, in the moon, or in imaginary regions of space ? We have forgotten our own infancy, and shall we know the infancy of the world ? and who will attest what no one has seen ? who will certify what no man comprehends ?

" Besides, what addition or diminution will it make to our existence to say yes or no to all these chimeras ? Hitherto neither we nor our forefathers have had the least notion of them, and we do not perceive that we have had on this account either more or less of the sun, more or less subsistence, more or less of good or of evil.

" If the knowledge of these things is so necessary, why have we lived as well without it as those who have taken so much trouble about it ? if this knowledge is superfluous, why should we burden ourselves with it to day ?" Then addressing himself to the doctors and theologians : " What !" said he, " is it necessary that we, poor and ignorant men, whose every moment is scarcely sufficient for the cares of life and the labors of which you take the profit, is it necessary for us to learn the numberless histories that you have related, to read the quantity of books that you have cited, and to study the various languages in which they are composed ? A thousand years of life would not suffice.—"

" It is not necessary," replied the doctors, " that you should acquire all this science : we have it for you.——"

" But even you," replied the simple men, " with all your science, you cannot agree, of what advantage then is your science ?

" Besides, how can you answer for us ? If the faith of one man is applicable to many, what need have even you to believe ? your fathers may have believed for you, and this would be reasonable, since they have seen for you.

" Further, what is believing, if belief influences no action ? And what action is influenced by believing, for instance, that the world is or is not eternal?"

"The latter would be offensive to God," said the doctors.— "How prove you that?" replied the simple men.—"In our books," answered the doctors—"We do not understand them," returned the simple men.

"We understand them for you," said the doctors.

"That is the difficulty," replied the simple men. "By what right do you constitute yourselves mediators between God and us?"

"By his orders," said the doctors.

"Where is the proof of these orders?" said the simple men.—"In our books," said the doctors.—"We understand them not," said the simple men; "and how came this just God to give you this privilege over us? Why should this common father oblige us to believe on a less degree of evidence than you? He has spoken to you, be it so; he is infallible, and deceives you not: but it is you who speak to us; and who shall assure us that you are not in error yourselves, or that you will not lead us into error? And if we should be deceived, how will that just God save us contrary to law, or condemn us on a law which we have not known?"

"He has given you the natural law," said the doctors.

"And what is the natural law?" replied the simple men: "If that law suffices, why has he given any other? If it is not sufficient, why did he make it imperfect?"

"His judgments are mysteries," said the doctors, "and his justice is not like that of men."—"If his justice," replied the simple men, "is not like ours, by what rule are we to judge of it? and moreover, why all these laws, and what is the object proposed by them?"

"To render you more happy," replied a doctor, "by rendering you better and more virtuous: it is to teach man to enjoy his benefits, and not injure each other, that God has manifested himself by so many oracles and prodigies."

"In that case," said the simple men, "there is no necessity for so many studies, nor of such a variety of arguments; only tell us which is the religion that best answers the end which they all propose."

Immediately on this, every group extolling its own morality above that of all others, there arose among the different sects a new and most violent dispute. "It is we," said the Mussulmen, "who possess the most excellent morals, who teach all the virtues useful to men and agreeable to God. We profess justice, disinterestedness resignation to providence, charity to our brethren, alms-giving and devotion; we torment not the soul with superstitious fears; we live without alarm and die without remorse."

"How dare you speak of morals," answered the Christian priests, "you whose chief lived in licentiousness and preached impurity? you whose first precept is homicide and war? For this we appeal to experience: since twelve hundred years your fanatical zeal has not ceased to spread commotion and carnage among the nations; and if Asia, once so flourishing, is now languishing in barbarism and depopulation, it is in your doctrine, that we find the cause: in that doctrine, the enemy of all instruction, which sanctifies ignorance, which consecrates the most absolute despotism in the governors, exacts the most blind and passive obedience from the people, has stupified the faculties of man, and brutalized the nations.

"It is not so with our sublime and celestial morals; it was they which raised the world from its primitive barbarity, from the senseless and cruel superstitions of idolatry, from human sacrifices,* from the shameful orgies of pagan mysteries; it was they that purified manners, proscribed incest and adultery, polished savage nations, banished slavery, and introduced new and unknown virtues, charity for men, their equality before God, forgiveness and forgetfulness of injuries, the restraint of all the passions, the contempt of worldly greatness, a life completely spiritual and completely holy."

"We admire," said the Mussulmen, "the ease with which you reconcile that evangelical meekness, of which you are so ostentatious, with the injuries and outrages with which you are constantly galling your neighbours. When you criminate so severely the great man whom we revere, we might fairly retort on the conduct of him whom you adore; but we scorn such advantages, and, confining ourselves to

---

* "From human sacrifices."—See the frigid declamation of Eusebius, Præp. Ev. lib. 1, p. 11. who pretends that, since the coming of Christ, there have neither been wars, nor tyrants, nor cannibals, nor sodomites, nor persons committing incest, nor savages devouring their parents, etc. When we read these early doctors of the church, we are astonished at their insincerity or infatuation. A curious work would be a small volume of their most remarkable passages, to expose their folly. The truth is that Christianity has invented nothing new in morals, and all its merit consists in putting into practice principles which owed their success to circumstances of the times; that is to say, the arrogant and cruel despotism of the Romans in the various branches, military, judiciary, and administrative, having exhausted the patience of nations, produced among the inferior or popular classes, a movement of reaction absolutely similar to that, which since twenty-five years, exists in Europe among the people against the oppression of the sacerdotal and feudal casts.

the real object in question, we maintain that the morals of your gospel have by no means that perfection which you ascribe to them: it is not true that they have introduced into the world new and unknown virtues: for example, the equality of men before God, that fraternity and that benevolence which follow from it, were formal doctrines of the sect of the Hermetics or Samaneans, from whom you descend. As to the forgiveness of injuries, the Pagans themselves had taught it: but in the extent you give it, far from being a virtue, it becomes an immorality, a vice. Your so much boasted precept of holding out one cheek after the other, is not only contrary to every sentiment of man, but is opposed to all ideas of justice: it emboldens the wicked by impunity; debases the virtuous by servility; delivers up the world to despotism and tyranny; and dissolves all society; such is the true spirit of your doctrines; your gospels, in their precepts and their parables, never represent God but as a despot without any rules of equity; a partial father, treating a debauched and prodigal son with more favor than his other respectful and virtuous children; a capricious master, who gives the same wages to workmen who had wrought but one hour, as to those who had labored through the whole day, one who prefers the last comers to the first; the moral is everywhere misanthropic and antisocial, it disgusts men with life and with society, and tends only to encourage hermitism and celibacy.

"As to the manner in which you have practised these morals, we appeal, in our turn, to the testimony of facts: we ask whether it is this evangelical meekness which has excited your interminable wars of sects, your atrocious persecutions of pretended heretics, your crusades against Arianism, Manicheism, Protestantism, without speaking of your crusades against us, and of those sacrilegious associations, still subsisting, of men who take an oath to continue them.* We ask you whether it be gospel charity which has made you exterminate whole nations in America, and annihilate the empires of Mexico and Peru; which makes you continue to dispeople Africa and sell its inhabitants like cattle, notwithstanding your abolition of slavery: which makes you ravage India and usurp its dominions; and whether it be the same charity which, for three centuries past, has led you to havoc the habitations of the people of three continents, of whom the most prudent, the Chinese and Japanese, were constrained

---

* "Men who take an oath to continue them."—The oath taken by the knights of Malta, was, to kill, or make prisoners the Mahometans, for the glory of God.

to drive you off, that they might escape your chains and recover their internal peace."

Here the Bramins, the Rabbins, the Bonzes, the Chamans, the priests of the Molucca islands and of the coast of Guinea, loading the Christian doctors with reproaches : " Yes !" cried they, " these men are robbers and hypocrites, who preach simplicity to surprise confidence ; humility, to enslave with more ease ; poverty, to appropriate all riches to themselves ; they promise another world, the better to usurp the present ; and while they speak to you of tolerance and charity, they burn in the name of God, the men who do not worship him in their manner."

" Lying priests," retorted the missionaries, " it is you who abuse the credulity of ignorant nations to subjugate them ; it is you who have made of your ministry an art of cheating and imposture ; you have converted religion into a traffic of cupidity and avarice. You pretend to hold communication with spirits, and they give for oracles nothing but your wills ; you feign to read the stars, and destiny decrees only your desires ; you cause idols to speak, and the gods are but the instruments of your passions : you have invented sacrifices and libations to collect for your own profit the milk of flocks, and the flesh and fat of victims : and under the cloak of piety you devour the offerings of the gods, who cannot eat, and the substance of the people who labor."

" And you," replied the Bramins, the Bonzes, the Chamans, " you sell to the credulous living, your vain prayers for the souls of the dead : with your indulgences and absolutions, you have usurped the power of God himself ; and making a traffic of his favors and pardons you have put heaven at auction, and by your system of expiations, you have formed a tariff of crimes which has perverted all consciences."*

" Add to this,' said the Imans, " that these men have invented the most insidious of all systems of wickedness ; the absurd and impious obligation of recounting to them the most intimate secrets

* "A tariff of crimes."—As long as it shall be possible to obtain purification from crimes and exemption from punishment by means of money or other frivolous practices ; as long as kings and lords shall suppose that building temples or instituting foundations, will absolve them from the guilt of oppression and homicide ; as long as individuals shall imagine that they may rob and cheat, provided they fast during Lent, go to confession, and receive extreme unction, it is impossible there should exist either a public or private morality, or salutary practical legislation. But to see the effects of these doctrines, it is only necessary to peruse the History of the Temporal Power of the Popes, 4th. edition.

of actions, and of thoughts (confession;) so that their insolent curiosity has carried their inquisition even into the sanctuary of the marriage bed,* and the inviolable recesses of the heart."

Thus by mutual reproaches the doctors of the different sects began to reveal all the crimes of their ministry, all the vices of their craft : and it was found that among all nations the spirit of the priesthood, their system of conduct, their actions, their morals were absolutely the same :

That they had everywhere formed secret associations, and corporations at enmity with the rest of society ; †

That they had everywhere attributed to themselves prerogatives and immunities, by means of which they lived exempt from the burdens of other classes ;

That they everywhere avoided the toils of the laborer, the dangers of the soldier, and the disappointments of the merchant ;

* "Even into the sanctuary of the marriage bed."—Confession is a very ancient invention of the priests, who did not fail to avail themselves of that means of governing.—It was practised in the Egyptian, Greek, Phrygian, Persian mysteries, etc. Plutarch has transmitted us the remarkable answer of a Spartan whom a priest wanted to confess. ' Is it to you or to God I am to confess?' ' To God,' answered the priest : ' In that case,' replied the Spartan, 'man, begone!' (remarkable sayings of the Lacedemonians.) The first Christians confessed their faults publicly, like the Essenians. Afterwards, priests began to be established, with power of absolution from the sin of idolatry. In the time of Theodosius, a woman having publicly confessed an intrigue with a deacon, bishop Necterius, and his successor Chrysostom, granted communion without confession. It was not until the seventh century that the abbots of convents exacted from monks and nuns confession twice a year ; and it was at a still later period that bishops of Rome generalized it. As to the Mussulmen, who abhor this practice, and who do not allow women a moral character, and scarcely a soul, they cannot conceive how an honest man can listen to the recital of the most secret actions and thoughts of a girl or a woman. May not we French, among whom our education and sentiments lender many women superior to the men, ask with astonishment, how can an honest woman consent to reveal them to the impertinent curiosity of a monk or a priest?

† " Corporations at enmity with the rest of society."—That we may understand the general feelings of priests respecting the rest of mankind, whom they always call by the name of the people, let us hear one of the doctors of the church. ' The people,' says bishop Synnesius (in Calvit., pag. 515.) 'are desirous to be deceived ; there is no acting otherwise with them.——Such were always the principles of the ancient priests of Egypt ; and for this reason they shut themselves up in their temples, and there composed their mysteries, out of the reach of the eye of the people. (And forgetting what he had just said, he adds:) for had the people been in the secret they might have been offended at the deception. In the meantime how is it possible to conduct one's self otherwise with the people, so long as they are the people? For my own part, to myself I shall always be a philosopher, but in dealing with the mass of mankind I shall be a priest '

That they lived everywhere in celibacy, to shun even the cares of a family;

That under the cloak of poverty, they possessed everywhere the secret of acquiring wealth and all sorts of enjoyments;

That under the name of mendicity they raised taxes to a greater amount than princes;

That in the form of gifts and offerings, they had established fixed and certain revenues exempt from charges;

That under pretence of retirement and devotion they lived in idleness and licentiousness;

That they had made a virtue of alms-giving, to live quietly on the labors of others.

That they had invented the ceremonies of worship, as a means of attracting the reverence of the people, while they were playing the parts of gods, of whom they styled themselves the interpreters and mediators, to assume all their powers; that with this design, they had, according to the degree of ignorance or information of their people, assumed by turns the character of astrologers, drawers of horoscopes, fortune-tellers, magicians, necromancers,* quacks, phy-

'A little jargon,' says Gregory of Nazianzus to St. Jerom, (Hieron ad Nep.) 'is all that is necessary to impose on the people. The less they comprehend, the more they admire.—Our forefathers and doctors have often said. not what they thought, but what circumstances and necessity dictated.'

'We endeavour,' says Sanconiathon, 'to excite admiration by means of the marvellous.' [Feæp. Ev., lib. iii.] Such was the conduct of all the priests of antiquity, and is still that of the Bramins and lamas who are the exact counterpart of the Egyptian priests. To justify this system of imposition and falsehood, we are told that it would be dangerous to enlighten the people, because they would abuse their information. Is it meant that instruction and deceit are synonymous? No, but as the people are unfortunate by the stupidity, ignorance and avarice of those who lead and instruct them, the latter want them to be hoodwinked; doubtless it would be dangerous to make a direct attack on the erroneous belief of a nation; but there is a philanthropic and medical art of preparing men's eyes for the light, as well as their arms for liberty. If ever a corporation is instituted in this sense, it will astonish the world by its success.

* "Magicians, necromancers."—What is a magician, in the sense in which people understand the word? A man who by words and gestures, pretends to act on supernatural beings and compel them to descend at his call and obey his orders. Such was the conduct of the ancient priests, and such is still that of all priests in idolatrous nations, for which reason we have given them the denomination of magicians. Now when a christian priest pretends to make God descend from heaven, to fix him to a morsel of leaven, and to render by means of this talisman, souls pure and in a state of grace, what is all this but a trick of magic? And where is the difference between him and a Chaman of Tartary who invokes the genii, or an Indian Bramin, who makes his Vichenou descend in a vessel of water to drive away evil spirits? But

sicians, courtiers, confessors of princes, always aiming at the great object to govern for their own advantage.

That sometimes they had exalted the power of kings and consecrated their persons to monopolize their favors or participate in the authority ;

That sometimes they had preached up the murder of tyrants (reserving it to themselves to define tyranny,) to avenge themselves of their contempt or their disobedience ;

And that they always stigmatized with impiety whatever crossed their interest; that they hindered all public instruction, to exercise the monopoly of science : that finally, in all times and in all places, they had found the secret of living in peace in the midst of the anarchy they created ; in safety under the despotism that they favored ; in indolence, amidst the industry they preached! and in abundance while surrounded with scarcity ! and all this by carrying on the singular trade of selling words and gestures to credulous people, who purchase them as commodities of the greatest value.*

Then the different nations, in a transport of fury, were going to tear in pieces the men who had thus abused them ; but the legislator, arresting this movement of violence, addressed the chiefs and doctors; " What ! " said he, " instructers of nations, is it thus you have deceived them ? "

And the terrified priests replied ; " O legislator ! we are men, the people are so superstitious ! they have themselves encouraged these errors."

such is the magic of custom and education, that we look upon as simple and reasonable in ourselves, what appears extravagant and absurd in others.

* " Commodities of the greatest value."—A curious work would be the comparative history of the Pope's agnuses and the pastils of the grand lama! It would be werth while to extend this idea to religious ceremonies in general, and to confront, column by column, the analogous or contrasting points of faith and superstitious practices, in all nations. There is one more species of superstition which it would be equally salutary to cure, blind veneration for the great; and for this purpose it would be only necessary to write a minute detail of the private life of those who govern the world, princes, courtiers and ministers. No work would be more philosophical than this : and accordingly we have seen what a general outcry was excited, when the anecdotes of the court of Berlin first appeared. What would be the alarm were the public acquainted with the private history of other courts? Did the people know all the crimes and all the baseness of this species of idol, they would no longer covet their specious pleasures, of which the plausible and hollow appearance disturbs their peace, and hinders them from enjoying the much more solid happiness of their own condition.

And the kings said; " O legislator ! the people are so servile and so ignorant ! they prostrated themselves before the yoke, which we scarcely dared to show them."

Then the legislator turning to the people : " People !" said he, " remember what you have just heard ; they are two indelible truths. Yes, you are yourselves the authors of the evils you lament ; it is you that encourage tyrants by a base adulation of their power, by an imprudent admiration of their false beneficence, by servility in obedience, by licentiousness in liberty, and by a credulous reception of every imposition ; on whom shall you wreak vengeance for the faults committed by your own ignorance and cupidity ? "

And the people, struck with confusion, remained in mournful silence.

CHAPTER XXIV.

SOLUTION OF THE PROBLEM OF CONTRADICTIONS

THE legislator then resumed his discourse, " O nations !" said he, " we have heard the discussion of your opinions ; and the different sentiments which divide you have given rise to many reflections, and furnished several questions which we shall propose to you to solve.

" First, considering the diversity and opposition of the creeds to which you are attached, we ask on what motives you found your persuasion ; is it from a deliberate choice that you follow the standard of one prophet rather than another ? Before adopting this doctrine rather than that, did you first compare ? did you maturely examine them ? Or have you received them only from the chance of birth, from the empire of education and habit ? Are you not born Christians on the banks of the Tiber, Mussulmen on those of the Euphrates, Idolaters on the Indus, just as you are born fair in cold climates and sable under the scorching sun of Africa ? And if your opinions are the effect of your fortuitous position on the earth, of consanguinity, of imitation, how is it that such a hazard should be a ground of conviction, an argument of truth ?

" Secondly, when we reflect on the mutual proscriptions and arbitrary intolerance of your pretensions, we are frightened at the consequences that flow from your own principles. Nations ! who reciprocally devote each other to the bolts of heavenly wrath, suppose that the universal Being whom you revere, should this moment descend from heaven on this multitude, and, clothed with all his power, should sit on this throne to judge you, suppose he should say to you : ' Mortals ! it is your own justice that I am going to exercise upon you. Yes, of all the religious systems that divide you, one alone shall this day be preferred ; all the others, all this multitude of standards, of nations, of prophets shall be condemned to eternal destruction ; this is not enough—among the particular sects of the chosen system, one only can be favored, and all the others must be condemned ; neither is this enough : from this little remnant of a group, 1 must exclude all those who have not fulfilled the conditions enjoined by its precepts : O men ! to what a small number of elect have you limited your race ! to what a penury of beneficence do you reduce the immensity of my goodness ! to what a solitude of admirers do you condemn my greatness and my glory ? '

" But," said the legislator rising : " no matter ; you have willed it so ; Nations ! here is an urn in which all your names are placed : one only is a prize—approach and draw this tremendous lottery.—" And the nations, seized with terror, cried : " No, no ; we are all brothers, all equal ; we cannot condemn each other."

Then said the legislator, resuming his seat : " O men ! who dispute on so many subjects, lend an attentive ear to one problem which you exhibit, and which you ought to decide yourselves." And the people giving great attention, he lifted an arm towards heaven ; and pointing to the sun, said : " Nations, does that sun which enlightens you appear square or triangular ? " " No," answered they with one voice, " it is round."

Then taking the golden balance that was on the altar : " This gold that you handle every day, is it heavier than the same volume of copper ? " " Yes," answered all the people, " gold is heavier than copper."

Then taking the sword : " Is this iron," said the legislator, " softer than lead ? " "No," said the people.

" Is sugar sweet, and gall bitter ?"—" Yes."

" Do you love pleasure, and hate pain ?"—" Yes."

" Thus then you are agreed in these points and many others of the same nature.

" Now, tell us, is there a cavern in the centre of the earth, or inhabitants in the moon ?"

This question occasioned an universal murmur; every one answered differently, some yes, others no; one said it was probable; another said it was an idle, ridiculous question; some, that it was worth knowing; and the discord was universal.

After sometime, the legislator having obtained silence, said: " Explain to us, O nations, this problem. We have put to you several questions which you have answered with one voice, without distinction of race or of sect; white men, black men, followers of Mahomet and of Moses, worshippers of Boudda and of Jesus, all have returned the same answer. We then proposed another question, and you are all at variance! Why this unanimity in one case, and this discordance in the other?"

And the group of simple men and savages answered and said: " The reason of this is evident: in the first case we see and feel the objects; and we speak from sensation: in the second, they are beyond the reach of our senses; we speak of them only from conjecture."

" You have resolved the problem," said the legislator " and your own consent has established this first truth:

" That whenever objects can be examined and judged of by your senses, you are agreed in opinion;

" And that you only differ when the objects are absent and beyond your reach.

" From this first truth flows another equally clear and worthy of notice. Since you agree on things which you know with certainty, it follows that you disagree only on those which you know not with certainty, and about which you are not sure; that is to say, you dispute, you quarrel, you fight for that which is uncertain, that of which you doubt. O men! is not this folly?

" Is it not then demonstrated that Truth is not the object of your contests? that it is not her cause which you defend, but that of your affections, and of your prejudices? that it is not the object, as it really is in itself, that you would verify, but the object as you would have it; that is to say, it is not the evidence of the thing that you would enforce, but your own personal opinion, your particular manner of seeing and judging. It is a power that you wish to exercise, an interest that you wish to satisfy, a prerogative that you arrogate to yourselves; it is a contest of vanity. Now, as each of you, on comparing himself to every other, finds himself his equal and his fellow, he resists by a feeling of the same right. And your disputes, your combats, your intolerance, are the effect of this right which you deny each other, and of the intimate conviction of your equality.

" Now, the only means of establishing harmony is to return to nature, and take for a guide and regulator the order of things which she has founded ; and then your accord will prove this other truth :

" That real beings have in themselves an identical, constant and uniform mode of existence ; and that there is in your organs a like mode of being affected by them.

" But at the same time, by reason of the mobility of these organs as subject to your will, you may conceive different affections, and find yourselves in different relations with the same objects ; so that you are to them like a mirror, capable of reflecting them truly as they are, or of distorting and disfiguring them.

" Hence it follows that, whenever you perceive objects as they are, you agree among yourselves and with the objects ; and the similitude between your sensations and their manner of existence, is what constitutes their truth with respect to you ;

"And on the contrary, whenever you differ in your opinion, your disagreement is a proof that you do not represent them such as they are, that you change them.

" Hence also it follows, that the causes of your disagreement exist not in the objects themselves, but in your minds, in your manner of perceiving or judging.

" To establish therefore an uniformity of opinion, it is necessary first to establish the certainty, completely verified, that the portraits which the mind forms are perfectly like the originals : that it reflects the objects correctly as they exist. Now, this result cannot be obtained but in those cases where the objects can be brought to the test, and submitted to the examination of the senses. Everything which cannot be brought to this trial is for that reason alone, impossible to be determined ; there exists no rule, no term of comparison, no means of certainty, respecting it.

" From this we conclude, that, to live in harmony and peace, we must agree never to decide on such subjects, and to attach to them no importance ; in a word, we must trace a line of distinction between those that are capable of verification, and those that are not, and separate by an inviolable barrier, the world of fantastical beings from the world of realities ; that is to say, all civil effect must be taken away from theological and religious opinions.

15*

" This, O people ! is the object proposed by a great nation freed from her fetters and her prejudices; this is the work which, under her eye, and by her orders, we had undertaken when your kings and your priests came to interrupt it.—O kings and priests ! you may suspend, yet for awhile, the solemn publication of the laws of nature: but it is no longer in your power to annihilate or to subvert them."

A general shout then arose from every part of the assembly ; and the nations universally, and with one voice, testified their assent to the proposals of the legislator : " Resume," said they, " your holy and sublime labors, and bring them to perfection ! Investigate the laws which nature, for our guidance, has implanted in our breasts, and collect from them an authentic and immutable code ; nor let this code be any longer for one family only, but for us all without exception ! Be the legislator of the whole human race, as you shall be the interpreter of nature herself; show us the line of partition between the world of chimeras and that of realities : and·teach us, after so many religions of error and delusion, the religion of evidence and truth !"

Then the legislator, having resumed his inquiry into the physical and constituent attributes of man, and examined the motives and affections which govern him in his individual and social state, unfolded in these words the laws on which nature herself has founded his happiness.

THE

LAW OF NATURE.

CHAPTER I.

OF THE LAW OF NATURE.

Q. WHAT is the law of nature ?

A. It is the constant and regular order of facts, by which God governs the universe; an order which his wisdom presents to the senses and to the reason of men, as an equal and common rule for their actions, to guide them, without distinction of country or of sect, towards perfection and happiness.

Q. Give a clear definition of the word law.

A. The word law, taken literally, signifies lecture,* because, originally, ordinances and regulations were the lectures, preferably to all others, made to the people, in order that they might observe them, and not incur the penalties attached to the infraction of them : whence follows the original custom explaining the true idea.

The definition of law is, " An order or prohibition to act, with the express clause of a penalty attached to the infraction, or of a recompense attached to the observance of that order."

Q. Do such orders exist in nature ?

A. Yes.

Q. What does the word nature signify ?

A. The word nature bears three different senses.

---

* From the Latin word lex, lectio. Alcoran likewise signifies lecture and is only a literal translation of the word law.

1st. It signifies the universe, the material world: in this first sense we say the beauty of nature, the richness of nature, that is to say, the objects in the heavens and on the earth exposed to our sight;

2dly. It signifies the power that animates, that moves the universe, considering it as a distinct being, such as the soul is to the body: in this second sense we say, " The intentions of nature, the incomprehensible secrets of nature."

3dly. It signifies the partial operations of that power on each being, or on each class of beings; and in this third sense we say, " The nature of man is an enigma; every being acts according to its nature."

Wherefore, as the actions of each being, or of each species of beings, are subjected to constant and general rules, which cannot be infringed without interrupting and troubling the general or particular order, those rules of action and of motion are called natural laws, or laws of nature.

Q. Give me examples of those laws

A. It is a law of nature, that the sun illuminates successively the surface of the terrestrial globe;—that its presence causes both light and heat;—that heat acting upon water, produces vapors;—that those vapors rising in clouds into the regions of the air, dissolve into rain or snow, and renew incessantly the waters of fountains and of rivers.

It is a law of nature, that water flows downwards; that it endeavours to find its level; that it is heavier than air; that all bodies tend towards the earth; that flame ascends towards the heavens;—that it disorganizes vegetables and animals; that air is necessary to the life of certain animals; that, in certain circumstances, water suffocates and kills them; that certain juices of plants, certain minerals attack their organs, and destroy their life, and so on in a multitude of other instances.

Wherefore, as all those and similar facts are immutable, constant, and regular, so many real orders result from them for man to conform himself to, with the express clause of punishment attending the infraction of them, or of welfare attending their observance. So that if man pretends to see clear in darkness, if he goes in contradiction to the course of the seasons, or the action of the elements; if he pretends to remain under water without being drowned, to touch fire without burning himself, to deprive himself of air without being suffocated, to swallow poison without destroying himself, he receives from each of those infractions of the laws of nature a corporeal punishment proportionate to his fault; but if on the contrary, he observes and practises each of those laws according to the regular and exact relations they have to him, he preserves his existence, and renders it as happy as it can be: and as the only and common end of all those laws, considered relatively to mankind, is to preserve, and render them happy, it has been agreed upon to reduce the idea to one simple expression, and to call them collectively the law of nature.

CHAPTER II.

CHARACTERS OF THE LAW OF NATURE.

Q. What are the characters of the law of nature?

A. There can be assigned ten principal ones.

Q. Which is the first?

A. To be inherent to the existence of things, and, consequently, primitive and anterior to every other law: so that all those which man has received, are only imitations of it, and their perfection is ascertained by the resemblance they bear to this primordial model.

Q. Which is the second?

A. To be derived immediately from God, and presented by him to each man, whereas all other laws are presented to us by men, who may be either deceived or deceivers.

Q. Which is the third?

A. To be common to all times, and to all countries, that is to say, one and universal.

Q. Is no other law universal?

A. No: for no other is agreeable or applicable to all the people of the earth; they are all local and accidental, originating from circumstances of places and of persons; so that if such a man had not existed, or such an event happened, such a law would never have been enacted.

Q. Which is the fourth character?

A. To be uniform and invariable.

Q. Is no other law uniform and invariable?

A. No: for what is good and virtue according to one, is evil and vice according to another ; and what one and the same law approves of at one time, it often condemns at another.

Q. Which is the fifth character ?

A. To be evident and palpable, because it consists entirely of facts incessantly present to the senses, and to demonstration.   •

Q. Are not other laws evident ?

A. No: for they are founded on past and doubtful facts, on equivocal and suspicious testimonies, and on proofs inaccessible to the senses.

Q. Which is the sixth character ?

A. To be reasonable, because its precepts and entire doctrine are conformable to reason, and to the human understanding.

Q. Is no other law reasonable ?

A. No: for all are in contradiction to the reason and the understanding of men, and tyrannically impose on him a blind and impracticable belief.

Q. Which is the seventh character ?

A. To be just, because in that law, the penalties are proportionate to the infractions.

Q. Are not other laws just ?

A. No: for they often exceed bounds, either in rewarding deserts, or in punishing delinquencies, and consider as meritorious or criminal, null or indifferent actions.

Q. Which is the eighth character ?

A. To be pacific and tolerant, because in the law of nature, all men being brothers and equal in rights, it recommends to them only peace and toleration, even for errors.

Q. Are not other laws pacific ?

A. No: for all preach dissension, discord, and war, and divide mankind by exclusive pretensions of truth and domination.

Q. Which is the ninth character ?

A. To be equally beneficent to all men, in teaching them the true means of becoming better and happier.

Q. Are not other laws beneficent likewise ?

A. No: for none of them teach the real means of attaining happiness; all are confined to pernicious or futile practices; and this is evident from facts, since after so many laws, so many religions, so many legislators and prophets, men are still as unhappy and as ignorant, as they were six thousand years ago.

Q. Which is the last character of the law of nature ?

A. That it is alone sufficient to render men happier and better, because it comprises all that is good and useful in other laws, either civil or religious, that is to say, it constitutes essentially the mora. part of them ; so that if other laws were divested of it, they would be reduced to chimerical and imaginary opinions devoid of any practical utility.

Q. Recapitulate all those characters.

A. We have said that the law of nature is,

1st.	Primitive ;	6th.	Reasonable ;
2d.	Immediate ;	7th.	Just ;
3d.	Universal ;	8th.	Pacific ;
4th.	Invariable ;	9th.	Beneficent : and
5th.	Evident ;	10th.	Alone sufficient ;

And such is the power of all these attributes of perfection and truth, that when in their disputes the theologians can agree upon no article of belief, they recur to the law of nature, the neglect of which, say they, forced God to send from time to time prophets to proclaim new laws ; as if God enacted laws for particular circumstances, as men do, especially when the first subsists in such force, that we may assert it to have been at all times and in all countries the rule of conscience for every man of sense or understanding.

Q. If, as you say, it emanates immediately from God, does it teach his existence ?

A. Yes, most positively : for, to any man whatever, who observes with reflection the astonishing spectacle of the universe, the more he meditates on the properties and attributes of each being, on the admirable order and harmony of their motions, the more it is demonstrated that there exists a supreme agent, an universal and identic mover, designated by the appellation of God ; and so true it is that the law of nature suffices to elevate him to the knowledge of God, that all which men have pretended to know by supernatural means, has constantly turned out ridiculous and absurd, and that they have ever been obliged to recur to the immutable conceptions of natural reason.

Q. Then it is not true that the followers of the law of nature are atheists ?

A No, it is not true ; on the contrary, they entertain stronger and nobler ideas of the Divinity than most other men ; for they do not sully him with the foul ingredients of all the weaknesses and passions entailed on humanity.

Q. What worship do they pay to him ?

A. A worship wholly of action ; the practice and observance of all the rules which the supreme wisdom has imposed on the motion of each being ; eternal and unalterable rules, by which it maintains the order and harmony of the universe, and which, in their relations to man, constitute the law of nature.

Q. Was the law of nature known before this period ;

A. It has been at all times spoken of: most legislators pretend to adopt it as the basis of their laws ; but they only quote some of its precepts, and have had only vague ideas of its totality.

Q. Why ?

A. Because, though simple in its basis, it forms in its developements and consequences, a complicated whole which requires an extensive knowledge of facts, joined to all the sagacity of reasoning.

Q. Does not instinct alone teach the law of nature ?

A. No ; for by instinct is meant nothing more than that blind sentiment by which we are actuated indiscriminately towards everything that flatters the senses.

Q. Why then is it said that the law of nature is engraved in the hearts of all men ?

A. It is said for two reasons : 1st., because it has been remarked, that there are acts and sentiments common to all men, and this proceeds from their common organization ; 2dly., because the first philosophers believed that men were born with ideas already formed, which is now demonstrated to be erroneous.

Q. Philosophers then are fallible ?

A. Yes, sometimes.

Q. Why so ?

A. 1st., Because they are men ; 2dly., because the ignorant call all those who reason, right or wrong, philosophers ; 3dly., because those who reason on many subjects, and who are the first to reason on them, are liable to be deceived.

Q. If the law of nature be not written, must it not become arbitrary and ideal ?

A. No: because it consists entirely in facts, the demonstration of which can be incessantly renewed to the senses, and constitutes a science as accurate and as precise as geometry and mathematics ; and it is because the law of nature forms an exact science, that men, born ignorant and living inattentive and heedless, have had hitherto only a superficial knowledge of it.

CHAPTER III.

PRINCIPLES OF THE LAW OF NATURE WITH RELATION TO MAN.

Q. Explain the principles of the law of nature with relation to man

A. They are simple; all of them are comprised in one fundamental and single precept.

Q. What is that precept?

A. It is self-preservation.

Q. Is not happiness also a precept of the law of nature?

A. Yes: but as happiness is an accidental state, resulting only from the developement of man's faculties and his social system, it is not the immediate and direct object of nature; it is, in some measure, a superfluity annexed to the necessary and fundamental object of preservation.

Q. How does nature order man to preserve himself?

A. By two powerful and involuntary sensations, which it has attached, as two guides, two guardian Geniuses to all his actions: the one, a sensation of pain, by which it admonishes him of, and deters him from, everything that tends to destroy him; the other, a sensation of pleasure, by which it attracts and carries him towards everything that tends to his preservation and the developement of his existence.

Q. Pleasure therefore is not an evil, a sin, as casuists pretend.

A. No, only in as much as it tends to destroy life and health, which, by the avowal of those same casuists, we derive from God himself.

Q. Is pleasure the principal object of our existence, as some philosophers have asserted?

A. No; not more than pain; pleasure is an incitement to live, as pain is a repulsion from death.

Q. How do you prove this assertion?

A. By two palpable facts; one, that pleasure when taken immoderately, leads to destruction; for instance, a man who abuses the pleasure of eating or drinking, attacks his health, and injures his

16

life. The other, that pain sometimes leads to self-preservation : for instance, a man who suffers a mortified member to be cut off, endures pain in order not to perish totally.

Q. But does not even this prove that our sensations can deceive us respecting the end of our preservation ?

A. Yes ; they can momentarily.

Q. How do our sensations deceive us ?

A. In two ways ; by ignorance, and by passion.

Q. When do they deceive us by ignorance ?

A. When we act without knowing the action and effect of objects on our senses : for example, when a man touches nettles without knowing their stinging quality, or when he swallows opium without knowing its soporiferous effects.

Q. When do they deceive us by passion ?

A. When, conscious of the pernicious action of objects, we abandon ourselves, nevertheless, to the impetuosity of our desires and appetites : for example, when a man who knows that wine intoxicates, does nevertheless drink it to excess.

Q. What is the result ?

A. It results that the ignorance in which we are born, and the unbridled appetites to which we abandon ourselves, are contrary to our preservation ; that consequently the instruction of our minds and the moderation of our passions are two obligations, two laws which derive immediately from the first law of preservation.

Q. But if we are born ignorant, is not ignorance a law of nature ?

A. No more than to remain in the naked and feeble state of infancy. Far from being a law of nature, ignorance is an obstacle to the practice of all its laws. It is the real original sin.

Q. Why then have there been moralists who have looked upon it as a virtue and a perfection ?

A. Because, from a whimsical or misanthropical disposition they have confounded the abuse of knowledge with knowledge itself : as if, because men abuse the power of speech, their tongues should be cut out : as if perfection and virtue consisted in the nullity, and not in the developement and proper employ of our faculties.

Q. Instruction is therefore indispensably necessary to man's existence.

A. Yes, so indispensable, that without it he is every instant assailed and wounded by all that surrounds him ; for if he does not know the effects of fire, he burns himself; those of water, he drowns himself; those of opium, he poisons himself; if, in the savage state, he does not know the wiles of animals, and the art of seizing game, he perishes through hunger; if, in the social state, he does not know the course of the seasons, he can neither cultivate the ground, nor procure nourishment; and so on, of all his actions, respecting all the wants of his preservation.

Q. But can man separately by himself acquire all this knowledge necessary to his existence, and to the developement of his faculties?

A. No, not without the assistance of his fellow men, and by living in society.

Q. But is not society to man a state against nature?

A. No: it is on the contrary a necessity, a law that nature imposed on him by the very act of his organization: for, 1st., nature has so constituted man, that he cannot see his species of another sex without feeling emotions and an attraction, the consequences of which induce him to live in a family, which is already a state of society; 2nd., by endowing him with sensibility, she organized him so that the sensations of others reflect within him, and excite reciprocal sentiments of pleasure and of grief, which are attractions, and indissoluble ties of society; 3rd., and finally, the state of society, founded on the wants of man, is only a further means of fulfilling the law of preservation: and to pretend that this state is out of nature, because it is more perfect, is the same as to say, that a bitter and wild fruit of the forest, is no longer the production of nature, when rendered sweet and delicious by cultivation in our gardens.

Q. Why then have philosophers called the savage state, the state of perfection?

A. Because, as I have told you, the vulgar have often given the name of philosophers to whimsical geniuses, who, from moroseness, from wounded vanity, or from a disgust to the vices of society, have conceived chimerical ideas of the savage state, in contradiction with their own system of a perfect man.

Q. What is the true meaning of the word philosopher?

A. The word philosopher signifies a lover of wisdom: wherefore, as wisdom consists in the practice of the laws of nature, the true philosopher is he who knows those laws extensively and accurately, and who conforms the whole tenor of his conduct to them.

Q. What is man in the savage state?

A. A brutal, ignorant animal, a wicked and ferocious beast, like bears and Ourang-outangs.

Q. Is he happy in that state?

A. No: for he only feels momentary sensations; and those sensations are habitually of violent wants which he cannot satisfy, since he is ignorant by nature and weak by being insulated from his species.

Q. Is he free?

A. No: he is the most abject slave that exists; for his life depends on everything that surrounds him; he is not free to eat when hungry, to rest when tired, to warm himself when cold; he is every instant in danger of perishing; wherefore nature offers but fortuitous examples of such beings; and we see that all the efforts of the human species, since its origin, solely tend to emerge from that violent state, by the pressing necessity of self-preservation.

Q. But does not this necessity of preservation engender in individuals egotism, that is to say self-love? and is not egotism contrary to the social state?

A. No: for, if by egotism you understand a propensity to hurt our neighbour, it is no longer self-love, but the hatred of others. Self-love, taken in its true sense, not only is not contrary to society, but is its firmest support by the necessity we lie under of not injuring others, lest in return they should injure us.

Thus man's preservation and the unfolding of his faculties, directed towards this end, are the true law of nature in the production of the human being: and it is from this simple and fruitful principle that are derived, are referred, and in its scale are weighed, all ideas of good and evil, of vice and virtue, of just and unjust, of truth or error, of lawful or forbidden, on which is founded the morality of individual, or of social man.

CHAPTER IV.

BASIS OF MORALITY; OF GOOD, OF EVIL, OF SIN, OF CRIME, OF VICE AND OF VIRTUE.

Q. WHAT is good, according to the law of nature?

A. It is everything that tends to preserve and perfect man.

Q. What is evil?

A. It is everything that tends to man's destruction or deterioration

Q. What is meant by physical good and evil, and by moral good and evil?

A. By the word physical is understood, whatever acts immediately on the body. Health is a physical good; and sickness a physical evil. By moral, is meant what acts by consequences more or less remote. Calumny is a moral evil; a fair reputation is a moral good, because both one and the other occasion towards us, on the part of other men, dispositions and habitudes,* which are useful or hurtful to our preservation, and which attack or favor our means of existence.

Q. Everything that tends to preserve or to produce is therefore a good?

A. Yes; and it is for that reason that certain legislators have classed amongst the works agreeable to the divinity, the cultivation of a field and the fecundity of a woman.

Q. Whatever tends to give death is therefore an evil?

A. Yes: and it is for that reason some legislators have extended the idea of evil and of sin even to the murdering of animals.

Q. The murdering of a man is therefore a crime in the law of nature?

A. Yes: and the greatest that can be committed: for every other evil can be repaired, but murder alone is irreparable.

Q. What is a sin in the law of nature?

A. It is whatever tends to trouble the order established by nature, for the preservation and perfection of man and of society.

Q. Can intention be a merit or a crime?

A. No: for it is only an idea void of reality; but it is a commencement of sin and evil, by the tendency it gives towards action

Q. What is virtue according to the law of nature?

A. It is the practice of actions useful to the individual and to society.

Q. What is meant by the word individual?

A. It means a man considered separately from every other.

Q. What is vice according to the law of nature?

A. It is the practice of actions prejudicial to the individual and to society.

---

* It is from this word habitudes, (reiterated actions,) in Latin mores, that the word moral, and all its family, are derived.

Q. Have not virtue and vice an object purely spiritual and **ab-**stracted from the senses?

A. No : It is always to a physical end that they finally relate, and that end is always to destroy or preserve the body.

Q. Have vice and virtue degrees of strength and intenseness?

A. Yes : according to the importance of the faculties which they attack or which they favor ; and according to the number of individuals in whom those faculties are favored or injured.

Q. Give me some examples.

A. The action of saving a man's life is more virtuous than that of saving his property ; the action of saving the life of ten men, than than that of saving only the life of one, and an action useful to the whole human race is more virtuous than an action that is only useful to one single nation.

Q. How does the law of nature prescribe the practice of good and virtue, and forbid that of evil and vice ?

A. By the very advantages resulting from the practice of good and virtue for the preservation of our body, and by the losses which result, to our existence, from the practice of evil and vice.

Q. Its precepts are then in action ?

A. Yes : they are action itself considered in its present effect and in its future consequences.

Q. How do you divide the virtues ?

A. We divide them into three classes, 1st. individual virtues, as relative to man alone ; 2d. domestic virtues, as relative to a family 3d. social virtues, as relative to society.

CHAPTER V.

OF INDIVIDUAL VIRTUES.

Q. WHICH are the individual virtues ?

A. They are five principal ones, to wit :—

   1st. Science, which comprises prudence and wisdom;
   2d. Temperance, comprising sobriety and chastity ;
   3d. Courage, or strength of body and mind;

4th. Activity, that is to say, love of labor and employment of time ;

5th. And finally, cleanliness, or purity of body, as well in dress as in habitation

Q. How does the law of nature prescribe science ?

A. Because the man acquainted with the causes and effects of things, attends in an extensive and sure manner to his preservation and to the developement of his faculties. Science is to him the eye and the light which enable him to discern clearly and accurately all the objects with which he is conversant, and hence by an enlightened man is meant a learned and well informed man. With science and instruction a man never wants for resources and means of subsistence ; and upon this principle a philosopher who had been shipwrecked said to his companions, that were inconsolable for the loss of their wealth ; " For my part, I carry all my wealth within me."

Q. Which is the vice contrary to science ?

A. It is ignorance.

Q. How does the law of nature forbid ignorance ?

A. By the grievous detriments resulting from it to our existence ; for the ignorant man, who knows neither causes nor effects, commits every instant errors most pernicious to himself and to others ; he resembles a blind man groping his way at random, and who, at every step, jostles or is jostled by every one he meets.

Q. What difference is there between an ignorant and a silly man ?

A. The same difference as between him who frankly avows his blindness and the blind man who pretends to sight ; silliness is the reality of ignorance, to which is superadded the vanity of knowledge.

Q. Are ignorance and silliness common ?

A. Yes, very common ; they are the usual and general distempers of mankind : more than three thousand years ago the wisest of men said, The number of fools is infinite ; and the world has not changed

Q. What is the reason of it ?

A. Because much labor and time are necessary to acquire instruction, and because men, born ignorant, and averse to trouble, find it more convenient to remain blind and to pretend to see clear.

Q. What difference is there between a learned and a wise man ?

A. The learned knows, and the wise man practises.

Q What is prudence ?

A. It is the anticipated perception, the foresight of the effects and consequences of every action ; by means of which foresight man avoids the dangers which threaten him, whilst he seizes on and creates opportunities favorable to him : he thereby provides for his present and future safety in a certain and extensive manner; whereas the imprudent man, who calculates neither his steps nor his conduct, nor efforts nor resistance, falls every instant into a thousand difficulties and dangers which sooner or later impair his faculties and destroy his existence.

Q. When the Gospel says " happy are the poor of spirit " does it mean the ignorant and imprudent ?

A. No : for at the same time that it recommends the simplicity of doves, it adds the prudent cunning of serpents. By simplicity of mind is meant uprightness, and the precept of the gospel is that of nature.

CHAPTER VI.

ON TEMPERANCE.

Q. What is temperance ?

A. It is a regular use of our faculties, which makes us never exceed in our sensations, the end of nature to preserve us ; it is the moderation of the passions.

Q. Which is the vice contrary to temperance ?

A. The disorder of the passions, the avidity of all kind of enjoyments, in a word, cupidity.

Q. Which are the principal branches of temperance ?

A. Sobriety, and continence or chastity.

Q. How does the law of nature prescribe sobriety ?

A. By its powerful influence over our health. The sober man digests with comfort ; he is not overpowered by the weight of aliments ; his ideas are clear and easy ; he fulfils all his functions properly ; he conducts his business with intelligence ; his old age is exempt from infirmity ; he does not spend his money in remedies, and he enjoys, in mirth and gladness, the wealth which chance and his own prudence have procured him. Thus, from one virtue alone, generous nature derives innumerable recompenses.

Q. How does it prohibit gluttony ?

A. By the numerous evils that are attached to it The glutton, oppressed with aliments, digests with anxiety; his head, troubled by the fumes of indigestion, is incapable of conceiving clear and distinct ideas : he abandons himself with violence to the disorderly impulse of lust and anger, which impair his health ; his body becomes bloated, heavy, and unfit for labor ; he endures painful and expensive distempers; he seldom lives to be old ; and his age is replete with n. firmities and sorrow.

Q. Should abstinence and fasting be considered as virtuous actions ?

A. Yes, when one has eaten too much ; for then abstinence and fasting are simple and efficacious remedies ; but when the body is in want of aliment, to refuse it any, and let it suffer from hunger or thirst, is delirium and a real sin against the law of nature.

Q. How is drunkenness considered in the law of nature ?

A. As a most vile and pernicious vice. The drunkard, deprived of the sense and reason given us by God, profanes the donations of the divinity : he debases himself to the condition of brutes ; unable even to guide his steps, he staggers and falls as if he were epileptic ; he hurts and even risks killing himself; his debility in this state exposes him to the ridicule and contempt of every person that sees him ; he makes, in his drunkenness, prejudicial and ruinous bargains, and injures his fortune ; he makes use of opprobrious language, which creates him enemies and repentance ; he fills his house with trouble and sorrow, and ends by a premature death or by a cacochymical old age.

Q. Does the law of nature interdict absolutely the use of wine ?

A. No; it only forbids the abuse ; but as the transition from the use to the abuse is easy and prompt amongst the generality of men, perhaps the legislators, who have proscribed the use of wine, have rendered a service to humanity.

Q. Does the law of nature forbid the use of certain kinds of meat, or of certain vegetables, on particular days, during certain seasons.

A. No : it absolutely forbids only whatever is injurious to health ; its precepts, in this respect, vary according to persons, and even constitute a very delicate and important science : for the quality, the quantity, and the combination of aliments have the greatest influence, not only over the momentary affections of the soul, but even over its habitual disposition. A man is not the same fasting as after a meal, even if he were sober. A glass of spirituous liquor or a dish of coffee, give degrees of vivacity, of mobility, of disposition to anger, sadness or gaiety ; such a meat, because it lies heavy on the stomach, engenders moroseness and melancholy ; such another, because it facilitates digestion, creates sprightliness, and an inclination to oblige and to love. The use of vegetables, because they have little nourishment, enfeebles the body, and gives a disposition to repose, indolence, and ease ; the use of meat, because it is full of nourishment, and of spirituous liquors, because they stimulate the nerves, creates vivacity, uneasiness and audacity. Now from those habitudes of aliment result habits of constitution and of the organs, which form afterwards different kinds of temperaments, each of which is distinguished by a peculiar characteristic. And it is for this reason, that, in hot countries especially, legislators have made laws respecting regimen or food. The ancients were taught by long experience, that the dietetic science constituted a considerable part of morality ; amongst the Egyptians, the ancient Persians, and even amongst the Greeks, at the Areopagus, important affairs were examined fasting ; and it has been remarked, that amongst those people, where public affairs were discussed during the heat of meals, and the fumes of digestion, deliberations were hasty and violent, and the results of them frequently unreasonable and productive of turbulence and confusion.

CHAPTER VII·

ON CONTINENCE.

Q. Does the law of nature prescribe continence ?

A. Yes : because a moderate use of the most lively of pleasures is not only useful, but indispensable, to the support of strength and health : and because a simple calculation proves that, for some minutes of privation, you increase the number of your days, both in vigor of body and of mind.

Q. How does it forbid libertinism ?

A.   By the numerous evils which result from it to the physical and the moral existence.   He who carries it to an excess enervates and pines away; he can no longer attend to study or labor; he contracts idle and expensive habits, which destroy his means of existence, his public consideration and his credit : his intrigues occasion continual embarrassment, cares, quarrels and lawsuits, without mentioning the grievous deep-rooted distempers, and the loss of his strength by an inward and slow poison : the stupid dulness of his mind, by the exhaustion of the nervous system; and, in fine, a premature and infirm old age.

Q.   Does the law of nature look on that absolute chastity so recommended in monastical institutions, as a virtue ?

A.   No : for that chastity is of no use either to the society that witnesses or the individual who practises it : it is even prejudicial to both.   First it injures society by depriving it of population, which is one of its principal sources of wealth and power; and as bachelors confine all their views and affections to the term of their lives, they have in general an egotism unfavorable to the interests of society.

In the second place, it injures the individuals who practise it, because it deprives them of a number of affections and relations which are the springs of most domestic and social virtues; and besides, it often happens, from circumstances of age, regimen, or temperament, that absolute continence injures the constitution and causes severe diseases, because it is contrary to the physical laws on which nature has founded the system of the reproduction of beings ; and they who recommend so strongly chastity, even supposing them to be sincere, are in contradiction with their own doctrine, which consecrates the law of nature by the well known commandment : increase and multiply.

Q.   Why is chastity considered a greater virtue in women than in men ?

A.   Because a want of chastity in women is attended with inconveniences much more serious and dangerous for them and for society; for, without taking into account the pains and diseases they have in common with the men, they are further exposed to all the disadvantages and perils that precede, attend and follow childbirth.   When pregnant contrary to law, they become an object of public scandal and contempt, and spend the remainder of their lives in bitterness and misery.   Moreover, the expense of maintaining and educating their fatherless children falls on them : which expense impoverishes them, and is every way prejudicial to their physical and moral existence. In this situation, deprived of the freshness and health that constitute their charms, carrying with them an extraneous and expensive burden, they are less prized by men, they find no solid establishment, they fall into poverty, misery, and wretchedness, and thus drag on in sorrow their unhappy existence.

Q.   Does the law of nature extend so far as the scruples of desires and thoughts?

A.   Yes, because in the physical laws of the human body, thoughts and desires inflame the senses, and soon provoke to action: now, by another law of nature in the organization of our body, those actions become mechanical wants which recur at certain periods of days or of weeks, so that at such a time the want is renewed of such an action and such a secretion; if this action, and this secretion be injurious to health, the habitude of them becomes destructive of life itself. Thus thoughts and desires have a true and natural importence.

Q.   Should modesty be considered as a virtue?

A.   Yes, because modesty, in as much as it is a shame of certain actions, maintains the soul and body in all those habits, sound to good order, and to self-preservation. The modest woman is esteemed, courted and established, with advantages of fortune which assure her existence, and render it agreeable to her, whilst the immodest, and prostitute, are despised, repulsed and abandoned to misery and infamy.

CHAPTER VIII.

ON COURAGE AND ACTIVITY.

Q.   ARE courage and strength of body and mind virtues in the law of nature?

A.   Yes, and most important virtues; for they are the efficacious and indispensable means of attending to our preservation and welfare. The courageous and strong man repulses oppression, defends his life, his liberty, and his property; by his labor he procures himself an abundant subsistence, which he enjoys in tranquillity and peace of mind. If he falls into misfortunes, from which his prudence could not protect him, he supports them with fortitude and resignation ; and it is for this reason that the ancient moralists have reckoned strength and courage amongst the four principal virtues.

Q. Should weakness and cowardice be considered as vices ?

A. Yes, since it is certain that they produce innumerable calamities. The weak or cowardly man lives in perpetual cares and agonies ; he undermines his health by the dread, oftentimes ill founded, of attacks and dangers : and this dread which is an evil, is not a remedy ; it renders him, on the contrary, the slave of him who wishes to oppress him ; and by the servitude and debasement of all his faculties, it degrades and diminishes his means of existence, so far as the seeing his life depend on the will and caprice of another man.

Q. But, after what you have said on the influence of aliments, are not courage and force, as well as many other virtues, in a great measure the effect of our physical constitution and temperament ?

A. Yes, it is true ; and so far, that those qualities are transmitted by generation and blood, with the elements on which they depend : the most reiterated and constant facts prove that in the breed of animals of every kind, we see certain physical and moral qualities attached to the individuals of those species, increase or decay according to the combinations and mixtures they make with other breeds.

Q. But then as our will is not sufficient to procure us those qualities, is it a crime to be destitute of them ?

A. No ; it is not a crime, but a misfortune : it is what the ancients call an unlucky fatality ; but even then, we have it yet in our power to acquire them : for, as soon as we know on what physical elements such or such a quality is founded, we can promote its growth, and accelerate its developements, by a skilful management of those elements ; and in this consists the science of education, which, according as it is directed, meliorates or degrades individuals or the whole race, to such a pitch, as totally to change their nature and inclinations ; for which reason it is of the greatest importance to be acquainted with the laws of nature, by which those operations and changes are certainly and necessarily effected.

Q. Why do you say that activity is a virtue according to the law of nature ?

17

A   Because the man who works and employs his time usefully, derives from it a thousand precious advantages to his existence. If he is born poor, his labor furnishes him with subsistence; and still more so, if he is sober, continent, and prudent, for he soon acquires a competency, and enjoys the sweets of life; his very labor gives him virtues; for, while he occupies his body and mind, he is not affected with unruly desires, time does not lie heavy on him, he contracts mild habits, he augments his strength and health, and attains a peaceful and happy old age.

Q.   Are idleness and sloth vices in the law of nature?

A.   Yes, and the most pernicious of all vices; for they lead to all the others. By idleness and sloth, man remains ignorant, he forgets even the science he had acquired, and falls into all the misfortunes which accompany ignorance and folly; by idleness and sloth, man, devoured with disquietude, in order to dissipate it, abandons himself to all the desires of his senses, which, becoming every day more inordinate, render him intemperate, gluttonous, lascivious, enervated, cowardly, vile and contemptible. By the certain effect of all those vices, he ruins his fortune, consumes his health, and terminates his life in all the agonies of sickness and of poverty.

Q.   From what you say, one would think that poverty was a vice?

A.   No: it is not a vice; but it is still less a virtue; for it is by far more ready to injure than to be useful; it is even commonly the result, or the beginning of vice; for the effect of all individual vices is, to lead to indigence, and to the privation of the necessaries of life; and when a man is in want of necessaries, he is tempted to procure them by vicious means, that is to say, by means injurious to society. All the individual virtues tend, on the contrary, to procure to a man an abundant subsistence; and when he has more than he can consume, it is much easier for him to give to others, and to practise the actions useful to society.

Q.   Do you look upon opulence as a virtue?

A   No; but still less as a vice: it is the use alone of wealth that can be called virtuous or vicious, according as it is serviceable or prejudicial to man and to society. Wealth is an instrument the use and employment alone of which determine its virtue or vice.

CHAPTER IX

ON CLEANLINESS

Q. WHY is cleanliness included amongst the virtues ?

A. Because it is, in reality, one of the most important amongst them, on account of its powerful influence over the health and preservation of the body. Cleanliness, as well in dress as in residence, obviates the pernicious effects of the humidity, baneful odors, and contagious exhalations proceeding from all things abandoned to putrefaction : cleanliness maintains free transpiration ; it renews the air, refreshes the blood, and disposes even the mind to cheerfulness.

From this it appears that persons attentive to the cleanliness of their body and habitations, are in general, more healthy, and less subject to disease, than those who live in filth and nastiness ; and it is further remarked, that cleanliness carries with it, throughout all the branches of domestic administration, habits of order and arrangement, which are the chief means and first elements of happiness.

Q. Uncleanliness or filthiness is therefore a real vice ?

A, Yes, as real a one as drunkenness, or as idleness from which in a great measure it is derived. Uncleanliness is the second, and often the first cause of many inconveniences, and even of grievous disorders ; it is a fact in medicine, that it brings on the itch, the scurf, tetters and leprosies, as much as the use of tainted or sour aliments ; that it favors the contagious influence of the plague and malignant fevers, that it even produces them in hospitals and prisons ; that it occasions rheumatisms, by incrusting the skin with dirt, and thereby preventing transpiration ; without reckoning the shameful inconvenience of being devoured by vermin, the foul appendage of misery and depravity.

Most ancient legislators, therefore, considered cleanliness, which they called purity, as one of the essential dogmas of their religions : it was for this reason that they expelled from society, and even punished corporally those who were infected with distempers produced by un cleanliness ; that they instituted and consecrated ceremonies of ablu tions, baths, baptisms, and of purifications even by fire and the aro matic fumes of incense, myrrh, benjamin, etc. ; so that the entire sys tem of ablutions, all those rites of clean and unclean things, degen erated since into abuses and prejudices, were only founded originally on the judicious observation, which wise and learned men had made, of the extreme influence that cleanliness in dress and abode exercises over the health of the body, and by an immediate consequence over that of the mind and moral faculties.

Thus all the individual virtues have for their object, more or less direct, more or less near, the preservation of the man who practises them ; and by the preservation of each man, they lead to that of families and society which are composed of the united sum of individuals.

CHAPTER X.

ON DOMESTIC VIRTUES.

Q. WHAT do you mean by domestic virtues ?

A. I mean the practice of actions useful to a family, supposed to live in the same house. *

Q. What are those virtues ?

A. They are economy, paternal love, conjugal love, filial love, fraternal love, and the accomplishment of the duties of master and servant.

Q. What is economy ?

A. It is, according to the most extensive meaning of the word, the proper administration of everything that concerns the existence of the family or house ; and as subsistence holds the first rank, the word economy is confined to the employment of money for the first wants of life.

Q. Why is economy a virtue ?

A. Because the man who makes no useless expenses acquires a suberabundancy which is true wealth, and by means of which he procures for himself and his family everything that is really convenient and useful ; without mentioning his securing thereby resources against accidental and unforeseen losses, so that he and his family

---

* Domestic is derived from the Latin word domus, a house.

enjoy an agreeable and undisturbed competency, which is the basis of human felicity.

Q. Dissipation and prodigality therefore are vices?

A. Yes; for by them man, in the end, is deprived of the necessaries of life; he falls into poverty and wretchedness; and his very friends, fearing to be obliged to restore to him what he has spent with or for them, avoid him as a debtor does his creditor, and he remains abandoned by the whole world.

Q. What is paternal love?

A. It is the assiduous care taken by parents to make their children contract the habit of every action useful to themselves and to society.

Q. Why is paternal tenderness a virtue in parents?

A. Because parents who rear their children in those habits, procure for themselves during the course of their lives, enjoyments and helps, that give a sensible satisfaction at every instant, and which assure to them, when advanced in years, supports and consolations against the wants and calamities of all kinds with which old age is beset.

Q. Is paternal love a common virtue?

A. No: notwithstanding the ostentation made of it by parents, it is a rare virtue; they do not love their children, they caress and spoil them; in them they love only the agents of their will, the instruments of their power, the trophies of their vanity, the pastime of their idleness: it is not so much the welfare of their children that they propose to themselves, as their submission and obedience; and if among children so many are seen ungrateful for benefits received, it is because there are among parents as many despotic and ignorant benefactors.

Q. Why do you say that conjugal love is a virtue?

A. Because the concord and union resulting from the love of the married, establish in the heart of the family a multitude of habits useful to its prosperity and preservation. The united pair are attached to, and seldom quit their home; they superintend each particular direction of it; they attend to the education of their children; they maintain the respect and fidelity of domestics; they prevent all disorder and dissipation; and from the whole of their good conduct, they live in ease and consideration; whilst married persons who do not love one another, fill their house with quarrels and troubles, create dissension between their children and the servants, leaving both in discriminately to all kinds of vicious habits; every one in turn spoils, robs and plunders the house : the revenues are absorbed without profit; debts accumulate, the married pair avoid each other, or contend in law-suits; and the whole family falls into disorder, ruin, disgrace, and want.

Q. Is adultery an offence in the law of nature ?

A. Yes : for it is attended with a number of habits injurious to the married, and to their families. The wife or husband whose affections are estranged, neglect their house, avoid it, and deprive it, as much as they can, of its revenues or income, to expend them with the object of their affections; hence arise quarrels, scandal, lawsuits, the neglect of their children and servants, and at last the plundering and ruin of the whole family : without reckoning that the adulterous woman commits a most grievous theft, in giving to her husband heirs of foreign blood, who deprive his real children of their legitimate portion.

Q. What is filial love ?

A. It is, on the side of children, the practice of those actions, useful to themselves and to their parents.

Q. How does the law of nature prescribe filial love ?

A. By three principal motives : 1st, by sentiment, for the affectionate care of parents inspires, from the most tender age, mild habits of attachment; 2dly, by justice, for children owe to their parents a return and indemnity for the cares, and even for the expenses they have caused them ; 3dly, by personal interest, fo , if they use them ill, they give to their own children examples of revolt and ingratitude which authorise them, at a future day, to behave to themselves in a similar manner.

Q. Are we to understand by filial love a passive and blind submission.

A. No . but a reasonable submission, founded on the knowledge of the mutual rights and duties of parents and children ; rights and duties, without the observance of which their mutual conduct is nothing but disorder.

Q. Why is fraternal love a virtue ?

A. Because the concord and union which result from the love of brothers, establish the strength, security and conservation of the family : brothers united, defend themselves against all oppression, they aid one another in their wants, they help one another in their misfortunes, and thus secure their common existence ; whilst brothers disunited, abandoned each to his own personal strength, fall into all the inconveniences attendant on an insulated state and individual weakness. This is what a certain Scythian king ingeniously expressed, when on his death-bed : calling his children to him, he ordered them to break a bundle of arrows ; the young men, though strong, being unable to effect it, he took them in his turn, and untying them, broke each of the arrows separately with his fingers. " Behold," said he, " the effects of union ; united together you will be invincible ; taken separately, you will be broken like reeds."

Q. What are the reciprocal duties of masters and of servants ?

A. They consist in the practice of the actions which are respectively and justly useful to them ; and here begin the relations of society ; for the rule and measure of those respective actions is the equilibrium or equality between the service and the recompense, between what the one returns and the other gives ; which is the fundamental basis of all society.

Thus, all the domestic and individual virtues, refer more or less mediately, but always with certitude, to the physical object of the amelioration and preservation of man, and are thereby precepts resulting from the fundamental law of nature in his formation.

CHAPTER XI

OF THE SOCIAL VIRTUES; OF JUSTICE.

Q What is society ?

A. It is every reunion of men living together under the clauses of an expressed or tacit contract, which has for its end their common preservation.

Q. Are the social virtues numerous ?

A. Yes : they are in as great number as the kinds of actions useful to society : but all may be reduced to one only principle.

Q. What is that fundamental principle ?

A. It is justice, which alone comprises all the virtues of society

Q. Why do you say that justice is the fundamental and almost only virtue of society ?

A. Because it alone embraces the practice of all the actions use-ful to it ; and because all the other virtues, under the denominations of charity, humanity, probity, love of one's country, sincerity, gene-rosity, simplicity of manners and modesty, are only varied forms and diversified applications of the axiom, Do not to another what you would not wish to be done to yourself; which is the definition of jus-tice.

Q.   How does the law of nature prescribe justice ?

A.   By three physical attributes inherent in the organization of man.

Q.   What are those attributes ?

A.   They are equality, liberty, and property.

Q.   How is equality a physical attribute of man ?

A.   Because all men having equally eyes, hands, mouths, ears, and the necessity of making use of them in order to live, have, by this reason alone, an equal right to life, and to the use of the aliments which maintain it ; they are all equal before God.

Q.   Do you suppose that all men hear equally, see equally, feel equally, have equal wants and equal passions.

A.   No ; for it is evident and daily demonstrated, that one is short and another long sighted ; that one eats much, another little ; that one has mild, another violent passions ; in a word, that one is weak in body and mind, whilst another is strong in both.

Q.   They are therefore really unequal.

A.   Yes, in the developement of their means, but not in the nature and essence of those means ; they are made of the same stuff, but not in the same dimensions ; nor are the weight and value equal. Our language possesses no one word capable of expressing the identity of nature, and the diversity of its form and employment.   It is a proportional equality ; and it is for this reason I have said, equal before God, and in the order of nature.

Q.   How is liberty a physical attribute of man ?

A.   Because all men having senses sufficient for their preservation, no one wanting the eye of another to see, his ear to hear, his mouth to eat, his feet to walk, they are all, by this very reason, constitut-ed naturally independent and free ; no man is necessarily subjected to another, nor has he a right to domineer over him.

Q.   But if a man is born strong, has he not a natural right to master the weak man ?

A.   No ; for it is neither a necessity for him, nor a convention between them ; it is an abusive extension of his strength ; and here an abuse is made of the word right, which in its true meaning implies, justice or reciprocal faculty.

Q. How is property a physical attribute of man ?

A. In as much as all men being constituted equal or similar to one another, and consequently independent, and free, each is the absolute master, the full proprietor of his body and of the produce of his labor.

Q. How is justice derived from these three attributes ?

A. In this, that men being equal and free, owing nothing to each other, have no right to require anything from one another, only in as much as they return an equal value for it ; or in as much as the balance of what is given is in equilibrium with what is returned : and it is this equality, this equilibrium which is called justice, equity ;* that is to say that equality and justice are but one and the same word, the same law of nature, of which the social virtues are only applications and derivatives.

CHAPTER XII.

DEVELOPEMENT OF THE SOCIAL VIRTUES.

Q. Explain how the social virtues are derived from the law of nature. How is charity or the love of one's neighbour a precept and application of it ?

A. By reason of equality and reciprocity : for when we injure another, we give him a right to injure us in return : thus, by attacking the existence of our neighbour we endanger our own, from the effect of reciprocity ; on the other hand, by doing good to others, we have room and right to expect an equivalent exchange ; and such is the character of all the social virtues, that they are useful to the man who practises them, by the right of reciprocity which they give him over those who are benefited by them.

Q. Charity is then nothing but justice ?

A. No ; it is only justice ; with this slight difference, that strict justice confines itself to saying, Do not to another the harm you would

* Æquitas, æquilibrium, æqualitas, are all of the same family.

not wish he should do to you ; and that charity, or the love of one's neighbour, extends so far as to say, Do to another the good which you would wish to receive from him. Thus when the gospel said, that this precept contained the whole of the law and the prophets, it announced nothing more than the precept of the law of nature.

Q. Does it enjoin forgiveness of injuries ?

A. Yes, in as much as that forgiveness is consistent with self-preservation.

Q. Does it prescribe to us, after having received a blow on one cheek, to hold out the other ?

A. No; for it is, in the first place, contrary to the precept of loving our neighbour as ourselves, since thereby we should love, more than ourselves, him who makes an attack on our preservation. 2d. Such a precept in its literal sense, encourages the wicked to oppression and injustice; the law of nature has been more wise in prescribing a calculated proportion of courage and moderation, which induces us to forget a first or unpremeditated injury, but which punishes every act tending to oppression.

Q. Does the law of nature prescribe to do good to others beyond the bounds of reason and measure ?

A. No; for it is a sure way of leading them to ingratitude. Such is the force of sentiment and justice implanted in the heart of man, that he is not even grateful for benefits conferred without discretion. There is one only measure with them, and that is to be just.

Q. Is alms-giving a virtuous action ?

A. Yes, when it is practised according to the rule first mentioned ; without which it degenerates into imprudence and vice, in as much as it encourages laziness, which is hurtful to the beggar and to society ; no one has a right to partake of the property and fruits of another's labor, without rendering an equivalent of his own industry.

Q. Does the law of nature consider as virtues faith and hope, which are often joined with charity ?

A No : for they are ideas without reality ; and if any effects result from them, they turn rather to the profit of those who have not those ideas, than of those who have them ; so that faith and hope may be called the virtues of dupes for the benefit of knaves.

Q Does the law of nature prescribe probity ?

A. Yes : for probity is nothing more than respect for one's own rights in those of another ; a respect founded on a prudent and well combined calculation of our interests compared to those of others

Q. But does not this calculation, which embraces the complicated interests and rights of the social state, require an enlightened understanding and knowledge, which make it a difficult science ?

A. Yes, and a science so much the more delicate as the honest man pronounces in his own cause.

Q. Probity, therefore, is a sign of extension and justice in the mind ;

A. Yes : for an honest man almost always neglects a present interest, in order not to destroy a future one ; whereas the knave does the contrary, and loses a great future interest for a present smaller one.

Q. Improbity, therefore, is a sign of false judgment and a narrow mind ?

A. Yes ; and rogues may be defined ignorant and silly calculators : for they do not understand their true interest, and they pretend to cunning : nevertheless their cunning only ends in making known what they are ; in losing all confidence and esteem, and the good services resulting from them for their physical and social existence. They neither live in peace with others, nor with themselves ; and incessantly menaced by their conscience and their enemies, they enjoy no other real happiness but that of not being hanged.

Q. Does the law of nature forbid robbery ?

A. Yes : for the man who robs another gives him a right to rob him ; from that moment there is no security in his property nor in his means of preservation ; thus, in injuring others, he, by a counter-blow injures himself.

Q. Does it interdict even an inclination to rob ?

A. Yes ; for that inclination leads naturally to action, and it is for this reason that envy is considered a sin.

Q. How does it forbid murder ?

A. By the most powerful motives of self-preservation ; for, 1st. the man who attacks exposes himself to the risk of being killed, by the right of defence ; 2d. if he kills, he gives to the relations and friends of the deceased, and to society at large, an equal right of killing him ; so that his life is no longer in safety.

Q. How can we, by the law of nature, repair the evil we have done ?

A. By rendering a proportionate good to those whom we have injured.

Q. Does it allow us to repair it by prayers, vows, offerings to God, fasting and mortifications ?

A. No : for all those things are foreign to the action we wish to repair : they neither restore the ox to him from whom it has been stolen, honor to him whom we have deprived of it, nor life to him from whom it has been taken away ; consequently they miss the end of justice ; they are only perverse contracts by which a man sells to another goods which do not belong to him : they are a real depravation of morality, in as much as they embolden to commit crimes through the hope of expiating them ; wherefore, they have been the real cause of all the evils by which the people amongst whom those expiatory practices were used, have been continually tormented.

Q. Does the law of nature order sincerity ?

A. Yes : for lying, perfidy and perjury create distrust, quarrels, hatred, revenge, and a crowd of evils amongst men, which tend to their common destruction ; whilst sincerity and fidelity establish confidence, concord, and peace, besides the infinite good resulting from such a state of things to society.

Q. Does it prescribe mildness and modesty ?

A. Yes : for harshness and obduracy, by alienating from us the hearts of other men, give them an inclination to hurt us ; ostentation and vanity, by wounding their self-love and jealousy, occasion us to miss the end of a real utility.

Q. Does it prescribe humility as a virtue ?

A. No : for it is a propensity in the human heart to despise secretly everything that presents to it the idea of weakness ; and self-debasement encourages pride and oppression in others ; the balance must be kept in equipoise.

Q. You have reckoned simplicity of manners amongst the social virtues ; what do you understand by that word ?

A. I mean the restricting our wants and desires to what is truly useful to the existence of the citizen and his family ; that is to say, the man of simple manners has but few wants, and lives content with a little.

Q. How is this virtue prescribed to us ?

A. By the numerous advantages which the practice of it procures to the individual and to society ; for the man whose wants are few, is free at once from a crowd of cares, perplexities and labors ; he avoids many quarrels and contests arising from avidity and a desire of gain ; he spares himself the anxiety of ambition, the inquietudes of possession, and the uneasiness of losses ; finding superfluity everywhere, he is the real rich man ; always content with what he has, he is happy at little expense ; and other men not fearing any competition from him, leave him in quiet, and are disposed to render him the services he should stand in need of.

And if this virtue of simplicity extends to a whole people, they assure to themselves abundance; rich in every thing they do not consume, they acquire immense means of exchange and commerce; they work, fabricate and sell at a lower price than others, and attain to all kinds of prosperity both at home and abroad.

Q. What is the vice contrary to this virtue?

A. It is cupidity and luxury.

Q. Is luxury a vice in the individual and in society?

A. Yes; and to that degree, that it may be said to include all the others; for the man who stands in need of many things, imposes thereby on himself all the anxiety, and submits to all the means just or unjust of acquiring them. Does he possess an enjoyment, he covets another; and in the bosom of superfluity, he is never rich; a commodious dwelling is not sufficient for him, he must have a beautiful hotel; not content with a plenteous table, he must have rare and costly viands: he must have splendid furniture, expensive clothes, a train of attendants, horses, carriages, women, theatrical representations and games. Now, to supply so many expenses, much money must be had; and he looks on every method of procuring it as good and even necessary: at first he borrows, afterwards he steals, robs, plunders, turns bankrupt, is at war with every one, ruins and is ruined.

Should a nation be involved in luxury, it occasions on a larger scale the same devastations; by reason that it consumes its entire produce, it finds itself poor even with abundance; it has nothing to sell to foreigners; its manufactures are carried on at a great expense, and are sold too dear; it becomes tributary for everything it imports; it attacks externally its consideration, power, strength, and means of defence and preservation; whilst internally it undermines and falls into the dissolution of its members. All its citizens being covetous of enjoyments, are engaged in a perpetual struggle to obtain them; all injure or are near injuring themselves: and hence arise those habits and actions of usurpation, which constitute what is denominated moral corruption, intestine war between citizen and citizen. From luxury arises avidity, from avidity, invasion by violence and perfidy; from luxury arises the iniquity of the judge, the venality of the witness, the improbity of the husband, the prostitution of the wife, the obduracy of parents, the ingratitude of children, the avarice of the master, the dishonesty of the servant, the dilapidation of the administrator, the perversity of the legislator, lying, perfidy, perjury, assassination, and all the disorders of the social state; so that it was with a profound sense of truth, that ancient moralists have laid the basis of the social virtues on simplicity of manners, restriction of wants, and contentment with a little; and a sure way of knowing the extent of a man's virtues and vices, is, to find out if his expenses are proportionate to his fortune, and calculate from his want of money, his probity, his integrity in fulfilling his engagements, his devotion to the public weal, and his sincere or pretended love of his country.

Q. What do you mean by the word country?

A. I mean the community of citizens who, united by fraternal sentiments, and reciprocal wants, make of their respective strength one common force, the reaction of which on each of them assumes the preservative and beneficent character of paternity. In society, citizens form a bank of interest; in our country we form a family of endearing attachments; it is charity, the love of one's neighbour extended to a whole nation. Now, as charity cannot be separated from justice, no member of the family can pretend to the enjoyment of its advantages, except in proportion to his labor; if he consumes more than it produces, he necessarily encroaches on his fellow citizens; and it is only by consuming less than what he produces or possesses, that he can acquire the means of making sacrifices and being generous.

Q. What do you conclude from all this?

A. I conclude from it that all the social virtues are only the habitude of actions useful to society and to the individual who practises them; That they all refer to the physical object of man's preservation; That nature having implanted in us the want of that preservation, has made a law to us of all its consequences, and a crime of everything that deviates from it; That we carry in us the seed of every virtue, and of every perfection; That it only requires to be developed; That we are only happy in as much as we observe the rules established by nature for the end of our preservation; And that all wisdom, all perfection, all law, all virtue, all philosophy, consist in the practice of these axioms founded on our own organization:

Preserve-thyself; Instruct-thyself; Moderate-thyself;
Live for thy fellow citizens, that they may live for thee.

CONTROVERSY

BETWEEN

DR. PRIESTLY AND VOLNEY.

FROM THE ANTI-JACOBIN REVIEW

In 1797, Dr. Priestly published a pamphlet, entitled, " Observa tions on the increase of infidelity, with animadversions upon the writings of several modern unbelievers, and especially the Ruins of Mr. Volney. The motto to this tract was,

" Minds of little penetration rest naturally on the surface of things. They do not like to pierce deep into them, for fear of labor and trouble ; sometimes still more for fear of truth."

The following Letter is an answer from Volney, taken from the Anti-Jacobin Review of March and April, 1799.

From the Anti-Jacobin Review, for March 1799.

VOLNEY'S ANSWER TO DR. PRIESTLY.

SIR,—I received in due time your pamphlet on the increase of infidelity, together with the note without date which accompanied it.* My answer has been delayed by the incidents of business, and even by ill health, which you will surely excuse : this delay has, besides, no inconvenience in it. The question between us is not of a very urgent nature : the world would not go on less well with or without my answer as with or without your book. I might, indeed, have dispensed with returning you any answer at all ; and I should have been warranted in so doing, by the manner in which you have stated the debate, and by the opinion pretty generally received that, on certain occasions, and with certain persons, the most noble reply is silence. You seem to have been aware of this yourself, considering the extreme precautions you have taken to deprive me of this resource ; but as, according to our French customs, any answer is an act of civility, I am not willing to concede the advantage of politeness—besides, although silence is sometimes very significant, its eloquence is not understood by every one; and the public which has not leisure to analyze disputes (often of little interest) has a reasonable right to require at least some preliminary explanations ; reserving to itself, should the discussion degenerate into the recriminative clamors of an irritated self-love, to allow the right of silence to him in whom it becomes the virtue of moderation.

I have read, therefore, your animadversions on my Ruins, which you are pleased to class among the writings of modern unbelievers ; and since you absolutely insist on my expressing my opinion before the public, I shall now fulfil this rather disagreeable task with all possible brevity, for the sake of economising the time of our readers

* Dr. Priestly sent his pamphlet to Volney, desiring his answer to the strictures on his opinions in his " Ruins of Empires." *Editor A. J. Review*

In the first place, sir, it appears evidently, from your pamphlet, that your design is less to attack my book than my personal and moral character; and in order the public may pronounce with accuracy on this point, I submit several passages fitted to throw light on the subject.

You say, in the preface of your discourses, p. 12, ' There are, however, unbelievers more ignorant than Mr. Paine, Mr. Volney, Lequino, and others in France say,' &c.

Also in the preface of your present observations, p. 20. ' I can truly say that in the writings of Hume, Mr. Gibbon, Voltaire, Mr. Volney—there is nothing of solid argument : all abound in gross mistakes and misrepresentations.' Idem, p. 38—' Whereas had he (Mr. Volney) given attention to the history of the times in which Christianity was promulgated. . . . he could have no more doubt . . . &c. it is as much in vain to argue with such a person as this, as with a Chinese or even a Hottentot.'

Idem, p. 119—' Mr. Volney, if we may judge from his numerous quotations of ancient writers in all the learned languages, oriental as well as occidental, must be acquainted with all; for he makes no mention of any translation, and yet if we judge from this specimen of his knowledge of them, he cannot have the smallest tincture of that of the Hebrew, or even of the Greek.'

And, at last, after having published and posted me in your very title page, as an unbeliever and an infidel ; after having pointed me out in your motto as one of those superficial spirits who know not how to find out, and are unwilling to encounter, truth ; you add, p. 124, immediately after an article in which you speak of me under all these denominations—

" The progress of infidelity, in the present age, is attended with a circumstance which did not so frequently accompany it in any former period, at least, in England, which is, that unbelievers in revelation generally proceed to the disbelief of the being and providence of God so as to become properly Atheists." So that, according to you, I am a Chinese, a Hottentot, an unbeliever, an Atheist, an ignoramus, a man of no sincerity ; whose writings are full of nothing but gross mistakes and misrepresentations. Now I ask you, sir, What has all this to do with the main question ? What has my book in common with my person ? And how can you hold any converse with a man of such bad connexions ? In the second place, your invitation, or rather, your summons to me, to point out the mistakes which *I think you have made with respect to my opinions,* suggest to me several observations.

1st. You suppose that the public attaches a high importance to your mistakes and to my opinions : but I cannot act upon a supposition. Am I not an unbeliever ?

2d. You say, p. 18, that the public *will expect it 'from me :* Where are the powers by which you make the public speak and act ? is this also a revelation ?

3d. You require me to point out your mistakes. I do not know that I am under any such obligation ; I have not reproached you with them : it is not, indeed, very correct to ascribe to me, by selection or indiscriminately, as you have done, all the opinions scattered through my book, since, having introduced many different persons, I was under the necessity of making them deliver different sentiments, according to their different characters. The part which belongs to me is that of a traveller, resting upon the ruins and meditating on the causes of the misfortunes of the humam race. To be consistent with yourself you ought to have assigned to me that of the Hottentot or Samoyde savage, who argues with the Doctors, Chap. xxiii, and I should have accepted it ; you have preferred that of the erudite historian, Chap. xxii, nor do I look upon this as a mistake ; I discover, on the contrary, an insidious design to engage me in a duel of self-love before the public, wherein you would excite the exclusive interest of the spectators by supporting the cause which they approve ; while the task which you would impose on me, would only, in the event of success, be attended with sentiments of disapprobation. Such is your artful purpose, that, in attacking me as doubting the existence of Jesus, you might secure to yourself, by surprise, the favor of every christian sect, although your own incredulity in his divine nature is not less subversive of Christianity than the profane opinion, which does not find in history the proof required by the English law to establish a fact : to say nothing of the extraordinary kind of pride assumed in the silent, but palpable, comparison of yourself to Paul and to Christ, by likening your labors to theirs as tending to the same object, p. 10, preface. Nevertheless, as the first impression of an attack always confers an advantage, you have some ground for expecting you may obtain the apostolic crown ; unfortunately for your purpose I entertain no disposition to that of martyrdom : and however glorious it might be to me to fall under the arm of him who has overcome Hume, Gibbon Voltaire and even Frederick II, I find myself under the necessity of declining your theological challenge, for a number of substantial reasons.

1st. Because, to religious quarrels there is no end, since the prejudices of infancy and education almost unavoidably exclude impartial reasoning, and besides, the vanity of the champions becomes committed by the very publicity of the contest, never to give up a first assertion, whence result a spirit of sectarism and faction.

2d. Because no one has a right to ask of me an account of my religious opinions : every inquisition of this kind is a pretension to sovereignty, a first step towards persecution ; and the tolerant spirit of this country, which you invoke, has much less in view to engage men to speak, than to invite them to be silent.

3d. Because supposing I do hold the opinions you attribute to me, I wish not to engage my vanity so as never to retract, nor to deprive myself of the resource of a conversion on some future day after more ample information.

4th. And because, reverend sir, if, in the support of your own theses, you should happen to be discomfited before the christian audience, it would be a dreadful scandal : and I will not be a cause for scandal, even for the sake of good.

5th. Because in this metaphysical contest our arms are too unequal ; you speaking in your mother tongue, which I scarcely lisp, might bring forth huge volumes, while I could hardly oppose pages ; and the public, who would read neither production, might take the weight of the books for that of reasonings.

6th. And because being endowed with the gift of faith, in a pretty sufficient quantity, you might swallow in a quarter of an hour more articles than my logic would digest in a week.

7th. Because again, if you were to oblige me to attend your sermons, as you have compelled me to read your pamphlet, the congregation would never believe that a man powdered and adorned like any worldling, could be in the right against a man dressed out in a large hat, *with straight hair*,* and a mortified countenance, although the gospel, speaking of the pharisees of other times, who were unpowdered, says that when one fasts he must annoint his head and wash his face.†

8th. Because finally, a dispute to one having nothing else to do, would be a gratification, while to me, who can employ my time better, it would be an absolute loss.

* Dr. Priestly has discarded his wig since he went to America, and wears his own hair.   Editor A. J. Review.
† St Matthew, Chapter VI. verses 16 and 17.

I shall not then, reverend sir, make you my confessor in matters of religion, but I will disclose to you my opinion, as a man of letters, on the composition of your book. Having, in former days, read many works of theology, I was curious to find out whether by any chymical process you had discovered real beings in that world of invisibles; unfortunately I am obliged to declare to the public, which, according to your expression, p. 19, " hopes *to be instructed, to be led into truth, and not into error by me,*" that I have not found in your book a single new argument, but the mere repetition of what is told over and over in thousands of volumes, the whole fruit of which has been to procure for their authors a cursory mention in the dictionary of heresies. You everywhere lay down that as proved which remains to be proved; with this peculiarity, that, as Gibbon says, firing away your double battery against those who believe too much, and those who believe too little, you hold out your own peculiar sensations, as to the precise criterion of truth; so that we must all be just of your size in order to pass the gate of that New Jerusalem which you are building. After this, your reputation as a divine might have become problematical with me; but recollecting the principle of the association of ideas so well developed by Locke, whom you hold in estimation, and whom, for that reason I am happy to cite to you, although to him I owe that pernicious use of my understanding which makes me disbelieve what I do not comprehend—I perceive why the public having originally attached the idea of talents to the name of Mr. Priestly, doctor in chymistry, continued by habit to associate it with the name of Mr. Priestly, doctor in divinity; which however is not the same thing : an association of ideas the more vicious as it is liable to be moved inversely.*
Happily you have yourself raised a bar of separation between your admirers, by advising us in the first page of your preface, that your present book is especially destined for *believers.* To cooperate, however, with you, sir, in this *judicious* design, I must observe that it is necessary to retrench two passages, seeing they afford the greatest support to the arguments of *unbelievers.*

You say, p. 15, " *What is manifestly contrary to natural*

* Mr. Blair, doctor of divinity, and Mr. Black, doctor in chymistry, met at the coffee house in Edinburg: a new theological pamphlet written by doctor Priestly was thrown upon the table, "Really," said Dr. Blair," this man had better confine himself to chymistry, for he is absolutely ignorant in theology:"—"I beg your pardon," answered Dr. Black, " he is in the right, he is a minister of the gospel, he ought to adhere to his profession, for in truth he knows nothing of chymistry."

reason cannot be received by it;"—and p. 62, " With respect to intellect, men and brute animals are born in the same state, having the same external senses, which are the only inlets to all ideas, and consequently the source of all the knowledge and of all the mental habits they ever acquire.

Now if you admit, with Locke, and with us infidels, that every one has the right of rejecting whatever is contrary to his natural reason ; and that all our ideas and all our knowledge are acquired only by the inlets of our external senses ; What becomes of the system of revelation, and of that order of things in times past, which is so contradictory to that of the time present ? unless we consider it as a dream of the human brain during the state of superstitious ignorance.—With these two single phrases, I could overturn the whole edifice of your faith. Dread not, however, sir, in me such overflowing zeal : for the same reason I have not the frenzy of martyrdom, I have not that of making proselytes. It becomes those ardent, or rather, acrimonious tempers, who mistake the violence of their sentiments, for the enthusiasm of truth ; the ambition of noise and rumor, for the love of glory ; and for the love of their neighbour, the detestation of his opinions, and the secret desire of dominion. As for me who have not received from nature the turbulent qualities of an apostle, and never sustained in Europe the character of a dissenter, I am come to America neither to agitate the conscience of men, nor to form a sect, nor to establish a colony, in which, under the pretext of religion, I might erect a little empire to myself. I have never been seen evangelizing my ideas, either in temples or in public meetings. I have never likewise practised that quackery of beneficence, by which a certain divine, imposing a tax upon the generosity of the public, procures for himself the honors of a more numerous audience, and the merit of distributing at his pleasure a bounty which costs him nothing, and for which he receives grateful thanks dexterously stole from the original donors.— Either in the capacity of a stranger, or in that of a citizen, a sincere friend to peace, I carry into society neither the spirit of dissension, nor the desire of commotion ; and because I respect in every one what I wish him to respect in me, the name of liberty is in my mind nothing else but the synonyma of justice ; as a man, whether from moderation or indolence, a spectator of the world rather than an actor in it, I am every day less tempted to take on me the management of the minds or bodies of men : it is sufficient for an individual to govern his own passions and caprices. If by one of these caprices, I am induced to think it may be useful, sometimes to publish my reflections, I do it without obstinacy or pretension to that implicit faith, the ridicule of which you desire to impart to me, p. 123. My whole book of the Ruins which you treat so ungratefully, since you *thought it amusing*, p. 122, evidently bears this character. By means of the contrasted opinions I have scattered through it, it breathes that spirit of doubt and uncertainty which appears to me the best suited to the weakness of the human mind, and the most adapted to its improvement, inasmuch as it always leaves a door open to new truths ; while the spirit of dogmatism and immovable belief, limiting our progress to a first received opinion, binds us at hazard, and without resource, to the yoke of error or falsehood, and occasions the most serious mischiefs to society ; since by combining with the passions, it engenders fanaticism, which, sometimes misled and sometimes misleading, though always intolerant and despotic, attacks whatever is not of its own nature ; drawing upon itself persecution when it is weak, and practising persecution when it is powerful ; establishing a religion of terror, which annihilates the faculties, and vitiates the conscience : so that, whether under a political or a religious aspect, the spirit of doubt is friendly to all ideas of liberty, truth, or genius, while a spirit of confidence is connected with the ideas of tyranny, servility, and ignorance. If, as is the fact, our own experience and that of others daily teaches us that what at one time appeared true, afterwards appeared demonstrably false, how can we connect with our judgments that blind and presumptuous confidence which pursues those of others with so much hatred ? No doubt it is reasonable and even honest, to act according to our present feelings, and conviction : but if these feelings and their causes do vary by the very nature of things, how dare we impose upon ourselves or others an invariable conviction ? How, above all, dare we require this conviction in cases where there is really no sensation, as happens in purely speculative questions, in which no palpable fact can be presented ? Therefore when opening the book of nature, a more authentic one and more easy to be read than leaves of paper blackened over with Greek or Hebrew, when I reflected that the slightest change in the material world has not been in times past, nor is, at present, effected by the difference of so many religions and sects which have appeared and still exist on the globe, and the course of the seasons, the path of the sun, the return of rain and drought are the same for the inhabitants of each country, whether Christian, Mussulmen, Idolaters, Catholics, Protestants, &c. I am induced to

Printed in Great Britain
by Amazon

44849383R00126